WINNING WITH WORDS

Rhetoric-The Art of Convincing in a Court of Law Exemplified by the O.J. Simpson Trial

Maria Louise Staffe

Published by **Washington House**
A division of Trident Media Company
801 N Pitt Street, Suite 123
Alexandria, VA 22314 USA

Wisdom without eloquence does too little for the good of states.

Cicero

I dedicate this book to my three children Katarina Ludmilla, Oliver Nicholas, and Isabella Rosa, as rhetoric is a gift to be passed on to future generations.

Preface

The first time I went and saw a trial unfold in court I was shocked. I realized that neither side had any idea of how to effectively argue to their audience, the jurors. Time and time again I watched lawyers shoot themselves in the foot and jeopardize their case. Even without knowing exactly what their case was about, the rhetorical blunders were obvious. Unfortunately this was not a single event. Every time I attended a court trial I saw the same thing unfold. When talking to lawyers about this, I realized that not only is rhetoric not taught in law school, lawyers in general had no idea what I was talking about. I decided to write this book in order to try to bring attention to the situation and provide lawyers with something more than just antidotal teaching offered by "successful" trial lawyers.

This knowledge, which stretches back through the centuries to ancient Greece, can benefit anybody that has a message that they want to communicate to and seek acceptance from others.

I chose to use the O.J. Simpson case to show the different rhetorical means at work, because it is a case that is so well known. The Simpson case had a very clear outcome and has been very well documented. Because the balance of strength between the lawyers was so unsymmetrical we also get to see some rhetorical techniques working in pure form.

Even a huge amount of evidence was not enough to secure victory for the prosecution when they were unaware of the means of rhetoric. This is a situation any lawyer can face if they are not aware of this ancient discipline.

First and foremost I would like to thank my husband Jeffrey for all his help. Without it I would not have been able to complete this book. As a fellow rhetorician, Margit Simonson has also come up with valuable comments in the process of creating this book. I would like to thank her for her insightful comments. I would also like to thank Johannes Mosegaard and Hovedstadenes Ordblindeskole. Johannes has been a great help and an admirable humanist. I would like to thank Judy Justus for helping me with my English writing. I would also like to thank Marie Heising for translating my original writings into English. Finally I would like to thank the professors at the Copenhagen University Institute of Rhetoric. Especially I would like to thank Charlotte Jørgensen, Merete Onsberg, Christian Kock, and Lone Rørbech for their inspiration that shows their love of rhetoric.

Contents

1. THE ART OF CONVINCING

Rhetoric is useful, because the true and the just are naturally superior to their opposites, so that, if decisions are improperly made, they must owe their defeat to their own advocates; which is reprehensible. Further, in dealing with certain persons, even if we possessed the most accurate scientific knowledge, we should not find it easy to persuade them by the employment of such knowledge. For scientific discourse is concerned with instruction, but in the case of such persons instruction is impossible; our proofs and arguments must rest on generally accepted principles...

Aristotle

On June 12, 1994, two people were murdered in Los Angeles, a man, Ron Goldman, and a woman, Nicole Brown Simpson. It was a brutal murder where both the victims had had their throats cut. The murders took place just outside Nicole Simpson's home. Nicole Simpson was in her midthirties and Ron Goldman was in his midtwenties, and they were both whites. In addition, Ron Goldman was Jewish.

From the start, the double murder stirred massive national media coverage due to the fact that Nicole Simpson had been married to the former football star and national celebrity, Orenthal James Simpson. The fact that O. J. Simpson was suspected of having committed the double murder did not reduce the media coverage. Neither did the fact that, when about to be taken into custody, O.J. Simpson tried to escape from the police, carrying with him a loaded gun, his passport, a disguise kit, and about $9,000 in cash.

The attempt ended with several police cars following O.J. in his white Ford Bronco, traveling along the expressway very slowly, with the police in contact by telephone, and the whole scene being broadcast live on CNN. The car chase ended at O.J. Simpson's home where he, via cellular phones, was talked out of shooting himself.

The evidence against O.J. Simpson was enormous. Yet the prosecution lost the case. *Why*?

Ever since the trial ended, there has been speculation about why it ended as it did, with Simpson being acquitted within a few hours after the jurors started their deliberation. The jurors have been accused of being dumb and racists, the judge of being lenient and starstruck, the police for being sloppy, the defense team for being manipulative, and the prosecution for being dumb. Often one hears the explanation that it all had to do with race, and that the outcome of the case therefore was inevitable because the majority of the jurors were black.

If we look at the trial from a rhetorical perspective, we will see that the outcome of the trial was not determined from the beginning. And that the jury was not dumb or racists, but that *their verdict was a natural and logical result of the rhetorical strategy employed in the case*. We are going to see that the verdict was a result of strategies employed by a defense with rhetorical knowledge, and a prosecution without rhetorical knowledge.

In a court of law, rhetoric can be your best friend, or your most dangerous enemy; in both cases it is worth knowing. This book's aim is to introduce some basic rhetorical means and show that rhetoric is a practical tool, a tool that can make the sole difference between winning and losing in a court of law.

This book is going to give you an understanding of argumentation that can be used to better your skills in any kind of discourse. We are going to see how the use of ancient rhetorical skills determined the outcome of the trial of the twentieth century-a trial where both the prosecution's, as well as the defense's, strategies and criteria for judging their argumentation are expressions of a misunderstanding, or a distortion, of what good rhetoric entails.

Rhetoric is the art of convincing, and can be used to create conviction by pointing at the convincing aspects in any case. Rhetoric is a humanistic science that bases itself on the premise that a person creates an opinion within another person when they come within any sort of contact. This can happen through the way one behaves or what one says. From this it follows that rhetoric can be used as a practical tool. This was the way the Romans and the ancient Greeks used rhetoric. By using the rules of rhetoric, a speaker could find ways to convince his audience.

We need rhetoric, because we usually don't have a black and white situation. We usually have to agree upon various problems. For example, in a court of law an agreement has to be reached as to how much compensation a person is entitled to, or what degree of culpability a person has in the crime charged. Contrary to what many think today, rhetoric is more than just a technique to dress up the language. Rhetoric is learning the techniques to find and analyze opinions and arguments in a way that is not just pleasing to listen to, but also rich in content and well argued. Rhetoric takes care of both content and form, since the combination of well-argued content and polished linguistic form is the best way to educate, entertain, and move one's audience.

Rhetoric and knowledge, in beneficial coexistence, are the true basis of a strong democracy.

There is a tremendous lack of knowledge about how people are affected and moved in their decision processes. This affects everybody who wants to communicate a message to other people, all the way from psychologists to preachers. This is especially tragic when it comes to lawyers, since they hold people's economy, freedom, and sometimes even lives in their hands. This is an indictment of the legal education system. Law schools have let not only lawyers but also society in general down by not teaching rhetoric to law students. We are using the O.J. Simpson case as a backdrop to look at the results of this lack of knowledge.

And It Works

It is always easier to determine what should have been done after the fact. We can therefore wonder if the rhetorical theories make a difference in determining the actual outcome of a case. Though it may be easier to determine what should have been done after the fact any given case presents a rhetorical situation that can be mapped out ahead of time. You can determine your best strategies and your opponent's. You can determine the optimal rhetorical response of each of the parties and prepare in advance. You know your opponent's best counterstrategies and weakest points of those strategies. And you can make adjustments as the trial progresses. This can be seen from a case that lent itself to a test of the effectiveness of the rhetorical argumentation theories.

The actual case was about a woman who went into the hospital to have a hysterectomy and came out without an arm. She lost her arm due to complications that occurred after the operation. After an operation you stay at the hospital for a certain time period, where you are under observation for possible complications. It was in this time period that a blood clot formed in her arm. Blood clots are one of the possible complications that can occur after an operation. The whole discussion then evolved around whether the hospital staff and doctors were negligent for not detecting the clot sooner and taking action to prevent having to amputate her arm.

What was unique about this case, was that it had been tried once before, and the plaintiff had lost the case. All eight jurors in the civil case agreed that there wasn't any liability on the part of the hospital.

The plaintiff was granted an opportunity to retry the case. In other words, we had a case that had been tried before against the same defendant, and in the same state and county. The only thing that was changed the second go around was the argumentation techniques applied in the case. The plaintiff's argumentation in the first trial was reviewed and modified by the application of some basic rhetorical techniques This alone changed the case from all jurors agreeing that there was no liability on behalf of the hospital, to all the jurors agreeing that the hospital was liable. This resulted in a verdict of $3.1 million dollars.[1]

FIRST TRIAL	SECOND TRIAL
Case	The Same
Facts	The Same
Lawyers	The Same
Jury Pool	The Same
Argumentation Techniques	Changed
8 jurors agree: No liability = $ 0.00	8 jurors agree: Liability $ 3.1 mil

In the first trial, the plaintiff's attorney's main problem was that he rambled, making it difficult to understand his point of view. At the same time, he accused almost everybody involved of wrongdoings, including the hospital's procedure in general. It is difficult to get ordinary people to believe that that many people failed at the same time. In the Simpson case, Cochran was aware of this, and therefore he didn't accuse all the police involved in the case of being totally bad.

Why The O.J. Simpson Case?

Though each case has its own rhetorical situation, that may change with time. There are certain rhetorical structures that are the same in every case. Rhetoric is a pragmatic way of thinking. We look at what can be done under the given circumstances. To understand which factors are important in a trial, you therefore need to look at a specific case. The O.J. Simpson case provides us with a rich source of information. This case is appropriate to look at, as it is a very well-documented case. It received a very clear outcome, and there was an enormous amount of evidence presented.

Even though there were several lawyers on each side, I have chosen to focus on Marcia Clark and Christopher Darden representing the prosecution, and Johnnie Cochran and Barry Scheck representing the defendant, as I believe they are essential to the general legal discussion. They were also the four people who delivered the closing arguments in the case. Since rhetoric is a pragmatic way of thinking we look at what can be done under the given circumstances. I am therefore not going to get into issues such as the competence, behavior, and possible bias of Judge Ito. I am only going to look at what is the optimal rhetorical response under the given circumstance. In other words, what would have been the best thing to do, under the given circumstances? From a rhetorical prospective it is not of great interest how it ought to have been. The question is, what can we do about it?

To a great extent, the O.J. Simpson case lacked symmetry as regards to the balance of evidence, the production of it, and the judicial outcome. Because of that, we were given the opportunity to witness some sheer rhetorical theories working in pure form.

In this connection, it is interesting to see what arguments some of America's most highly paid lawyers and consultants can produce. "The People against O.J. Simpson" is a case worth reviewing because it was won by the defense, despite the fact that it had all odds against it from the beginning. Viewed in this context, it is fundamentally of minor importance whether the accused O.J. Simpson was guilty or not. The evidence against O.J. Simpson must be said to have been overwhelming.

In addition, from this case which attracted so much attention from the American public, we can learn much about American society and the American way of thinking. The interesting component of this case is the great impact it has produced on Americans' sense of justice, since this case was both very public and very controversial.

Finally, this case tells us something about the role of rhetoric within the legal system. We get the opportunity to see the importance rhetoric *can have* in a legal action and thereby look at the importance rhetoric *should have* in a legal action. We may say that the rhetorical aspect of this case is so strong that it has detached itself from its linkage to the law itself as well as to the specific case. The case detached itself from the legislative basis by changing the focus from being a murder case, to being a case about racism. The case also detached itself from the specific case in the sense that it changed from being about what *actually* happened, into being about previous injustices and the thoughts of what *might* happen in the future.

Taking into account the time aspect, one can say that neither the prosecution nor the defense came out of the trial as marked winners. This is due to the fact that both the prosecution and the defense devised wrong objectives and quality criteria for their argumentation. The prosecution essentially considered good rhetoric to be *logical argumentation* and the defense considered good argumentation to be *effective argumentation*. We can in this respect say that both the prosecution's as well as the defense's strategies and criteria for judging their argumentation are expressions of a misunderstanding or a distortion of what good rhetoric includes. If you think that your argumentation should only be logical, you completely ignore your audience, and the time and place where your argumentation is taking place. If you think that your argumentation should only be effective, you completely ignore the long-term consequences of your actions, and the ethical aspect of what you are doing.

The defense argued that Simpson had been framed, and that the evidence was contaminated.

Facts defeating the framing theory: Blood matching Simpson's DNA was found at the murder scene before any blood had been drawn from Simpson.

Dozens of people of different races, who did not know each other would have to have collaborated in an attempt to frame Simpson in a racially motivated plot, or as the defense team also claimed, in order to cover up their own incompetence.

Facts defeating the contamination and degradation theory: If Simpson was not the killer, contamination of the five blood drops found at the murder scene with Simpson's blood, drawn at the police station, would have resulted in two DNA profiles in the blood drops - Simpson's and the real killers. But only Simpson's DNA profile was found in the blood drops. Degradation, the breaking down of DNA into smaller pieces of DNA, does not change a person's DNA type; it remains the same. The degradation would have had to be so severe that the DNA of the real killer not only totally disappeared, but disappeared in five separate samples. Then each of those separate samples would have had to be contaminated with Simpson's blood. At the same time the control test, the purpose of which was to determine if the blood had been contaminated (these tests were carried out at the same time and location) would have had to escape contamination. This scenario had to be repeated five separate times. No one of these three events total degradation, a transfer of DNA, and failure of five control tests is a strong possibility. There was also a more traditional test performed on one of the blood drops from the murder scene that was not susceptible to contamination. This test also came out with Simpson's profile on one of the blood drops. This was powerful proof that there had been no contamination.

Many people ask themselves how defense attorneys like Cochran and Scheck could argue with such vigor to free Simpson. It is important here to realize that most people look at the Simpson case as a murder case. Scheck and Cochran, the two defense attorneys that I have focused upon, look at another picture that allowed them to put the murder case secondary to their greater aim.

Scheck is fighting for the civil rights of the prosecuted. Scheck is at war against the legal system, which he sees as putting far too many innocent people behind bars. We see this in "The Innocent Project," where Scheck and his partner Peter Neufeld, with the help of law students, are trying to free the wrongly convicted by the use of the newly developed DNA testing. In the Simpson case, Scheck is arguing more against the system, sloppy corrupt police officers, and jumping to quick decisions, than he is arguing Simpson's innocence. It is the indictment of the system more than the specific case that matters. As is often the case in war, the aims come before the means.

Cochran is at war against the L.A. police department. He is fighting racism and police misconduct, and tries to get at the police department any way he can. This is best exemplified by previous cases Cochran handled. A good example is the white truck driver that got beaten nearly to death by blacks in a Los Angeles riot. Cochran did not sue the black folks that nearly beat the white truck driver to death, but instead sued the L.A.P.D for being racist, by not providing enough officers to the poor black district.

If one reads Cochran's book *Journey to Justice*, one will also see that it almost doesn't mention the Simpson case, but talks mostly about Cochran's journey to justice, meaning Cochran's struggle against the

Los Angeles police department. This is Cochran's version of Hitler's "Mein Kampf," in the sense that it lays out Cochran's personal struggles and agenda. What the two authors have further in common, is that they put the *aims* before the *means*. Among other things, this results in that they use many of the same argumentation techniques when they address their audience, techniques that in both cases were extremely successful, since their opponents were unaware of the rhetorical techniques used, and therefore unable to stop the process.

An overview of the difference in the ways the defense and the prosecution looked at the case would look something like this:

	Paradigm	**Issue**	**Aim**
Prosecution	Logical / Mathematical	Murder Case	Justice for Two People
Defense	Rhetorical / Probability	Civil Rights Case	Bigger Picture

Basically, the case went from being a *murder case* to being a *civil rights case*, and the prosecution was not able to turn it back into a murder case. When Cochran kept repeating; "racist liar,"the prosecution was soon staggering behind claiming; "We are not racist liars." This is called stealing the agenda, and can be very effective.

The Historical Background of the O.J. Simpson Case

O.J. Simpson is a former American football star. Being forty-seven years old at the time of the murders (1994) he was one of the first black Americans to achieve stardom in the U.S. He was brought up in poverty and achieved wealth and fame. So he was not only the epitome of the American dream, he was also a positive example to many black Americans. Many poor Afro-Americans dream of rising from the slum by becoming sports stars, going for a career in sports rather than getting an education. (Although only one in 10,000 high school athletes will become a professional athlete, 66 percent of black males between age thirteen and eighteen believe they can become a professional athlete. Such unrealistic expectations have led many African American youths to focus on sports, at the expense of education.[2])

After he set aside football, O.J. Simpson knew how to please white society. He changed and polished his speech. He played golf with highly esteemed businessmen and officials and appeared in innumerable commercial spots for various products. He has appeared in a number of family TV-series, and his public image and professional appearance were charming and chivalrous.

Nicole Brown met O.J. Simpson in 1978 and shortly after they were married. Just one year later O.J. became violent towards Nicole. This led to several visits by the police and trips to the doctor for her. The documented list of his battering through the next thirteen years is very extensive. In 1992 Nicole Brown Simpson was granted a divorce from O.J. Simpson.

Ron Goldman was an acquaintance of Nicole Simpson. On the night of the murders, Nicole Simpson had been dining out with her mother at the restaurant where Ron Goldman worked as a waiter. Nicole's mother forgot her glasses in the restaurant, and she called the restaurant to see if they had found them. Ron Goldman decided to deliver them to Nicole on his way home from work. It is therefore most likely a coincidence that Ron Goldman was at the house at exactly the time at which the murderer struck.

After Nicole Simpson and Ron Goldman were found murdered, O.J. Simpson was charged with having committed the murders. The evidence against O.J. Simpson was overwhelming. The following is just some of the evidence against Simpson:

- He said he had dreams of killing Nicole.
- Blood from the victims was found in his bedroom and in his car.
- Simpson's hair and blood were found at the scene of the crime.
- A black man of the same height and build as Simpson's was seen entering his house shortly after the murders were committed, dressed in an all black outfit.
- A black knit cap was found at the crime scene, with hair that matched Simpson's.

- A pair of black socks was later found inside the house with traces of blood matching Ron and Nichole's DNA.
- A set of keys to Nicole's house, which had been stolen for a week before the murders, was also found in O.J.'s house.
- A glove identical to the one found at the crime scene was found on Simpson's property. On it was blood from the victims and fibers from Simpson's carpet in his Bronco.
- Simpson was bleeding all over his house the night of the murders. He was bleeding from cuts
  from his left hand. The murderer lost his left hand glove at the scene of the crime.
- Nicole gave the same kind of gloves as the one found at the crime scene to Simpson as a Christmas gift.
- Simpson had the same size shoes, size twelve, as the murderer. Only 12 percent of the male population wears a size twelve.

Three months into the trial Johnny Cochran, Simpson's trial lawyer, changed his theory from *My client was framed*, to *My client was framed because he is black*. Johnnie Cochran had earlier claimed that the evidence was falsified and that this was part of a conspiracy against O.J. Simpson, but not that the source of such a conspiracy was racism directed towards O.J. Simpson and black people in general. Even though the media took an immediate interest in the case, it was not until Cochran introduced the racial aspect that this issue was taken up by the media with a vengeance, making headlines again and again. It divided the American public into a predominantly white part, which was convinced of Simpson's guilt; and a mainly black part, which was convinced of Simpson's innocence.

The racial issue touches a very basic aspect in American society. Since Ron Goldman was not only white but also Jewish, it is worth noting that in addition to the tensions between blacks and whites in American society, anti-Semitic tendencies are found in parts of the black population. In this perspective, it is highly suggestive that Johnnie Cochran chose to rely on a character like Louis Farrakhan, the leader of Nation of Islam. This almost seventy-year-old organization, in addition to being a religious organization, is a black separatist movement. The members undergo severe discipline and strongly respond to real and supposed racism. Anti-Semitic outpourings from the present leader of the organization, Louis Farrakhan, and his ostentatious visits to dubious characters such as Libya's Muammar Gaddafi, stem both from a wish to demonstrate against white America and from old clashes between the Jewish and black populations of the cities.

The way Cochran relies on Farrakhan is by being seen publicly with him, embracing and shaking hands, and so forth. By merely associating with Farrakhan, Cochran also lends credibility to his conspiracy theory, since Farrakhan emphasizes conspiracy theories at his events. Cochran here uses the media, especially television, to get this to the jurors, by way of friends and relatives visiting the jury members during the one year-long trial. But most importantly, Cochran arrives at court with Farrakhan, and is seen with him in the presence of the jurors. Cochran used every means available during the trial to transform the case into a case about racism, such as when he spoke to the Congressional Black Caucus conference in Washington, D.C. where he compared the Simpson case to Brown vs. Board of Education, a landmark civil rights case. During and after his speech, he received a standing ovation.

When the aspect of the case changed from being one single event to being about racism within the Los Angeles police force (LAPD), the general interest in the case also changed. The case was brought from the gossip columns into the front pages of serious journalism, and thereby to the attention of the ordinary American. This changed the rhetorical situation. It went from being a *legal* case to being a *political* case. It is here important to keep in mind that this trial was taking place in Los Angeles, a city that had had several race riots. This city, a few years before, had experienced a riot after some white male officers had been acquitted for the beating of Rodney King, a black man stopped for a traffic violation and suspicion of drug use. Rodney King resisted arrest, and the police officers tried to beat him into submission. This whole incident was caught on videotape and shown in the media.

That the O.J. Simpson trial took place in the atmosphere of racial tensions was also seen from the fact that the announcement of the sentence was postponed so they could get the police ready, in case of a riot. Nobody had expected the jurors to come back with their verdict in just a couple of hours since the trial had lasted for almost nine months. No riots took place, but on television were shown groups of students at colleges and universities grouped together according to race, waiting to hear the verdict. After the verdict the whites mourned and the blacks celebrated the verdict. In order to understand this reaction, we have to gain some general understanding of the connection between rhetoric and law.

2. TIMELESS RHETORIC IN A CHANGING WORLD

If it is argued that one who makes an unfair use of such faculty of speech may do a great deal of harm, this objection applies equally to all good things except virtue, and above all to those things which are most useful.

Aristotle

The combination of rhetorical argumentation theory and legal argumentation has been both interesting and neglected within recent rhetorician research, where the combination of politics and rhetoric has attracted far greater attention. Paradoxically, this is unlike the emphasis given to it in classical rhetoric and the emergence of rhetoric as an independent discipline. In ancient Greece, the highest emphasis was given to the combination of rhetoric and law because they understood that their security and life depended upon an adequate understanding of the connection between law and rhetoric. Rhetoric was one of the most basic disciplines in school, not least because everyone at that time had to be his own lawyer. In ancient Greece you were not allowed to be represented by a third person, as we are today. So you represented yourself as well as your abilities allowed. The ironic thing is that today we are represented by lawyers with little, if any, knowledge and education in rhetoric, and, when it comes to creating a winning argument, are worse off than an ordinary citizen in ancient Greece. The Greeks at least had some basic knowledge or advice in how to address jurors in a convincing and effective way.

The argumentation theory from ancient Greece and Rome is compatible to our contemporary American courtroom. This is because the audience is similar when it comes to jury trials. In both cases, a citizen from the local community is judged by his or her peers. The concerns and interest of Cicero's audience were basically the same as for the American trial lawyer's audience. They are both addressing ordinary citizens, not experts. This means that the same fundamental principles and techniques of communication and acceptance are applied, as was the case when Gorgias and Cicero addressed their jurors in Athens and ancient Rome. That the amount of jurors in ancient Greece was around 150 and consisted only of free male citizens is, in this connection, not so important. It is still the same kind of feelings and concerns that you have to address, whether we are talking to twelve people or 150. It is under these circumstances that rhetoric developed into a science, and was considered one of the most basic and important traits to acquire

Viewed in this perspective it is striking that we today don't even educate the lawyers that will represent us in trial, in the basics of rhetoric. It has been sadly neglected not only by the law schools, but also by the rhetoric faculties.

That law and rhetoric has been divided as scholarly and practical disciplines is due to a total misunderstanding of rhetoric as being a superficial and manipulative technique, and a misunderstanding of the way we reason and make decisions as human beings.

Nothing is wrong with good argumentation and presentation techniques. It is only a problem where the balance of strength lacks symmetry to such an extent that it is possible to make people give their support on the basis of a delusion. In other words, where people are deceived. One of the alarming examples of how wrong matters may go was seen in Germany before and during the Second World War. In Germany they have indeed taken note of this and understand the implications of disavowing rhetoric. Therefore Germany, has one of the finest rhetoric studies in Europe.

It is no exaggeration to say that the interest in rhetoric following the Second World War has grown explosively, such as in Germany. There, like in other places, past demoniacal effects have been comprehended and the painful lesson has been learned. If we let rhetoric die, we run the risk of dying ourselves.

A skilled rhetorician without ethics is dangerous to society, if most people are ignorant of his ways. This is why it is so crucial that we educate people in rhetoric, and at least teach rhetoric to lawyers in law school. Unfortunately the way lawyers are taught to reason in law school is not the basis upon which most people make their decisions. Lawyers are taught to reason within the mathematical logical paradigm that is based upon a syllogism. A theoretical example could be:

Human beings are mortal
Socrates is a human being
Therefore Socrates is mortal

The syllogism deals with absolutes.

Jurors reason within the rhetorical paradigm that is based upon the enthymeme. This could sound something like this:

Bill is usually late
Today is a particular busy day for Bill
Bill is probably going to be late today

The enthymeme deals with probabilities.

In law school lawyers are taught to talk to other lawyers, but not to people outside their profession. We teach lawyers to think in one way, while the ones that are going to make the decision, the jurors, are thinking in another way. Lawyers think in legal terms, and the jury thinks in rhetorical terms.

If we want to keep the jury system, where one is judged by one's peers, lawyers have to know how to communicate with a jury. You cannot teach people one thing in law school, and have this high ideal about ordinary people making the decisions, and then not teach them how ordinary people reach decisions.

With Descartes and the huge success of the natural sciences, the mathematical paradigm has spread into areas were it doesn't belong, such as ethics, religion or everyday events that one is not able to squeeze into a mathematical formula. You cannot determine religion nor ethics solely on a logical basis. The way you argue and make decisions in everyday life is not the same way a scientist works. In natural science the man or the scientist is irrelevant, and the logic is everything. This is why in the O.J. Simpson case we saw a prosecution team that kept on applying logical evidence even though the source of this evidence had been compromised.

Rhetoric with its emphasis on probability is a counterweight to both dogmatism and pure relativism. It is the way we go about making decisions in everyday life. We are faced with having to make up our mind about something, even though we cannot be totally sure of what has happened or what it will amount to. We therefore have to base our decision on probability. In that respect the legal system is profoundly rhetorical, which is seen in the use of the expression "beyond reasonable doubt." It may be illustrated thus:

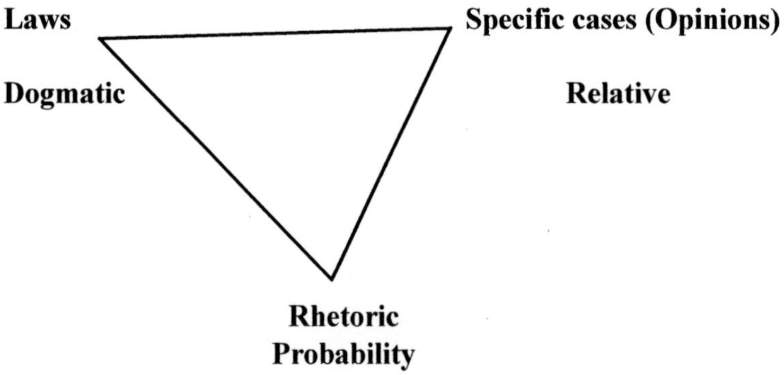

Laws reflect the dogmatic way of thinking in the sense that they are universal and apply always and everywhere. They are relatively unalterable if you look at them within a limited period of time and based on a specific case. They are the base or skeleton around which we build our society. And like the skeleton in our bodies, they are therefore the most nonyielding parts of our social structure. Like our bodies where the main and most vulnerable parts are protected by bone structure, the most basic structures of our society are protected by basic laws, such as the Constitution. It has, in addition a built-in protection against changes.

The specific cases reflect the lives we live, the way our reality unfolds. It is reality as it expands, all that fills up our society. In it we find a wide spectrum of opinions and interpretations of events. Truth is relative depending on whose eyes it is seen through, and where we are in time and place.

In this interaction we find the humanistic basis of the law. Rhetoric here blends together universal validities (*laws*) and specific situations (*events*) in a concrete decision. In practice, law is indeed an encounter between more or less universal opinions and the real world with its concrete cases that are often found in the gray area somewhere between black and white, that area of gray that can only be determined from an encounter between probabilities and attitudes. Nevertheless, it calls for a decision and an active response. It is here we meet life with all its differences and varieties and it is especially here that we need rhetoric, rhetoric as our way of understanding, interpreting, and evaluating our surroundings. The combination of law and rhetoric is in fact close to the classical humanistic ideal, by placing the individual at the center. Rhetoric is the very basis of human reasoning and relationship with others. The law is a safeguard of what we have hereby jointly achieved.

Law and rhetoric need each other. Rhetoric needs law to back and secure what has been agreed upon, and law needs rhetoric to make the general laws and specific cases come together! The combination of law and rhetoric is interesting to consider not only because we get a straightforward response to the effect of our reasoning, but also because legal arguments are an element in the creation of the rules and regulations on which we build our society. Not least in America, law is a contributory factor in keeping together a multicultural society, which finds its pivot point in the courtroom.

Americans meet in court. Political battles take place in court. The main characters in books, movies, and TV series are lawyers. If you are bored, you can always turn on the TV and watch a live trial. And when intellectuals meet to cross swords, then the debate is about literary interpretations of the law. Law has become Americans' ideology number one, a common frame of references in a multicultural, liberal society where the only thing that counts is, *my rights*. Conflicts in American society are, to a great extent, solved within the legal system.

Historically there has been an effort to suppress the knowledge of rhetoric because it has been perceived as twisting words in order to manipulate people. To focus on the ways in which rhetoric may be abused is like not seeing the forest for the trees. If we did not have rhetoric with its aspects of probability and opinion, we would not be able to act or make decisions in our dealings with each other. Rhetoric is what makes us able to act on a collective mind. Law and rhetoric with their pragmatic and humanistic bond are therefore inextricably linked to each other. Consequently, it is no surprise that they emerged at the same time in ancient Greece as the world's oldest scholarly disciplines. This development was able to take place in Greece because democracy is the foundation for law and rhetoric evolving as scholarly disciplines. If you have a tyranny, the law is what the ones in power decide and they basically don't need to justify it.

One of the reasons that we have not wanted to accept rhetoric's influence on our thoughts, actions, and decision processes is that we have not been willing to accept that we, to a great extent, are each other's fate. It interferes with our ideal of equal opportunities for all, and not least our feeling of being in control of our own life.

We are never in contact with another human being without holding a part of that person's life in our hands. In the relationship between the adult and the child we see this to its fullest extent. This is why behavioral scientists have been able to acknowledge it. This is true to a further or lesser extent in any relationship. *One never interacts with another person without holding part of their life in one's hand.* It can be just a passing emotion, or all the way to whether the other person succeeds in life.

Nonetheless, we have a strong and unconscious perception that a person's life is private, and the rest of us don't really belong within it. We feel that the other person lives in a world of his or her own, where the rest of us stand outside and only from time to time touch it. Therefore we usually see the encounters between people as their world touching each other's and later continuing on unaffected and intact. We think that only in an exceptional situation when a person, by mistake or intentionally, breaks into somebody else's world is there a great deal at stake.

This is not true. To a greater or lesser extent, we are each other's fate and every interaction counts. This is why rhetoric is so important. It is the means by which we communicate with each other.

It has been said that irrespective of the type of argumentation put forward in the Simpson case, the outcome of the case would have been the same. This is because some people believe the case was decided along racial lines. There is, however, no unambiguous evidence to support this attitude since the case was not about racism at the beginning. On the contrary, it was turned into a case about racism by Johnnie Cochran and his colleagues on the defense team. That was what the rhetorical situation called for in order to have the man acquitted. It was then the responsibility of the prosecution headed by Marcia Clark to give an adequate response to the defense team's full utilization of the rhetorical situation. This did not happen.

We clearly witnessed a imbalance of strength between prosecutor and defense. This imbalance opened up the possibilities for manipulation and an optimum utilization of the rhetorical situation.

A decisive difference in recipient awareness is seen in the reasoning of the prosecution and the defense, respectively; the defense was able to tailor their argumentation to their target group, the twelve jurors. They were able to utilize the jurors collective experience and prejudice, calling forth a collective Afro-American memory of assault, injustices, and abuse. Vindication and power came through the acquittal of O.J. Simpson, a man who had become the symbol of all previous injustices committed against black Americans. Johnnie Cochran's comparison of Mark Fuhrman to Hitler contributed in directing thoughts towards racially pure ideals, and thereby indirectly to Mark Fuhrman's statements that he would find something that would get a black man into trouble if he had a relationship with a white woman.

The jurors in the Simpson case were *not* racist but Cochran *used* racism to *create* doubt. He used racism as a foundation upon which he could build the rest of his arguments. He used a topic that was feasible to the audience as the foundation for the rest of his argumentation. It didn't matter how much additional evidence the prosecution team was able to present, since the evidence no longer had any relevance to the jurors in their decision.

The evidence had *no foundation*, because the defense team had cut away the ethos foundation for the prosecution's reasoning. The prosecution's evidence of spousal abuse had *no connection* to the murder case, because the issue of spousal abuse had been cut away from the issue of guilt. The prosecution's direct evidence had *no relevance*, because the defense team went in and created another case. *It was no longer a murder case, but a civil rights case. Fuhrman was convicted in the civil rights case, in order for Simpson to walk free in the murder case.*

It is easy to see why there has been an effort to suppress rhetoric. If you are a good rhetorician, you can literally get away with murder.

Based on this trial, it is easy to conclude that rhetoric is a terrible, manipulative art, which must be kept down to the furthest extent possible. It is exactly this way of thinking that brought about the situation we have just witnessed. The more we try to keep rhetoric down, the easier it is to manipulate people and take people to places where they do not want to go -- *where they commit themselves on a wrong basis*. Even the Greeks considered this; they called it the principle of "*ne-ars-appereat*," which means that art must be hidden in order for it to have optimum effect.

In this context, rhetoric is understood very narrowly as argumentation. We can of course not shed rhetoric as such as it is part of human behavior, thinking, and communication.

As earlier stated, nothing is wrong with good argumentation and presentation technique. It is only a problem where the balance of strength lacks symmetry to such an extent that it is possible to make people give their support on the basis of a delusion. In other words, where people are deceived.

It is a completely mistaken tactic to try and hide rhetoric and keep people ignorant of how it is used. First of all, we cannot prevent people from reading books or in some other way acquire this knowledge. Secondly, people with innate talents in this field, like Hitler, will always exist. The only thing you achieve by suppressing the knowledge of rhetoric is to turn the public at large into ignorant voters who can be led blindly.

If something had been done to corret the Simpson prosecution and make them realize that good reasoning does not keep within the bounds of the logical, mathematical paradigm, the trial would probably have turned out completely different. If they had been aware of the rhetorical concepts that are being presented in this book, such as *logos*, *ethos*, and *pathos*, not to say an understanding of the concepts of *claim*, *reasoning*, and *warrant*, the defense would have been much more limited in the extent they could deploy their tactics, because it does take a lot more energy to distort or hide "the truth" than to say things as we believe them to be.

We must not forget that rhetoric is the basis of our humanity and peaceful coexistence. Only through rhetoric can we reach a common ground for what we regard as true and ethically acceptable. Rhetoric is one of the key cornerstones of humanism.

Rhetoric's humanistic view is based on the individual's relations to his own life which he cannot experience through others. In addition, the rhetorical way of viewing man is based on the whole person. In this respect, classical psychology operated with a tripartition of the mind, cognition, feeling, and will. Immanuel Kant and his contemporary, Johann Tetens, distingusted between cognition and feeling. The result has been a widespread powerlessness towards and disavowal of feelings and the actual control it has over the decision and persuasion processes. Therefore, propaganda has had an easier job than necessary.

Since most lawyers are not knowledgeable in the area of rhetoric they are not confident that they can persuade a jury to their client's position. Therefore it has become fashionable to put a huge emphasis on voir dire. Voir dire is the jury selection process. The thought is that if you can pick a jury that already agrees with your position, you don't need to be as persuasive. Voir dire has its place in weeding out extremes. If your client, for example, is black, you of course need to get rid of a hard core white racist. But basically you get the jury you got based on coincidence and demographics. That there is such an emphasis on voir dire is probably due to a lack of understanding of the basis upon which conviction, belief, and acceptance are created and thereby a feeling of being out of control and powerless, when it comes to moving a jury.

If the attorneys in the Simpson case had been on a more-or-less equal level in their rhetorical understanding and abilities, the inherent strength of "truth" would have been able to turn the outcome of the agumentation in a direction many would have considered closer to the truth. We can allege that Cochran knew that his client was guilty and that he therefore had to put more energy into defending him than if he simply had to tell the truth as he saw it. More energy is used to say something you do not mean, than simply to say how things are as you perceive them. This is one of the reasons why it is possible to use lie detectors.

In a rhetorical sense, truth must be found in a smaller or larger area within which we can accept an interpretation of events as being true. Therefore, one can talk of a truth concept within rhetoric in relationship to a certain amount of relativity.

Even though rhetoric may be a factor in manipulation, we can say that in time, rhetoric will move towards a truer perception of our surroundings. "Truth" has an inherent strength, and therefore, over time, rhetoric will tend towards truth, unless the untruthful arguments are continuously provided new energy from the outside. Rhetoric is an encounter between complete relativism and dogmatism.

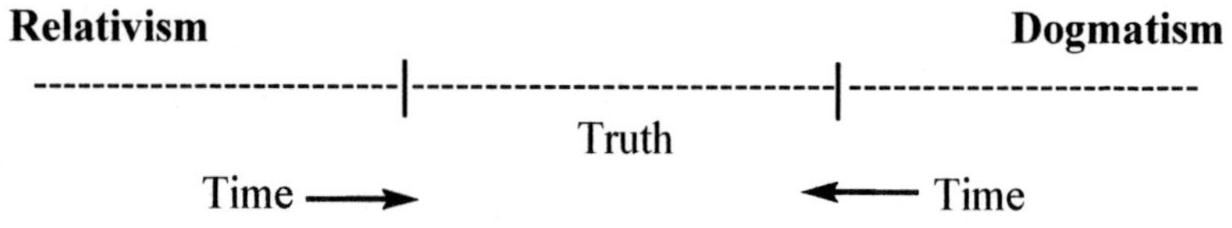

The prosecution's unambiguous acceptance of the logical, mathematical paradigm as the yardstick of correct and effective argumentation prevented them from understanding what the new rhetorical situation called for. They were not able to accept nor fully comprehend the new rhetorical situation.

After the trial, the prosecutors lost their confidence in the legal system made apparent when Christopher Darden and Marcia Clark left their positions as public prosecutors. We see how law does not work without rhetoric. It takes a minimum of rhetorical insight on the part of the prosecutor, as well as on the part of the defense lawyer, to do justice to the inherent strength of truth in the Aristotelian sense. The closest we can get to the truth is to make sure that both parties have a certain amount of rhetorical knowledge that will result in a reduced number of these extreme decisions that many feel lie too far from what they can call the truth.

The answer to the problem is not to keep people ignorant of rhetorical means. In other words, it is not the defense lawyers that had too much rhetorical insight, but rather the prosecutors that had too little. The answer is not to try and hide rhetoric, for the only thing achieved by so doing is an increase in the opportunities for deceiving ordinary people. On the contrary, rhetoric must unfold and flourish by ensuring that people, such as lawyers, have a certain knowledge of rhetoric to open up the possibilities of getting as close as possible to the truth.

3. COMPOSITION OF THE JURY

...in public speaking it is less worth while to talk of what is outside the subject, and that deliberative oratory lends itself to trickery less than forensic, because it is of more general interest. For in the assembly the judges decide upon their own affairs, so that the only thing necessary is to prove the truth of the statement of one who recommends a measure, but in the law courts this is not sufficient; there it is useful to win over the hearers, for the decision concerns other interests than those of the judges, who, having only themselves to consider and listening merely for their own pleasure, surrender to the pleaders but do not give a real decision. That is why, as I have said before, in many places the law prohibits speaking outside the subject in the law courts, whereas in the assembly the judges themselves take adequate precautions against this.

Aristotle

What is interesting about the Simpson case is that the arguments were directed towards a jury of so-called "ordinary" people that were randomly chosen from a specific geographic area. It says in the American Constitution that a trial by a jury of one's peers is each individual's right. Jurors are usually chosen at random among the registered voters. A result is that a person convicted of a felony, i.e., sentenced to more than one year's prison, cannot become a juror for he loses his right to vote as a consequence of the imprisonment.

In the Simpson case the jury consisted of ten black and two white Americans. They were a reflection of the demographic composition in a specific area. We are dealing with laymen without any particular knowledge of the legal system. In his or her reasoning the lawyer has to appeal to some universally accepted beliefs (topoi), that can become the basis of the argumentation, and certain accepted ways of reasoning. This opens up the possibility of a more direct use of the rhetorical argumentation theory. If we had been dealing with experts, people holding a specific knowledge of the law, it would have been necessary to take into account their legal background in relationship to the type of legal discourse they were used to hearing.

Topoi are the places where one finds grounds for one's reasoning. Within any aspect of life, there are some common accepted themes, *topoi*, upon which one can build one's argumentation. As an example: the way we often use events that have taken place in the past to support our argumentation.

There are three general topoi through which we can view a present question, if we want to use history in our argumentation:

1) **We should learn from the mistakes made in the past.**
2) **History repeats itself.**
3) **It is a step in a long development.**

In a sense, these themes in themselves lend foundation to our argumentation, if they are generally accepted among one's audience. What topos you choose of course depends on what your aim is. A topos is used as the ground foundation, the common shared belief, from where we build our arguments further to support our main claim.

Examples of topoi that are pretty common for most cultures is "age and wisdom" or "youth and madness." If we were defending a young person, we could use the topos "youth and madness". We could then say that we all do stupid things when we are young and that we should give someone a break so he has a chance to grow up to become a reasonable person, and so on. We could then use the topos "age and wisdom," and say, that he would probably not have done such a stupid thing if he had been a little older. And that the ones to blame were the people that had helped him, since they were twice his age, and they should have known better.

Another topos could, for example, be "the decline of the youth." This has been mourned since before Christ. It comes around at certain intervals in public discussions: young people today can't read or write, and so on.

In theory, the fact that jurors are chosen at random is suppose to mean that they constitute a representative segment of the population in exactly that area where the case is heard. But, as we are "only" dealing with twelve people, the groups of people we are dealing with are statistically quite varied. Both the defense and the prosecution have the possibility of rejecting possible jurors if it turns out that they hold certain preconceived opinions, are prejudiced or are in some other way connected to the case itself which may have a preferential influence on their verdict. In addition, the lawyers may refuse a certain number of jurors without grounds.

On this selection basis, the jurors need not be persons with a special interest in the overall social structure or people whose opinions as such are otherwise paid attention to publicly or privately. The legal discourse is conducted at a much more fundamental, universally accepted level, where absorption in the legal and factual details is not necessarily advantageous to the one seeking acceptance for his argument. The factual and legal details are not of great importance to the ordinary citizen compared to the essentials or the broad perspective of the case. This has not necessarily anything to do with the jurors' weak mental abilities, but with the way in which we reason and find our bearings in everyday life. Most of the decisions we have to make in our everyday life cannot be based on scientific and mathematically correct conclusions. It has to be based on intuition, probability, and experiences.

That jurors are a broad variety of people, and not judges or other kinds of legal experts, means that the outcome of a case tends to tilt in favor of the actual case, compared to the legislative basis. In everyday life, we as individuals, to a larger extent, base our decisions on actual events rather than on a dogmatic idealistic basis. This means that we are more inclined to change the law based on want has happened to a single individual. As an example we can take Megan's law, where a convicted sex criminal moved into a new neighborhood and killed a little girl. This resulted in a new law, stating that they have to register with the local police. This means that you can now look up people and see if they have ever been convicted of a sex crime.

The reason why the ancient Greek and Roman rhetorician theory is so appropriate to use in the contemporary American court room, is that it deals with basically the same kind of audience.

In ancient Greece, a jury picked at random among the citizens of the community also decided legal matters. Even though only the free male citizens were allowed to vote and serve as jurors, you still have to apply the same rhetorician means, in order to win acceptance for your cause. This is because in both cases we are dealing with ordinary people that make decisions based on the way they reason in their everyday life, not based upon legal training, codes, and ethics. They have a personal interest in the community in general, and are therefor mostly interested in how the case affects them personally. At the same time, the jurors are not directly involved themselves and therefore can be seen as granting the involved party a favor. I will explain this further in chapter 9, "Identification and Persuasion."

We view the world through ourselves, and it is therefore of extreme importance to know our audience. If we want to get through with our message, there is not, like in math, one right answer or one correct way to do it. The optimal rhetorical response depends upon the audience. This is seen in the way that different segments of the population have responded to the O.J. Simpson verdict.

In general, black men and women claimed that the judicial system is biased against blacks and is too often used as an instrument of oppression. They therefore heralded the verdict as the first step in a grassroots reform to right a racially biased institution. White women complained that the defense counsel unfairly played the race card to trump the prosecutor's domestic violence card. White men complained that the entire judicial system was broken.[3]

There is no doubt that the makeup of the jury played a decisive part in determining what kind of argumentation was going to be the most successful. This is why it is not a good idea to slavishly employ universal, logical, deductive reasoning as the only "true" form of reasoning.

The example of how the mayor of Washington, DC. fired one of his aides for using the word "niggardly" shows how important it is to tailor your argumentation and speech towards your audience, and not base it on universal standards. The word "niggardly" means to be petty and grudginge in spending or giving. The word was used by the mayor' aide when he talked to his staff about cutbacks in the budget. The word was used by him to describe the way he was going to act when dealing with the upcoming budget. One of the employees misunderstood the use of the word and saw it as a derogatory racial statement.

We see the importance of not using words that the receivers don't understand, that offends them, bores or confuses them. It must be viewed as fatal if the effect one seeks is not achieved, is prevented, or if one's statement creates greater harm in another direction. In this case, the man not only didn't get his message through, he ended up getting fired.

Jury Selection

The philosophy and controversy behind either picking jurors at random from the local community or picking the jurors selectively is stated very clear in theses two sayings:

A) In almost any kind of a job situation, we seek people with certain credentials. But when we want to determine something really serious, such as a man's liberty, life or death, we are satisfied with just collecting twelve of the people that happen to be standing around.

B) State a moral case to a plowman and a professor. The former will decide it as well, and often better than the latter, because he has not been led astray by artful rules.[4]

These two views concerning the jury system, jury trial vs. trial to the court, appointed jurors vs. juries selected from the voting pool, is built on different virtues:

A) Intelligence

B) Common sense

What constitutes wisdom is up to the individual. Often wisdom is viewed as a mixture of these two concepts.

This is why it is so important for lawyers to build their argumentation on common sense, and not solely on logic, since common sense is the virtue the American jury system is built upon.

Or as a juror in the Simpson case stated: "One of the first things you realize when you're listening to all this testimony is that you have to keep using your common sense."[5] "If I've said it once, I've said it ten times: Don't leave your common sense outside the door. Bring in your gut feeling. Somehow I think Marcia felt we hadn't, and I think that was her downfall. If she would have trusted us and kept her common sense, I think maybe it would have gone a different way."[6]

Knowing the importance of appealing to common sense, Cochran stated to the jury: "Something is wrong with the prosecution's case, and your common sense is never going to let you fall for it."

One of the things that leads us in common sense decisions is what analogy we can make. Often the winning party is the one that can come out with the most believable analogy supporting their point of view. A good example of this is a case in Sweden where a man was injured in a car accident, and sought compensation for future lost wages. Shortly after the accident he got an ulcer that prohibited him from working. The question was if he still was entitled to compensation for the initial accident. The case went all the way to the Swedish Supreme Court. The first two times the case was tried in the lower courts, he was found entitled to compensation, but the Supreme Court said that he wasn't. It turned out that the case had finally been determined by which analogy the Supreme Court had found most compatible. If the ulcer could be seen as a new injury, this should not have any effect upon his ability to collect compensation for the auto accident. If, on the other hand, the ulcer could be seen as equal to a slowly progressing normal event such as getting pensioned, then the other driver could not be held responsible for this taking place. The Supreme Court favored the last analogy, that the ulcer was equal to the slowly progressing aging process, and rendered a verdict against the plaintiff.

The outcome of the different cases rests upon the lawyer's ability to select and present a convincing analogy. In this case it could be argued that the accident was a contributing factor in producing the ulcer, that he could have had many years of active work, if the accident hadn't contributed in the outbreak of the ulcer. In other words, just because you have provoked two injuries, you can't use one to make the other go away. Your analogy could then be that, because somebody suffers from osteoporosis doesn't mean that barring an accident they would break their leg.

DEMANDS AND CONSTRAINTS

Our understanding of our surroundings is, to a greater or lesser extent, based on our own perceptions. Where our immediate sympathies lie is often linked to the way we perceive ourselves. In the Simpson case the sympathy of the jurors was connected to which type of injustice the jurors were most likely to consider might happen to them; in other words, a manifestation of what we fear. What demands and constraints this imposes on the prosecution and the defense are therefore connected to whether the individual juror sees himself as a potential victim of violence, or whether he finds it more likely that he will become the victim of a miscarriage of justice.

As the majority of the jurors were black, we must examine this question by looking at how ethnic and racial minorities view their legal rights in general. On this subject statistical data exist showing that members of ethnic minorities in the U.S. do not believe that they receive a fair treatment within the American legal system. This is documented from this research made in the state of California:

> After six years of gathering and analyzing data, the California Judicial Council Advisory Committee on Racial and Ethnic Bias in the Courts has concluded that racial and ethnic minorities in California are convinced they do not get a fair shake in the courts... Some members of the public believe that there is no sharp delineation between the

> authority of the police, the prosecutor, the public defender, and the judge.[7]

As is seen, part of these minority groups do not find that there is a sharp distinction between the executive and judicial branches. They lump together the police, the public prosecutor, the public defender, and the judiciary. This can only be viewed as disastrous mistrust of the legal system. It also helps explain how Cochran won support for his conspiracy theory and how he succeeded in mixing the image and credibility of the police, the prosecution, and the judges. In addition, Cochran vaguely hinted that Judge Ito took part in "the great conspiracy." In other words, that he somehow participated in trying to frame O.J. Simpson for the double murders of Nicole Brown and Ron Goldman.

It would be interesting to know whether these minority groups feel that they are more or less likely to become victims of violence or other kinds of crime than the rest of the American population. A look at the statistics shows that there is a high probability that the black jurors would know somebody close to them that had been in conflict with the law, as nearly one in three black men in their twenties in America are behind bars or elsewhere in the justice system.[8] This in itself could make one skeptical about the justice system.

This comment clearly shows how and why many blacks differ from many whites in their view of the police:

> How and why do blacks differ from whites in the perception of criminal justice? All Americans are rightly concerned about crime, and support the distinct possibility that the police suspect brought to trial is in fact the guilty culprit. But black America has special concerns about human error and prejudice in law enforcement and police investigation in part because blacks are disproportionately subjected to criminal justice. Blacks, therefore, are more likely to suffer the oppression from the distinct and inevitable possibility of erroneous or rogue police investigations. As comedian Richard Pryor used to say: When blacks go to criminal court expecting "justice" we notice it's "just us." Both the historical

> as well as the current political aspects of criminal justice in America give black Americana a substantial basis to look upon police authority with healthy distrust a distrust of government, incidentally, which libertarians champion as against all exercises of government power. Black distrust of police confrontations is contrary to the cozy assumption of unassailable credibility that white America bestows upon the police force the "thin blue line" that maintains the separation between civility and incivility.[9]

That people hold biased opinions and views does not mean that the legal verdict is preconceived right from the start. It does, however, mean *that their biases are taken into account when the argumentation to the jurors is formulated*. If you sense that the jurors are against your position from the start, it is necessary to get them to identify with you and your client. This means that they realize that they in some way, shape or form might find themselves in this situation. Moreover, it is crucial that the argumentation be able to move people's opinion and not just mobilize the ones that already share your opinion. We can divide argumentation into two categories, the kind that *moves votes*, and the kind that *gathers votes*. When you move votes, you change people's opinion. When you gather votes, you strengthen people's opinion in what they already believe in.

These are some of the characteristics of the vote gathering argumentation.[10] We can in general say that these traits will be most effective when we are addressing people that to a certain degree already agree with our position:

Gathering votes:

- *ideological argumentation, when one uses general and superior arguments in connection with what is being discussed*
- *narrative and visual expressions*
- *sharp, short, and marked expressions*

If we look at the defense team in the Simpson case, we see that Cochran, in the last part of his closing statement, uses mainly vote gathering argumentation. This is because he presumes that he now has a favorable audience.

These are some of the characteristics of the vote moving argumentation. These traits are more appealing to your audience if they don't already share your opinion, and you therefore have to move them from one opinion to another:

Moving votes:

- *concrete, informative argumentation, in other words argumentation that mainly tries to highlight the theme of what is actually being discussed*
- *high amount of information*
- *a few well-chosen key arguments*
- *well-defined, precise claims*
- *moderate, calm, and polite speech and gestures*
- *persistent, prolonged, and dogged use of arguments*

Barry Scheck uses mainly vote moving arguments. This is because he is the one that has to change the jury's opinion about the significance of the evidence.

Generally, when we are addressing a jury, it is no use directing our appeal to those that already have "seen the light." We must make sure that we present good reasons in support of our claim and not express ourselves too aggressively or categorically. We must be sympathetic and understanding about what worries the jurors, and deal with this problem in our reasoning. It is vital to find a common basis of values and beliefs that is shared by the jurors and then build our reasoning on that. It would be a good idea to come through with many examples and comparisons with which the jurors can identify. This can connect their sense of reality and previous experience with the point of view that we are advocating.

If we, on the other hand, believe that the jurors are sympathetic to our case, it might be more beneficial, and have a greater impact, to mobilize and rile up the people that already, to an extent, believe in us. This might, for example, affect the extent of the toughness of the verdict or the amount of money given in compensation. In any case, this adds to the possibilities of which type of argumentation may be used. Of course, it is also possible during the trial to go from trying to change people's opinions to mobilize the ones that agree with your position, if we believe we have "carried the jurors along with us." To a certain extent this it what Cochran and the rest of the defense team did in their defense of Simpson.

Based on the progress of the trial and the verdict itself, we see that the predominantly female jury identified more with the race issue than the gender issue. There are several ways in which we might look at this conflict. The three most obvious groupings are: *black against white, rich against poor, male against female*. I have in this connection chosen to disregard the conflict of rich against poor as this theme was not particularly dominate in the argumentation. On the other hand, the two other opposites were preeminent during the trial where the defense leveled their interpretation of the case as a demonstration of whites against blacks and the prosecution stressed the wife battering and dominance themes, a struggle between the sexes as opposed to a war between blacks and whites.

We can establish that the race aspect proved to have a more fundamental appeal than the gender aspect. There is a hierarchy of needs. We first seek to fulfill our most fundamental needs, such as food, shelter, and sleep. When these needs are fulfilled, we seek security, and so on. In the top of the pyramid we find the need for self-fulfillment.

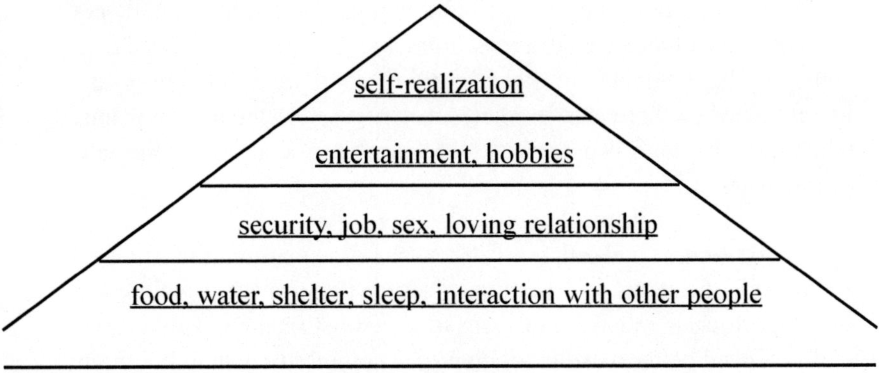

Hierarchy of needs.

In that connection the survival of the race is more basic than achievement of equality between men and women. In his closing speech Cochran, indirectly, predicted the wiping out of the black race by mentioning Hitler, and that nobody took him seriously either. In other words, if the jury members didn't stop Mark Fuhrman and associates now, it might evolve into a personal threat to the jury members. The prosecution did not draw any similar analogies showing that women in general have a reason to feel that their existence is threatened by Nicole being murdered.

During the appointment hearings for Supreme Court Justice Clarence Thomas, a black woman and former associate of Clarence Thomas, Anita Hill, was called to testify concerning allegations of sexual harassment perpetrated by Clarence Thomas against her. The black population, in general, disregarded the allegations and supported him, as it was most important for them to get a black man appointed in this position. Black women are still in the process of securing the race. Therefore, they don't have the resources to focus on the gender issue.

A polarized picture of the world has the strongest impact on us when we actually feel that "the others" control our fate, as when minority groups feel they do not get fair treatment within the legal system.

There are times when we are more inclined to magnify the differences between those we define as "ourselves" and those we define as "other." The tendency to favor the in group over the out-group increases, when there is an explicit similarity within the in-group, and when the out-group is perceived to be capable of controlling the fate of the in-group.

In addition, it is worth considering that those arguing in favor of a change in the status quo are up against the persuasive "principle" of *inertia,* which is our built-in resistance against change. This means that you need better reasons for changing something than to maintain things as they are. In this case you may consider Simpson's innocence and freedom as the status quo, whereas a conviction of Simpson is a change in his status and thereby of the status quo. This contributes to the fact that the arguments in favor of convicting an accused must be weightier than those to acquit him.

The reason why we have a built-in resistance against change is that we take a risk when we decide to change the way things are. That is why we demand better reasons to change things than to maintain them the way they are.

It is important to note that the fear of being framed by the police is not taken out of thin air. There have been cases where people have been convicted of a crime and it later was discovered that they had been framed by the police and public authorities. This is presumed to be the case in Illinois, where the prosecutors have been charged with falsifying evidence in a murder trial. An innocent man sat on death row for eleven years, before the real killer was linked to the murder by the use of DNA tests. In this case the police thought that they had the right man, and therefore presumably thought that it was okay to falsify the evidence.[11] It should here be mentioned that it was a very emotional case, a little girl had been murdered by a stranger. He had broke into her home in the middle of the day, while she was home alone, and the man convicted for the crime had sent a ransom note.

In this connection it is also important to keep in mind the latest scandal from Los Angeles, where a whole division of the police department in one of the poorest districts in the city was accused of severe police misconduct, reaching all the way from planting drugs and guns on suspects, to shooting unarmed handcuffed citizens.[12]

This knowledge should be put on top of the feeling that many blacks have of not being treated equally. If we look at traffic violations there is a saying, "Driving while black." This term has come about because police have ticketed blacks and other minority groups more frequently for traffic violations than whites, even though there is no statistical difference in the way blacks and whites drive.[13]

Several police officers claim that this is not an expression of a racist or evil intent. They claim that it is an unfortunate byproduct of sane police work, since certain crimes are more frequent among some minority groups. Police reason that since minority groups commit a disproportionate share of certain crimes, it makes sense to stop a disproportionate share of them.

An alleged traffic violation can be just an excuse to look for other things, such as drugs.

This criminalization of certain minority groups is offensive, annoying, and at times frightening to law-abiding citizens of these minority groups. The fear can be seen in the way some black parents advise their teenaged sons to act when they are stopped by the police, compared with the type of advise given by white parents to their children. Many white parents will advise their children to be cordial and not to aggravate the police officers when they are stopped for a traffic violation to minimize or avoid a ticket. The advice many black parents give to their children is how to survive being stopped by the police, then how to avoid a ticket. One black women said to her son, "Being black and being male, you've got two strikes against you. Keep your hands on the steering wheel, [and] make sure you get out of that situation alive"[14]

This fear of being shot is a result of the police officers' fears and prejudgments of the driver which can make police officers more likely to overreact in certain situations.

The selective targeting of minority groups is a self-fulfilling prophecy that helps maintain certain stereotypes. Where you look, you will also find. If we, for instance, took white male lawyers and stopped them more frequently than other citizens, their statistic of traffic violations would go up compared to the rest of the country. If you concentrate your efforts in one place, you won't look at other places.

If we take these facts and means of selective police work into account, it is not strange or unlikely for the black population to believe that O.J. was being targeted or framed because he was black. If upstanding citizens are treated like criminals by the police, they will not trust those same officers as investigators of crimes or as witnesses in court.

Our experiences shape our opinions, as the following quote shows:

> Even growing up in Charleston, as an "All-American boy," far from the large urban battlefields, my opinions have been shaped by my own experiences of being treated differ-

> ently by the police from the way my non-black friends were treated. I was often stopped by the police here in Charleston, for no apparent reason other than because I was a black kid in the car with other black kids.
>
> I was stopped at gunpoint by a police officer beneath the window of my mother's office as I strolled within the Capitol Complex on afternoon break from my summer job, handling tens of thousands of dollars daily, selling license plates for the Department of Motor Vehicles during the peak month of July. The policeman had stopped me - 6 feet, 3 inches, clothed in business attire - because a 5-foot, 8-inch black man had robbed the Rite Aid down the street of $63.21.
>
> We don't have to go far to see the danger of a prosecution team zealously rushing in behind a corrupt and lazy police investigation.[15]

It seems that a majority of whites now also believe that blacks are being targeted more frequently by the police than whites, and that they are not getting a fair treatment.[16] This type of racial discrimination is bad for the sense of justice, not only amongst minority groups, but the general population's sense of justice. If everybody is suppose to be equal under the law, and there is a general sense among the population that certain groups are being targeted more frequently by the police because of their race, it undermines the general belief in the police and the justice system.

This is a problem for all Americans that base their belief in the American society and the justice system. It also complicates aspects when you go to court. This is because there now is a new topic in society that says: In general not everybody is treated equal by the police and authorities. Or as a twenty-one year old university senior stated, "I'm overjoyed and I'm surprised. I didn't think we, as black males, could achieve justice in the system."[17] This is a new topos, which you can base your argumentation on. It not only enhances the amount of topics in a case, it can also undermine many of the other arguments traditionally presented in a court case.

We see these views expressed by one of the male jurors in the Simpson case, while talking to Judge Ito in his chambers. He said he had been enraged one time when a female deputy had told him to get off the patio of the hotel when she allowed several white jurors to remain. As a result, he said:

> "I'm to the point where I don't really trust anybody involved here. I mean, no disrespect to you, Your Honor, I don't even trust you, sir. I mean, I don't trust anybody." The experience with the deputy, Cryer said, reminded him of some other things. "Tell me about that," Ito prompted. "About police and, well, I, you know, I have no problems with police officers myself, but it kind of reminds me of why so many black men in America have such a problem with being confronted with white police officers in situations like when they are operating their cars, and they become very defensive about it, and just kind of made me realize that those situations do exist, and you don't really have to be doing anything for them to take it upon themselves to be harassing toward you."[18]

This comment illustrates in a nutshell how the jury ended up perceiving the case, and what key points the defense stressed to create a coherent version of the events that had taken place in the case:

> The prosecution's evidence consisted of old police reports, which chronicled some instances of domestic violence during the marriage. In addition, the Los Angeles Police Department produced blood and fibers, found at the crime scene, that matched those of O.J. Simpson, and blood and fiber evidence from the victims found at O.J. Simpson's home. The defense countered that the Los Angeles Police Department personnel assigned to this case were driven by a volatile mix of racial hatred, greed, and fear of repeated failure in high profile cases, and therefore they directed their attention exclusively to O.J. Simpson and bolstered the considerable circumstantial evidence by cross-pollinating blood and fiber evidence in trekking back and forth between O.J. Simpson's house and the crime scene. Once O.J. Simpson became the police suspect, the defense further

argued an institutional code of silence and shoddy professionalism swelled up to reinforce the frame-up.[19]

We see here that a coherent view of the police's motivation for framing O.J. Simpson has been created. This is backed by logical argumentation concerning the possibility of cross-pollinating the police's evidence. Supposedly the same police officers that show up at the crime scene were the ones that went directly over to Simpson's house to inform him of the murders and notify him that his two small children were at the police station. Since nobody answered the doorbell, they entered Simpson's estate. The police claimed that they were concerned for Simpson's safety, since they spotted blood drops inside Simpson's car parked outside his home. They claimed that they were concerned that whoever killed Nicole, could be going after him.

Since they had not secured a warrant to enter Simpson's house, the police could not claim that they were investigating Simpson.

The defense claimed it showed two things:

1) That no one other than Simpson was ever considered as a possible suspect
2) That the evidence had been planted

What claim the defense stressed depended on which theme they were putting forward in their argumentation. The defense basically went back and forth between the police had framed Simpson and the police had been incompetent. It was easier to prove sloppy police work than a frame up, therefore the incompetence could be applied were it was not possible to use the frame up theme.

There is no doubt that the police officers' decision to go straight from the crime scene to a former relative and possible suspect's house and enter his property without permission was not police work done according to the book. This gives a nice foundation for the defense's incompetence theory.

This foundation can then be used to support further allegations of incompetence against the police, as was the case with the police forensic laboratory. This comment showed how this could lead to the overall disbelief in the evidence:

> The jury's quick vote for acquittal signaled that the prosecution's claim of a mountain of evidence actually amounted to a molehill in the eyes of the jurors. In the collective minds of the jurors, the defense proved the existence of reasonable doubt by demonstrating two major faults with the prosecution's case. First, the most active homicide detective on the case, Mark Fuhrman, was a racist and the chief detective, Phillip Vannatter, was a liar. Second, the defense also conclusively demonstrated that Dennis Fung, the lead criminalist, and Andrea Mazolla, his entry-level assistant, exercised shoddy evidence collection techniques. The existence of blind cover-ups and shading of evidence was plainly evident. [20]

Or as one of the jurors stated:

> I think it might have been reasonable to suspect Mr. Simpson, based on the past history he had, but they weren't straight with us about why they chose to do what they did, and that made us suspect everything else we heard from them. That's the thing with Vannatter when he was saying O.J. was not the prime suspect. Why would he even get up there with that lie? Why didn't he just tell the truth?[21]

As the majority of the jurors in the Simpson case were black, the defense's argumentation was tailored towards them. This fine-tuning towards the main audience is seen in the result of the first vote that the jurors conducted in the deliberation room. It came out ten to two in favor of Simpson's innocence. This is equal to the number of blacks and whites on the jury. We know that the one guilty vote came from the one white woman on the jury. That the blacks on the jury voted not guilty is not due to a racist attitude amongst the black jury members. It is due to the defense's argumentation which was tailored towards them.

That the defense teams argumentation in general seemed feasible to the entire jury can be seen by the fact that the two remaining jurors were convinced within a very short time.

4. ARGUMENTATION MODEL AND MAIN ALLEGATIONS

Rhetoric then may be defined as the faculty of discovering the possible means of persuasion in reference to any subject whatever.
Aristotle

In principle, we can distinguish between two types of reasoning, reasoning in defense and reasoning in offense. The borderline between defensive and offensive reasoning is in practice rather vague. The parties in a case often change their positions more-or-less imperceptibly and it is a well-known fact that being on the offense may be the best defense. In this connection we may say that Marcia Clark's main reasoning was predominantly an attack, which the role as prosecutor calls for. Later we will look at how Johnnie Cochran succeeded in turning the tables and placing the prosecutor in a predominantly defensive position.

If we look at the build-up of an argumentation model,[22] we can see why it is so important to base your claim on a shared conviction. You back your claim with your reasoning, but underneath it lie opinions and value norms that your audience has to share with you in order to accept your reasoning and ultimately your claim. This is called your warrant. If our audience doesn't share the warrant with us, our argumentation has no foundation.

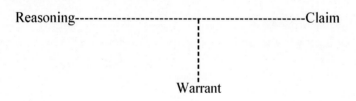

Reasoning---Claim

Warrant

Often the warrant is not mentioned in the discourse, as it is presumed to be too basic or obvious. It is often basic beliefs that you presume that you have in common, such as that you should not kill another human being, or that you should not steal. The argument could then sound like this:

Claim: You should not take that bag.
Reasoning: It belongs to somebody else.

Sometimes one can mention the warrant and leave the reasoning unsaid. This could be:

Claim: You should not take that bag.
Warrant: It is not right to steal other people's things.

The difference between warrant and reasoning is that the warrant is more basic than the reasoning. This means that what was the warrant in one argument can easily become the reasoning in another argument. This is often the case if you build your argumentation up one argument resting upon another. In this example it could be:

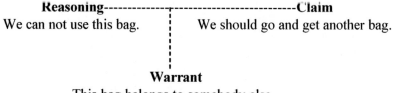

Reasoning------------------------------------**Claim**
We can not use this bag. | We should go and get another bag.

Warrant
This bag belongs to somebody else

Reasoning------------------------------------**Claim**
This bag belongs to somebody else. | We should not take that bag.

Warrant

It is not right to take other people's things.

This is called an argumentation hierarchy, where one argument rests upon another. One can also talk about argumentation rows. Here different arguments that are not connected are put forth in support of an issue, such as when one states all the reasons why something is a good idea.

In order for a claim to be an argument, either the reasoning or the warrant needs to be mentioned, otherwise it is only an assertion. Even though parts of the argument are left unsaid, all arguments at a minimum contain a claim, a reasoning, and a warrant as shown in the argumentation model. This is the minimum that an argumentation has to contain. If we look at an expanded version of the argumentation model, it would also contain a stressor, a refutation, and a backup. It looks like this:

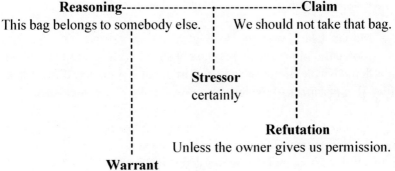

Reasoning — **Claim**

This bag belongs to somebody else. — We should not take that bag.

Stressor

certainly

Refutation

Unless the owner gives us permission.

Warrant

It is not right to take other people's things.

Back up

You should not do to others what you don't want them to do to you.

The stressor is a statement or a word that either weakens or strengthens the claim. In our example it could be the word certainly. The statement would then be: You should certainly not take that bag. The stressor is used to refine one's statement, and make it sound less categorical. It is within the stressor that you can see the strength of the warrant. *You find the stressor by asking how sure you are of your claim.*

The refutation is used to refute your claim. This is used to take your precautions in case something unexpected or unlikely should happen. In our example it could be: Unless the owner gives you permission. The refutation modifies your statement, and opens it up for other solutions or end results. It predicts certain objections/counterarguments that your receiver may have. *You find refutation by asking in what cases your claim would not hold true.*

The back-up strengthens your warrant by coming with the concrete reasons for the general rule of the warrant. This is something you would do if your warrant is not generally accepted. In our example it could have been: You should not do to others what you don't want them to do to you. *You find your back-up by asking what is the foundation for the general rule of the warrant.*

Marcia Clark was the lead prosecuting attorney in the O.J. Simpson case. In her closing argument she alleged that O.J. Simpson murdered Nicole Simpson and Ron Goldman. To support this she had fifty-five instances of evidence or, as she put it "55 coincidences."

Marcia Clark stated in her closing argument, "I like the 'just because' argument. The defense tells you that just because he cut himself doesn't mean he's the murderer. Just because he left a trial of blood at Rockingham doesn't mean he's guilty. Just because he was behaving strangely at the recital the night of the murder doesn't mean he's guilty." And she continued with a list of each of the fifty-five "coincidences."[23] Of these fifty-five instances she had eight which she considered to be the principal ones.

If we place Marcia Clark's main allegation in the argumentation model, it looks as follows:

Claim: O.J. Simpson murdered Ron Goldman and Nicole Simpson.

Reasoning:

1) A pair of socks was found in O.J. Simpson's home with remnants of blood from the two bodies.

2) A leather glove with remnants of Ron and Nicole's blood was found outside Simpson's house.

3) A knit cap was found at the scene of the murder with hair remnants matching O.J. Simpson's and fibers identical to the carpet in O.J. Simpson's car were found.

4) Blood from Nicole Simpson and Ron Goldman was found in O.J.'s car.

5) Blood from Ron and Nicole was found in and outside O.J. Simpson's home.

6) The murderer left his footprint in the victims' blood and on the ground outside the house. The shoe size is that of O.J. Simpson, a shoe size that only fits approx. 10 percent of the American male population; in addition, the shoe prints were made with Bruno Magli shoes, a rare and expensive fashionable shoe brand.

7) O.J. Simpson's blood was found at and around the scene of the murder.

8) Remnants of hair matching that of O.J. Simpson were found on Ron Goldman's shirt.

Warrant: So much circumstantial evidence cannot be accidental. It is therefore proven beyond reasonable doubt that O.J. Simpson is the murderer.

Here Marcia Clark made the mistake of assuming that this basic conviction, *warrant*, is shared by the audience. Had she put more emphasis on backing her warrant, the probability of finding a common ground of consent between her point of view, as a district attorney, and the individual juror's would have been greater. To back-up your warrant means to support or strengthen the foundation of your argumentation, which in this case is that so much circumstantial evidence cannot be accidental.

By backing up her warrant Marcia Clark could have prevented, or made more difficult, Cochran's attempt to destroy the basis of the prosecution's reasoning. To support and back up their reasoning it would be obvious to claim that to falsify all this evidence is impossible, and that, if at all possible, it would have called for a conspiracy in which more than a dozen different people would have to be involved. All this to convict a man to whom the police for years had turned a blind eye, when it came to battering his wife. The prosecution did put forward the improbability of a conspiracy but it was lost in the other evidence. This should have been brought forward clearly and distinctly during the trial. There had been plenty of opportunities for strengthening and supporting their point of view, if the prosecution had realized the possibilities of backing up their underlining convictions, *warrant*.

There may be several reasons why they did not do this. However, it was primarily due to the lack of symmetry in the balance of strength between the prosecutor and the defense. This is due to an unsymmetrical balance of strength between the two parties when it came to argumentative skills. It is the difference between a defense team consisting of a group of highly paid skilled rhetoricians, against the prosecution consisting of a group of lawyers with no apparent knowledge or training of argumentation theory.

It may also be due to the fact that the prosecution was not able to put itself in the place of its audience.

The ability to reason is linked to the ability to think in opposite directions.

This is one of the reasons why it is important to be able to question critically one's own position and reasoning no matter how enthusiastic one is about the matter.

It may be what happened in this case. Marcia Clark may simply have been carried away by her feelings and thereby lost the ability to see the case from other positions. It seems that Johnnie Cochran, to a larger extent, controlled his feelings and thereby to a larger extent was able to use the different forms of appeal towards the jury.

If Clark had backed her warrant it would also have provided her with a strong base against Johnnie Cochran's attack on the morals and image, *ethos*, of the police and thereby indirectly the validity of her warrant.

Conviction is built upon three things:

1) The speaker's credibility.
2) The content of what is said.
3) The audience's state of mind.

This is why we have three different forms of appeal: *ethos*, *logos*, and *pathos*, where ethos is our belief in the speaker, logos is the logical appeal connected to the issue itself, and pathos is the emotional appeal to the audience.

You need logos to build the foundation for your argumentation. You need ethos to make what you say and your person credible. You need pathos, the emotional response, to fuel the interest and action of your recipients.

<u>**Logos**</u>

Logos is the appeal to rational reasoning. When one tries to obtain support on the basis of logos, one sticks to the issue and concentrates one's efforts on the factual and matter-of-fact parts of one's case. The argumentation seems logical, since the issue is mainly kept on the facts in the case and strives to be objective.

Logos is characterized linguistically by a neutral wording and a bland style. The form and delivery is subdued and contained. A pure logical appeal shows its strength in a clear and strict thought pattern, and its weaknesses by being overly detailed and boring.

Ethos

When you apply through ethos you apply through personal traits. This can either be favorable traits of your own, or negative traits of your opponent that are to one's advantage. When one uses the ethos appeal to try to obtain support, one bases this support from the audience on the trust they have in you as a person. The importance of ethos is seen from the fact that if you don't believe in the man, you don't believe in his message either.

Because ethos has to do with the orator's total personality, the emotional appeal is not tied to the particular situation. The feelings that ethos appeals to in the audience can exist before, in the present, or after the event. An orator that already has a good reputation among his audience has an easier time getting support than the one that the audience doesn't know. He has good will that he brings from one case to another. When orators are unknown to the audience, they can, by the way they carry themselves, or by recommendations create a believable image of themselves, and thereby use the ethos appeal. The cornerstone within the concept of ethos is that the impression the receiver gets of the orator has to have validity outside the specific situation.

The important difference between the word *image* and *ethos* is that image is often connected to a business approach where, due to a nice surface, one sells a person or a company as merchandise that looks appealing. Ethos also has to do with appearance, but the cornerstone of what ethos stands for is a person's character and integrity. Ethos has more to do with the *inner* than the *outer* qualities of a person.

Just like one can take about a bad image, one can talk about a person's ethos as being good or bad, high or low. Ethos plays a big roll in practical argumentation. If a person's ethos has been damaged, it is very difficult to get support for one's position.

This comment is a good example of how a very emotional speech, if it has no ethos foundation, easily gets viewed as fake or hysterical. If a person doesn't seem very credible, an abundant display of emotions may easily seem fake:

> Having argued successfully to suppress evidence of all but the smallest hint of Mark Fuhrman's character, Marcia Clark demonstrated nothing less than unmitigated gall when she remarked in closing argument, like Captain Renault in the classic, Casablanca, that she was "shocked, shocked to learn" that her key witness had admitted to casual observers that he could not stand blacks, especially those involved in interracial relationships, that he would fabricate reasons to setup and harass blacks, and, most significantly, that cops needed to lie and plant evidence to meet trial evidentiary standards.[24]

It is easy to see how many black Americans could view Marcia Clark's remarks as something out of *Gone with the Wind.* If you are very emotional but don't have a firm ethos foundation, you seem fake, as if you are acting. This is also why many white Americans, on the other hand, thought it was a good speech. We can here see how the same speech can be viewed entirely differently, depending upon how much credibility one has with the audience.

Pathos

When one tries to gain support by the help of pathos, one involves the audience and bases the argumentation on their feelings and emotions in the particular situation. One can try to appeal to the anger, happiness, pity, or excitement of one's audience. The importance of pathos is best illustrated by the fact that everything we do has an emotional reason. It is, you could say, the fuel our engine is running on. Even in the driest study, there is an emotional reason for us doing it.

Contrary to ethos, which deals with the more long-term emotions, pathos deals with the more spontaneous feelings that occur at the spur of the moment. Pathos is therefore, out of the three forms of appeal, the one that is most connected to the specific situation. This means that pathos is closely connected to the time and place where the specific situation takes place, and may not easily be understood when it is taken out of its context. The result of pathos can sometimes even be heard in applause and expressions of disapproval, such as booing, whistling, laughter, stomping, and so on. Because it is so tightly connected to the specific situation, pathos, of the three forms of appeal, is the hardest to contain in a written format. Different speeches that have functioned well in specific situations by stressing the pathos appeal often seem hollow in later review.

If you don't get the pathos appeal, the immediate emotional appeal, in your argumentation, the jurors will lack interest in your case. They will not have any fuel to go either one way or another. This means that they will keep the status quo because it takes better reasons for people to change something than to maintain things as they are. In other words, they will not award anybody any money or send somebody to jail because this would be a change in the status quo.

Pathos will show itself by an extraordinary style and an often very emotional choice in words. Sometimes one can achieve the strongest pathos effect if one uses understatements instead of emotionally charged words. Using a trembling voice and big arm movements can easily make the audience laugh where they were supposed to cry.

It is often seen as something positive if one uses a logical argumentation. At the same time, the two other forms of appeal are looked upon as less proper forms of argumentation. Within rhetoric this way of evaluating the different forms of appeal is a total misconception. In most cases, one would expect that logos was the dominating form of appeal, but ethos, and in many cases also pathos, has to be present in order for the argumentation to succeed. It would not matter how appropriate the argumentation was viewed from a logos standpoint, if the one arguing doesn't seem trustworthy. On the other hand, one would be willing to believe in what somebody says if this person on other occasions has been trustworthy. Ethos therefore can be used to build logos.

Johnnie Cochran's reasoning is mainly an attack: "The police and public authorities are corrupt and incompetent, therefore you can't trust the police and the prosecution." That is to say, a rejection of the authority of the prosecution. Cochran bases his attack on the police especially on one man, a police officer by the name of Mark Fuhrman. Later he expands this to include the prosecution. Mark Fuhrman participated in the collection of evidence against Simpson. Mark Fuhrman's dishonesty consists in his assertion under oath in front of the jurors that he had not used the insult "nigger" for the past ten years. In addition, the defense makes him testify that those saying that he has racist points of view are liars. This is later refuted when tape recordings of Fuhrman come to light where he uses the word "nigger" several times and in addition makes highly derogatory remarks about blacks. Among other things he was quoted by a witness as saying that he always stops mixed couples where the man is black and the woman white, and if they have done nothing wrong, he makes up something.

If we put Cochran's main allegation into an argumentation model,[25] it looks like this:

Claim:	You can't trust the police or the prosecution.
Reasoning:	Fuhrman is a proven liar (Mark Fuhrman's racist statements on tape).
Warrant:	Those who lie about minor things also lie about major things. Or, if any one person has lied about one thing, you can no longer trust anything of what is said by any of the parties involved.

In his speech Johnnie Cochran repeatedly puts forward another allegation:

Claim:	You can't convict O.J. Simpson of the double murder of Nicole Simpson and Ron Goldman.
Reasoning:	Because not all the evidence seems to be reliable.

Warrant: If some of the evidence does not seem reliable, you cannot accept any of the evidence.

This then leads to Cochran's main allegation:

Claim: You can't convict this man of murder.

Reasoning: Because the evidence is not to be counted on.

Warrant: You cannot convict a man of a crime if you have no certain evidence that he committed the crime.

We can see here that Cochran bases his basic reasoning on the loss of credibility. It is Mark Fuhrman's loss of ethos that is expanded and transformed into the ethos of the police, public prosecutors, and public authorities in general.

The first thing the prosecution should have done was to stop the expansion and transformation of the lost credibility from Fuhrman to the entire public authorities. This could have been done by pointing out only one person was responsible for Fuhrman's thoughts and actions, and that was Fuhrman himself. Not the forty people that happened to work with him. The prosecution could have asked the jury members how they would feel if they were called a thief, because somebody at the place they worked had stolen something. They could be asked if this attitude wasn't as prejudiced as being a racist.

In the O.J. Simpson case, it would have been beneficial for the prosecution to have backed up their warrant by stressing the concrete reasons for their warrant. If you lack the basis for your warrant, you loose your entire argument.

The practical use of the argumentation model is mainly that it can be used to find the strong and weak sides of one's own and one's opponent's argumentation.

By using the argumentation model it becomes much easier to draw out from the text or speech what our opponent is actually saying and what reasoning supports this view. This means that we then know where we should apply our counterarguments, since we can determine our opponent's weakest argumentation. We often dig up something that has been unsaid or implicit. By getting it out in the open a good counterargument is often revealed.

When it comes to our own argumentation, the argumentation model can be used to strengthen and focus our argumentation. By using the model, we can see if what we say either falls under or supports our main argument. If not it is outside our focus and we don't want it in our argumentation since too many different arguments can weaken our main argumentation by taking the attention away from our strongest argumentation.

Another important aspect of a strong and effective argumentation is that one is able to reason in a way that draws a red thread through the entire argumentation that one's audience is able to follow. In other words make sure to explain how the things you say fit in or support your main argument. The argumentation model can here be used to check if what you said is connected to your main argumentation. The biggest mistake lawyers generally make when they address a jury is that they think that the jurors understand the significance of what they are saying in connection with the bigger picture.

We see this as a very prominent difference between the prosecutions and the defense argumentation in the Simpson case. This can be seen in the way the prosecution stacks up the evidence of domestic violence committed by O.J. Simpson against Nicole Brown Simpson, but neglects to connect this to the bigger picture in a way so that the jurors can see the relevance of these events.

Not only is the defense able to connect all of what they are saying to their overall claim, they are also able to utilize this weakness in the prosecution's argumentation and go in and cut the connection totally between the spousal abuse and the murders. Therefore, this issue is no longer relevant for the jurors in their decision.

We have already seen how the defense succeeded in *dismissing the blood and fiber evidence by cutting the ethos foundation* for the prosecution's argumentation. We are now going to look at how the defense succeeded in *dismissing the spousal abuse issue by cutting the logos foundation* for the prosecution's evidence.

If one focuses only on the probative value of battering in the Simpson case, as opposed to the question whether domestic violence is a serious social problem, then data on the prevalence of domestic violence would seem to help the defense, not the prosecution. The more widespread the incidence of domestic violence, the more likely a husband picked at random would have a history of it, and the less probative it would be in marking out O.J. Simpson as more dangerous than other husbands. The defense seemed to realize that much, for it also cited statistics indicating that domestic violence was widespread. Not content with that, however, it added a highly misleading statistical argument. It maintained that battering was a poor predictor of murder because fewer than one-tenth of one percent of batterers kill their spouses, so that using battering to diagnose murder is like saying that marijuana use leads to heroin. The argument was put in its most vivid form in the national media when one of the authors of the defense brief, Alan Dershowitz, appeared on the Today show and called the evidence massively irrelevant:[26]

I've been studying the subject and teaching it for 30 years, and I think we've learned a lot about spousal violence in the last 20 or 30 years that we didn't know before. It's much more widespread than we ever believed. Gloria Allred will tell you that there are more than two million, maybe as many as five million cases of spousal abuse every single year. But there are only about 1,500 cases of spousal murder every year, which means that 99.9 percent of all people who engage in spousal abuse don't then turn to murder. Yesterday, I ran into Stephen J. Gould, the world famous scientist, and he said it's the most fundamental fallacy of social science research to assume that just because killers may have engaged in battery, that it follows that batterers will kill. It's like the old marijuana-heroin fallacy; namely, just because everyone who ended up using heroin started with marijuana, it still isn't true that many people who start with marijuana turn to heroin.

Because the prosecution was not effectively able to counter this skillful use of statistics, the defense succeeded in cutting the connection between the spousal abuse and the murder. This means that the defense didn't necessarily have to deny or diminish the fact that spousal abuse had taken place, because the relevance of it would be gone.

This time it is not the ethos foundation for the prosecution's circumstantial evidence that is gone, but the logos foundation for the spousal abuse issue. The foundation for the prosecution's argumentation is again cut, leaving their two major areas of reasoning groundless.

This argument that the defense put forward, carried to its logical conclusion, would mean that evidence of a love triangle would be "massively irrelevant" in a murder case because only a tiny percentage of lovers ever kill their rivals.

It states the probability that a woman will be murdered by her husband, given that we know he battered her but nothing else. A more useful statistic would be the probability that a woman was murdered by her husband, given that *we know he battered her and that we also know she was murdered.* That probability can be derived by comparing the number of women murdered by battering husbands with the total number of women murdered. Using Dershowitz's statistics and some figures from the *World Almanac*, the statistician I. J. Good came up with a probability of one-third to one-half that a battering husband murdered his wife, given that we have no information other than that he battered her and she was murdered. Of course, the probability would change if additional incriminating or exculpatory evidence came to light.[27]

It is of course difficult to say how effective the prosecution was able to counter this use of statistics regarding the relevance of the spousal abuse. We can only say that it doesn't seem like the prosecution was able to counter this in the minds of the jurors.

This can be seen clearly in the comments given by the jurors after the verdict. As Brenda Moran, a juror in the Simpson case, said: "They disregarded Simpson's record as a wife beater, finding it a waste of time."

5. APOLOGIA STRATEGIES

...vengeance previously taken upon one person appeases anger against another, even though it be greater. Wherefore Philocrates, when someone asked him why he did not justify himself when the people were angry with him, made the judicious reply, " Not yet." "When then?" "When I see someone accused of the same offense"; for men grow mild when they have exhausted their anger upon another, as happened in the case of Erguphilus. For although the Athenians were more indignant with him than with Callisthenes, they acquitted him because they had condemned Callicrates to death on the previous day.

Aristotle

In an attempt to determine which strategies where available for the defense lawyers to choose between in their defense of O.J. Simpson, it may be interesting to look at the different theoretical self-defense strategies (apologia). I say chose between, not knowing if they were even aware of all the options.

It is important to establish that the type of self-defense strategies we are dealing with here are not an individual making his own speech to defend himself, but a legal defense. There are, however, many similarities between the legal defense and true self-defense, which in my opinion warrants the use of the so-called apologia strategies in this specific example. Primarily because O.J. Simpson remained silent and let his defense lawyers speak for him. This was probably done because his own testimony was deemed to have an adverse effect on his case. The defense lawyers thereby took the place of Simpson and pled his case. There was indeed a certain distance between the case and the person making the statement, but still the overall defense strategy was often the same.

In a self-defense there are four general defense strategies to choose between[28]:

1) Denial
2) Support
3) Differentiation
4) Transcendence

Let's have a look at an outline of the four general defense strategies:

Denial is the possibility of denying statements, facts, points of view, objects or circumstances. The denial strategies are of course only useful to a speaker to the extent that these denials do not constitute an obvious perversion of the truth or distortion of realities or up to the point where any distortion conflict with the audience's other convictions. It is therefore not possible to use a well-known manipulation strategy. It would have been difficult to use the conspiracy and racism argumentation towards certain jurors in a court trial taking place shortly after the O.J. Simpson trial. Denial is reformatory, which means that it corrects people's view on things, trying to reform and improve our opinion of what happened, not, fundamentally change our opinion about what it is all about. The intention is not to change the audience's opinion or affect what the case is about. Denial consists of mere disavowal of responsibility on the part of the speaker for any participation in or sympathetic attitude towards what repels the audience.

The support strategy is best seen as the opposite of denial. Support refers to any rhetorical strategy whatsoever that reinforces existing facts, feelings, objects or circumstances. When supporting, the speaker tries to identify himself with something that the audience sees as favorable. An attempt is not made at changing the audience's basic understanding of the case but at bringing into focus another aspect of the case instead. If, for example, you are accused of having killed another person, you can claim that you acted in self-defense. Like denial, the support strategy is reformatory in the sense that the speaker does not make up a total new identification and neither does the speaker try to change the audience's feelings towards the original emphasis in the case. The support and denial strategies are reformatory in the sense that they do not change the audience's basic understanding of the individual elements of the case. In this case an attempt is not made at changing the audience's opinion on killing another person.

Differentiation and transcendence are, by contrast, both transformatory. Differentiation is comprised of strategies the purpose of which are to dissociate some facts, feelings, objects or circumstances from a wider context in which the audience put them earlier. It is possible to change the view on an assault if you look at each of the components that led to the course of events and why they triggered the subsequent reaction. If the division of the old context into two or more new perceptions of reality is to have any effect, it must be accompanied by a change in the audience's opinion on what the case is about. At least one of the new constructions must by the division assume a new conclusive meaning substantially different from how it was regarded in its original context. In our example it might be that a single act rather than being an indication of an evil intent indicates that the assailant felt threatened and scared.

Differentiation therefore consists of the strategies that represent a division of the original understanding of the course of events. You try to make the audience look at specific parts of the case as opposed to an overall understanding of the case. This strategy is only effective to the extent that the new view and the old view each provides the audience with radically different interpretations of the situation. Hair-splitting over the meaning of definitions will hardly help the accused, but strategies that put what repels the audience into a new perspective can often benefit the accused in his self-defense.

Transcendence comprises all strategies where facts, feelings, objects or circumstances are combined with a wider context in which they have not been put earlier by the audience. As is the case with differentiation, transcendence is transformatory in the sense that this strategy influences the audience's opinion on what the case is about.

It could be, as we will see later that the evidence collected is no longer seen as an indication of the accused's guilt, but as an indication of a conspiracy.

To sum up, the transcendence strategies are a change in the way we understand the actual meaning or significance of an event. Transcendence strategies psychologically move the audience away from the details of the specific issue towards an overall, general consideration of the accused's character. Such strategies are effective in apologia-type discourse to the extent that the speaker's new interpretation of the case, in the audience's mind, proves to be in agreement with the new context. In our example this implies that the audience is able to picture the evidence collected as an element in a conspiracy. Innumerable speeches in self-defense include transcendence either as a result of complex combinations of strategies or as a consequence of the speaker's relatively obvious attempts at identifying the course of events with a new context.[29] If you arrange it in a table, it looks as follows:

	Reformatory	Transformatory	Emphasis on Details	Emphasis on the General
DENIAL	X		X	
SUPPORT	X		X	
DIFFERENTIATION		X		X
TRANSCENDENCE		X		X

	Negation	Identification	Tends towards the concrete	Tends towards the abstract
DENIAL	X			
SUPPORT		X		
DIFFERENTIATION			X	
TRANSCENDENCE				X

Johnnie Cochran's defense strategy was, in this case, a mix of denial and transcendence. In order for Simpson not to be convicted of the double murder of Ron Goldman and Nicole Brown Simpson, it is necessary to deny that Simpson committed the murders. The interesting and brilliant elements of this defense are that denial is combined with transcendence. This makes Cochran able to deal with all the facts in the case. At the same time he can enrage the jurors using themes concerning the justice system and life in general.

This is of course also where his theory should be attacked, to prevent him from using this tactic, and expose him as a manipulator, not the protector of truth and justice, as he builds himself up to be. This opens up an attack on the man, to discredit his ethos. In other words, it opens up the possibility of an attack on Cochran's ethics and credibility, and thereby the ability to undermine everything he says.

Cochran's speech is both reformatory and transformatory. For Cochran does not try to change our opinion on committing murder, but, on the other hand, tries to change our opinion on what this case is really about. Cochran's tactics are to psychologically move the jurors away from the details of the case, the evidence, etc. towards a more abstract general consideration, not the accused's character, but of the prosecutor's character. He did this with the use of rhetorical questions like: "And so Fuhrman wants to take all black people now and burn them and bomb them ... That is genocidal racism ... Do you think he talked to his partners about it? Do you think his commanders knew about it? Do you think everybody knew about it and turned their heads?"

A rhetorical question is a question you pose to your audience, as part of your speech. The difference between an ordinary question and a rhetorical question is that the audience, when faced with a rhetorical question, answers the question in their own minds. The audience becomes involved in the subject, as if it were a regular conversation. The audience feels that it is taking part in what is said. It makes them think about the aspects of the issue that the speaker wants them to focus on. If the speaker takes it one step further and answers the question it is called a rhetorical conversation.

By putting the rhetorical question to the jurors of whether they think that Fuhrman's colleagues knew of Fuhrman's racist views, he indirectly incriminates the rest of the police force by implicating them as accessories to Fuhrman's statements. Cochran by the use of rhetorical questions paves the way for an overall accusation against the police. Cochran was forced to lump together the police, with Fuhrman, to legitimize his conspiracy theory. To legitimize the conspiracy theory it required that, among other things, various persons within the police department had racist motives and were cooperating in attempting to have Simpson unlawfully convicted. To strengthen his allegation, Cochran made use of both colleague and sexual linkages as is seen from this quotation: "Male officers get together to cover up for each other, don't tell the truth, hide, turn their heads, cover. You can't trust this evidence. You can't trust the messenger. You can't trust this message."

From there Cochran proceeded to also involve the prosecution with Marcia Clark and Christopher Darden, the leading prosecutors, as accessories to Fuhrman's racist statements and conviction by stating, "His misdeeds go far beyond this case because he speaks of a culture that's not tolerable in America. Clark and Darden knew about Mark Fuhrman, and they weren't going to tell you. Marcia made him a 'choir boy' on the stand, all the while knowing he was a liar and a racist."

Cochran built up his argumentation step by step to become more and more all-encompassing. This makes Cochran's allegations seem less far-fetched and over-reacted. Indeed, Cochran starts by insinuating incompetence by the police before he advances his conspiracy theory. This makes it possible for him to rely on the accusations of incompetence whenever the conspiracy theory is weak. This is seen in this quotation which was made shortly prior to those mentioned above: "They allowed this ... investigation to be ... *infected* by a ... *dishonest* and corrupt ... *detective*. They never, *ever* looked for ... anyone else. We think if they *had* done their job, as we have done, Mr. Simpson would have been eliminated early on."

In the previous quotes one can see that Cochran comes up with a third accusation that lies somewhere in between incompetence and a conspiracy. That accusation was that the police, prosecutors, and other authorities would cover up for or turn their heads when it came to racism, unlawful acts, and incompetence committed by their colleagues. This connection between incompetence and a regular frame-up makes it easier to slide back and forth between incompetence and a conspiracy theory when necessary. It also can cause confusion and muddy the waters when it has to do with *how many people were involved in the frame-up*, contrary to *how many would have to be involved*. Used skillfully by the defense and not accurately countered by the prosecution, this can be taken all the way to convincing the jurors that Simpson was innocent at the same time as they believe that there was no conspiracy. As can be seen by these statements from the jurors:

> I think it was sloppiness. I don't think it was a conspiracy at all. I think it started out bad so they immediately started covering up some of this stuff.[30]

> I think what happened is a lot of people just got too caught up in the moment and didn't do their jobs properly. I just thought he was sloppy. If there was any type of conspiracy that he was more or less involved in, I thought it was just trying to correct some of the things he may have done wrong to start with, such as documenting the evidence properly, rather than trying to frame anybody.[31]

This argument between incompetence and a conspiracy goes all the way from: No one ever tried to frame anybody, but that they were just trying to boost their case and hide the initial mistakes that they made, to somebody tried to frame Simpson, and the rest just turned their heads, or covered up for them. If certain facts are muddied up sufficiently, this can be a very coherent way to view the events.

The reason that this argumentation appeals more to blacks versus whites, is that the assertion (topos) that certain groups in society would turn their heads or cover up for their colleagues and pals has been a more significant concern among minority groups than among mainstream whites.

The extent of the argumentation looks something like this:

	Ways of explaining away the evidence
	--
Willful intent	*The Big Conspiracy*-O.J. was being framed by all the police. *The Code of Silence*- not all police officers were involved in framing O.J. but those that were not were either *covering up* for those that were and/or *turning their heads.* *Evidence Manipulation*-The police were either *boosting their case* by planting additional evidence or *covering up for incompetence.*
No intent	The police were *incompetent.*

The brilliant part of Cochran's argumentation is that he has insured himself against a breakdown in the coherent worldview he is presenting for the jurors. No hole is left open. Everything can be explained away, to prevent any doubts to enter into the jurors' minds. We here see Cochran's skill and intuition in the way he is able to mix the accusations of incompetence with the conspiracy theory. We then see his superiority in his ability to mix them in the right amount to make the jurors accept it.

6. THE RHETORICAL SITUATION AND THE RELEVANT TOPOI

[Rhetoric's] function is not so much to persuade, as to find out in each case the existing means of persuasion. The same holds good in respect to all the other arts. For instance, it is not the function of medicine to restore a patient to health, but only to promote this end as far as possible; for even those whose recovery is impossible may be properly treated.

Aristotle

A rhetorical situation is any situation that calls for a response where you can effect or change a person's actions or attitude. You do not create the rhetorical situation yourself; each rhetorical situation calls for an answer.[32] By this I mean that you do not independently create the arguments, but rather you respond to, react to a need or answer the call. The way in which you choose to reason in order to carry your point may be more or less optimum.

So it is not so much us that, to begin with, create the particular rhetorical situation; rather, we choose if or how we wish to respond to what the rhetorical situation calls for. It is not before you respond to what the situation demands that you actively take part in changing and framing the particular situation. The optimum answer to the rhetorical situation must be seen in relation to what we wish to achieve from the situation. The optimum rhetorical answer to an event in the Simpson case was not the same for Johnnie Cochran as it was for Marcia Clark. The optimum rhetorical answer in a given situation must be seen as an ideal to strive for that can be approached from many different angles. Whether our answer to the rhetorical situation is adequate is entirely dependent on the ability of our opponent, i.e., how much is needed in order for our reasoning to be successful and then, of course, whether it takes into account the further consequences of our statements, whether there are personal consequences or reactions from the surrounding world. By personal consequences, I mean that the statements do not go below one's own ethical and moral level. By the reactions from the surrounding world, I mean the consequences of our statements over a longer period of time. What, for example, are the consequences in the long run of imposing our will unduly?

Just because a rhetorical situation calls for an answer, an answer is not necessarily given to it. An answer to a rhetorical situation may be given too early or too late, and thus the discourse does not get the optimum effect. This is because the rhetorical situation has a life cycle in which it develops, matures, and then fades away. We all know the situation where we did not say what we wanted to say and if we say it now it will no longer have the same effect, since the situation no longer calls for it.

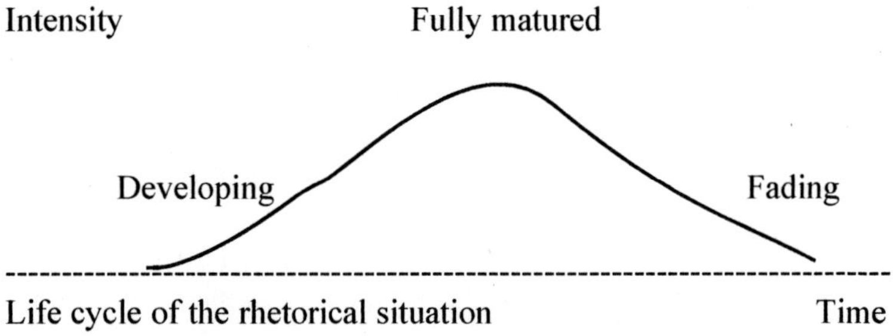

In this sense rhetoric is always pragmatic. Rhetoric is an act that intends to change our surroundings. Even linguistic acts with no apparent meaning, such as talking about the weather with a stranger at a bus stop has a meaning. In that case the intention is to relax the tension of the situation and become more comfortable in each other's company. In this sense rhetoric is always persuasive, since you always try to change a situation.

The rhetorical situation is made up of three elements: a problem, an audience, and a number of facts and limitations that have to be taken into account in the particular situation. If we view the Simpson case in this light, we can say that the problems were that two people had been murdered, and that Simpson had been accused of committing the murders. What your problem is depends on whether you are the prosecutor or the defense lawyer. The audience is the jurors as they are the only ones with power to change the status quo. The facts and limitations of the case may be the jurors' biased opinions and the legal demands made on the statements of the case.

It, for example, puts some constraints on your argumentation if you have to factor in the jurors' biases against your client. If you, in this case, were the prosecution, you would have to factor in the jurors' biases against the police. Johnny Cochran had to take into consideration the legal demands and limitations that the law put on him, when he transformed the case into something else.

Success depends on our interest in the case, our skills as rhetoricians, and our background knowledge not only of the case, but our recipient audience. By background knowledge of our recipient audience is meant, e.g., insight into the jurors' ways of reasoning and how they perceive the world. The rhetorical situation can change at any time. If the circumstances for the case change the rhetorical situation would therefore call for another response. In a legal case this could happen if one of the parties provided additional information or chose to change their tactics.

We can basically only reach an agreement if we already share most of the value norms and beliefs with our audience.

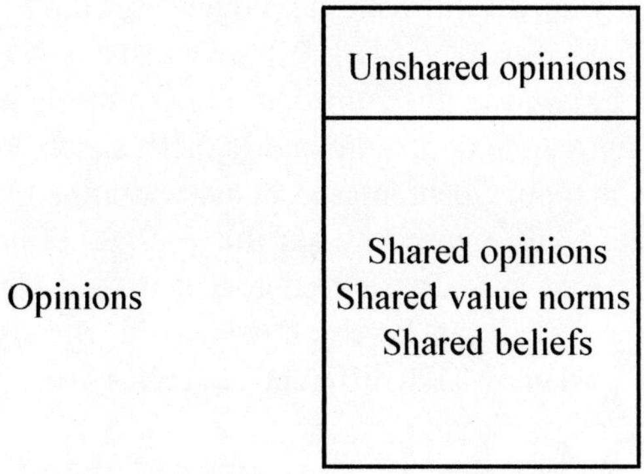

Fortunately our disagreements are often only scratching the surface of an otherwise homogenic foundation. In order to reach our audience, we have to reach down into the beliefs we share with our audience, and use this as a foundation upon which we build our reasoning. These beliefs are, in our minds, categorized under different topics or themes. These are within rhetoric, as previously mentioned, called topoi.

The prosecution's and the defense's understanding of the rhetorical situation showed itself in the type of topic (topoi) they chose to make use of in their reasoning. Cochran's sense of the rhetorical situation was obvious from his choice of topoi he built his argumentation upon. "This is about racism" was the topoi from which he got the basis of his overall reasoning.

Originally, it was not a case about racism, but it was made to be one by Johnnie Cochran. The rhetorical situation called for this if he was to have any hope of getting Simpson acquitted. The aspect of racism did not become an active element in the case until Cochran advanced it three months into the trial, when he accused Mark Fuhrman of planting the evidence, because he was a racist.[33] It is, in this situation, not so important if this strategy was Cochran's or planned out from the beginning by all the members of the defense team. This was the time when the rhetorical situation changed, and demanded another response from the prosecution team.

There had been a thorough research of the police officers' background in order to dig up anything incriminating. A strategy that must be said to have been fully successful with the provision of the Mark Fuhrman tapes, a taped interview with Mark Fuhrman made by a film writer. These tapes were played in the courtroom in front of the jury. On these tapes Mark Fuhrman makes some highly racist statements.

It turned out that the topoi Cochran used in his reasoning made it possible to reconcile in the jurors' minds the charges brought against Simpson in the trial and the new context that focused on racism and incompetence. Cochran hereby changed the rhetorical situation, which demanded new and different strategies from the prosecution.

From being a murder case the case was converted into a case about racism and incompetence on the part of the police. It becomes a struggle against evil itself as symbolized by Hitler. As Cochran says: "There was another man not long ago in the world who had these same views, who wanted to burn people. ... People said he was just crazy. He was just a half-baked painter. They didn't do anything about it. ... This man, this scourge, became one of the worst people in the history of this world, Adolf Hitler, because people didn't care, or didn't try to stop him." Cochran used this phrase to compare Fuhrman with Hitler, and implied that Fuhrman could evolve into the next Adolf Hitler. Cochran is here not only able to carry through this fierce amplification but he also managed to personify the abstraction of evil. The evil forces in the world are symbolized by Hitler, the great anti-hero of our time. And not only does he personify the concept, he is at the same time successful in presenting Mark Fuhrman, one of the top detectives and investigators in the O.J. Simpson case, as synonymous with Hitler.

In this connection it should be mentioned that no precedents or proofs have been found that show that Mark Fuhrman actively acted with prejudice or outright illegality because of his racist opinions. In addition, Mark Fuhrman on the tape recordings is assisting a film writer in creating a fictitious work. It has also been suggested that he tried to make an impression on the young writer. Mark Fuhrman had previously received psychiatric treatment for suffering from violent fantasies and delusions of previous events. This is to be seen in the contents of, the tapes' claims, that he together with other police officers had beat up suspects in order to get them to confess. The alleged incidences have been investigated, and no proof has ever been found that any of this had actually taken place.

Another distinctive topos that Cochran used was: "In reality this is about a conspiracy." Cochran's amplifications and exaggeration prove successful partly through the strength they add to the speech situation. Deliberate overestimation by the speaker of the strength of the argument he advances generally tends to increase its strength. For him to put forward a conclusion as more certain than he himself considers it to be is to engage his personage and use the prestige attached to it, thus adding an extra argument to those already advanced. This procedure is a middle state between that of evil consciousness and pure tenacity.[34]

The topos Marcia Clark and Christopher Darden used in their overall reasoning was: "This is about wife battering and ultimate dominance." We are dealing with a violent murder of passion. They try to substantiate this with an enormous amount of evidence of the wife battering, Simpson's behavior, and his presence at the scene of the murder. They provide instances of this through blood, hair, and fiber remnants found at the scene, in Simpson's car, and in his home. Consequently, it is a mix of a psychological, motive-seeking reasoning and logically deductive evidence. This does not strike a chord with this jury in the same way as Cochran's racial conspiracy theory, since racial inequality is a part of the jury's personal experiences and the conspiracy theory resembles a feeling of helplessness towards strong and unknown powers that control the course of one's life. This tendency to view events as signs of a conspiracy is a common way of reasoning when you do not feel in control of your own life, and when you are not able to overview the totality of the events. The prosecution team's tactics basically remained the same throughout the trial, and they therefore did not answer the new rhetorical situation.

If the jury had come from another economic and educational segment of the population, the psychological motive-seeking reasoning could very well have struck a chord with the jury's way of viewing and explaining the world. This is why it is so important to know your audience. This may sound as though trial lawyers would have to hire a psychologist to adequately present their case. This is in most cases not necessary. You just have to use some common sense, and apply some more general aspect topics and ways of reasoning, so you can tie some strings of identification between your client and the jury members. At the same time you need to attack the strings of identification your opponent is trying to tie between his client and the jury members. If you at the same time try to heighten your own, and your client's credibility, while you attack your opponent and his client's credibility, you have the formula for success that has been used successfully by trial lawyers such as Cochran and Gerry Spence.

In this case it could have been done by saying that when you are as rich as O.J. Simpson, race and skin color doesn't matter anymore, it is a question of money and power. That the victims, by being poor, had more in common with the jury members than O.J. Simpson. One could have said that Cochran was only there to serve his pocketbook and the rich. At the same time the prosecution could have claimed that they were there to serve the people of California, and would have been there whether the accused was rich or poor.

An important part of being a skilful rhetorician is to know where the weak points are in your argumentation. You are then able to strengthen and plan your counterpoints in these areas. The defense team was aware that the topos, rich against poor, was their weak point, as can be seen by this statement:

> Shortly before the final arguments were to commence, the California Supreme Court handed down a decision upholding a conviction despite the defense objection that the prosecutor improperly used a biblical passage in his final argument. The passage was from Chapter 24 of Proverbs, stating that it is wrong to convict the poor and let the rich go free. When we read the decision and passed it around the table at one of the defense team strategy meetings, a collective groan was heard.[35]

Cochran then decided to incorporate another part of the Proverbs into his closing statement to counter this. Cochran moved to strengthen his weak point, in order to be able to withstand the anticipated attack. Since the prosecution was not aware that this was their best topos, they did not utilize this opportunity. This in a nutshell shows the difference in the prosecution and the defense teams' rhetorical abilities. The defense team was so good that they were able to detect their weak points in advance, and strengthen them. The prosecution's rhetorical abilities were so poor, that they weren't able to utilize this opportunity, assuming they even considered it.

7. FORMS OF APPEAL AND THE ETHICAL REQUIREMENT

And since sufferings are pitiable when they appear close at hand, while those that are past or future, ten thousand years backwards or forwards, either do not excite pity at all or only in a less degree, because men neither expect the one nor remember the other, it follows that those who contribute to the effect by gestures, voice, dress, and dramatic action generally, are more pitiable; for they make the evil appear close at hand, setting it before our eyes as either future or past.

Aristotle

The issues connected to the ethos aspect such as personal goodwill, ethics, and image were fundamental to the case throughout the whole trial. Johnnie Cochran's defense of Simpson was an attack on the goodwill, ethics, and image of the police and the authorities in general. The spotlight was no longer turned to Simpson's actions, but to the actions of the police and the authorities. It is seen here when he says, "They allowed this ... investigation to be ... *infected* by a ... *dishonest* and corrupt ... *detective*. They never, *ever* looked for ... anyone else. We think if they *had* done their job, as we have done, Mr. Simpson would have been eliminated early on."

The prosecution suffers during the trial two severe losses of credibility, which weakens their ethos considerably. They suffer the first and probably worst loss of ethos when Mark Fuhrman takes the stand and under oath asserts that he is not a racist and that he has not used the word "nigger" in the last ten years. Whereupon the defense plays a recording in which Mark Fuhrman talks to a film writer. In the course of this conversation he uses the word "nigger" countless times and, in addition, states that all blacks should be eliminated. More specifically, they should be round up and burned. This obviously is not something that has a reassuring effect on the jurors who, except two, are black. This must be seen in connection with the fact that Mark Fuhrman collected essential parts of the incriminating evidence against O.J. Simpson, such as the glove found on Simpson's estate, on which traces of Ron and Nicole's blood were found.

Against this massive loss of credibility the prosecution's counter reasoning is lost on the jurors. The prosecution states in this connection that, logically, it would not be possible for Mark Fuhrman to plant all this evidence. Johnnie Cochran's unearthing of Mark Fuhrman's racist statements plays on some basic strings in these black Americans' memory. From a collective mind the memories of exploitation and injustice are revived. This makes the jury furious about the racist statements and is a conclusive breach of confidence between the jurors and the prosecution.

The other serious loss of ethos suffered by the prosecution in the course of the trial was when they ask O.J. Simpson to try on a blood-stained glove, which is part of the evidence against him. It makes a strong impression that the glove appears not to fit Simpson. The prosecution then presents pictures that showed Simpson wearing a pair of similar gloves, and produces expert evidence that a leather glove may well shrink after being soaked in blood. However, this explanation seems somewhat far-fetched and thin to the jurors. It is debatable to what an extent Simpson did not fit the glove and to what an extent Simpson obstructed the fitting by bending his fingers. You can also discuss to what degree the defense exaggerated the event; in any case, it was a pointless chance to take. If Simpson's hand fit the gloves, it didn't prove anything, but if the gloves didn't fit him, it proved everything.

It is characteristic that the prosecution in this case was staggering behind Johnnie Cochran's reasoning and, as a result, they used a lot of time on defensively rejecting Cochran's arguments. Cochran was able to set the agenda during the main part of the argumentation and thereafter kept the attention on aspects such as racism and incompetence.

Why is it so damaging to suffer a loss of ethos? How is it that a relatively insignificant circumstance is the cause of rejecting everything a person says even though it is contrary to common sense and logical thinking?

Under normal circumstances we believe what people say; we

place our immediate trust in people as a gift. What happens if this trust is betrayed? What happens if it is proved that you have lied? What happens if doubt is raised as to your sincerity and thereby produces a consequential loss of the image and morals one upholds?

The immediate and fundamental trust with which we meet complete strangers is the basis on which our language is built. Without this trust our language would be meaningless. To display trust means to give yourself away. That is why our reactions are so strong when our trust is betrayed even though there wasn't much at stake. Often the betrayal of trust consists in the trust being used against the one who displayed it. That is bad enough. But what is worse is not the embarrassment or trouble which the betrayal of trust may cause, but the fact that the other did not accept it. In order for the other one to betray our trust, it must have left him cold. Fundamentally, he did not want to accept it no matter how much he did on the face of it, in order to betray it. And the question is whether the coldness of the betrayal of trust much more than the actual embarrassment in which the one that was trustful is brought in is the reason for the reaction.[36]

In this case there is no doubt that the jurors felt betrayed, not least by Mark Fuhrman, who had lied right to their faces. That it was more the lie in itself, than the importance of what the lie was about, was undoubtedly one of the reasons for the strong reaction. That is a factor in explaining why the use of an insult like "nigger" gets such a huge impact. Implicit in this specific case was also that the laying bare of the rancorous attitudes towards blacks evidenced in the theory that a miscarriage of justice was about to be committed against Simpson, and that in reality we are not dealing with a murder case. However, it is still a weak piece of evidence compared to the weight of the evidence.

Even when these things are taken into consideration, it is still a fierce reaction created by one man's use of an insult and racist statements a reaction which is not comparable to the offense. According to an opinion poll published in *Time* magazine shortly after the judgment in the civil case, where Simpson was found liable for the murders, 68 percent of the white population believed that Simpson had committed the murders. The same poll showed that only 18 percent of the black population believed that Simpson had murdered Nicole Simpson and Ron Goldman.[37]

Johnnie Cochran used predominantly the ethos and pathos forms of appeal. Ethos, as mentioned, is the image morals and goodwill a person holds, and pathos is the more short-term and immediate emotions such as anger and happiness. He strengthened, relatively, Simpson's ethos by attacking the ethos of the police and the prosecution. At the same time he tried to strengthen his own ethos by comparing himself to black civil rights campaigners like Malcolm X and Louis Farrakhan, by using a style and wording found in speeches by these well-known individuals. In this way he strengthens his own ethos, and was better able to succeed in carrying through his use of emotions. God and the devil, Malcolm X and Hitler, are concepts and persons useful in making things appear in a black/white perspective. This at the same time helps elevate the speech to an emotional level.

Of course, both the defense and the prosecution used logos and ethos, forms of appeal, respectively, in their speeches. Cochran used the logical form of appeal when he rebuked specific elements in the evidence against Simpson. He argued that blood from Simpson found at the scene of the murder, in Simpson's car, and near Simpson's house was planted. He based this on the way in which the trails of blood were shaped and on the fact that microscopic remnants of chemicals were found in the blood samples, chemicals that are also used for preparing the inside of glass that is used for preserving blood tests. It must be noted that remnants of this chemical may originate from a number of other sources.

The prosecution did attack Simpson's ethos by emphasizing Simpson's battering of his wife. But it was not the predominant form of appeal in their closing statement.

Another way to build ethos is through the use of maxims. Maxims are potent expressions of an ethical or philosophical nature that claim to express a universal truth. Cochran used concise common sentences (maxims) which acted as constant reminders or summing-up to the jurors of his major arguments. At the same time they had a positive effect on Cochran's ethos. For example: "The ones that lie in small things also lie in big things" or, "If it doesn't fit you must acquit."

In a speech, maxims are part of the rhetorical decoration. In legal speech, maxims are often used to remind and sum up the issue to the jury or judge. Proverbs can often be used as maxims. Another important part of addressing a jury is the body language and the nonverbal communication one projects to the jury members. The reason this issue is so important is that if there is a good balance between contents and expression we, as listeners, believe that the speaker's inner soul lies open to us, since it is only the good person that dares let us look all the way into the soul.

It is also a lot more difficult to deceive people with one's body language and tone of voice then with words, because these traits are closely linked to our personality and feelings. We all consciously or unconsciously know this. This is why we always believe the tone of voice, contrary to the words, if the message is conflicting. Since the expression comes from within, body language is not something that, taken apart from the contents, can be glued upon a person as images. A rehearsed gesture will almost always seem mechanical and artificial. In these cases, the unconscious gestures the person makes, will usually speak louder. It is not just a single gesture that makes a difference, but a whole pattern of gestures. A person's voice and body language have to come from within as a natural expression of the person's opinions and personality. This in a way is a confirmation of the person's trustworthiness and good character.

Even though you are not able to glue gestures upon a person, you are able to weed out bad traits. In this sense, it would be beneficial to look at which nonverbal traits are winning traits, and which are losing traits. The basics that determine the effect of a person's nonverbal communication can be seen in these two columns.[38]

Voice and Body

Winning traits:
-vivid and diversified voice
-clear and energetic articulation
-intense look that holds the receiver captivated

-physical energetic readiness
-eager gesticulation
-firm and directing gestures
-eye contact

Loosing traits:
-monotone voice
-loose articulation
-downcast eyes

We can now compare these trait with the perception the jury had of Marcia Clark and Christopher Darden, and the conclusions that they drew. One of the jury members stated about Marcia Clark: "...the prosecution believed that they had a strong case but they were showing signs of stress and frustration. A lot of times Marcia would sigh and make gestures with her hands as though she were throwing in the towel. That didn't help her."[39] We here see that the verbal and the nonverbal messages conflict, and that the nonverbal message wins. If we look at our list, this more precisely correlates to a lack of physical energetic readiness. The effect of these conflicting messages can also be seen in this quote from one of the jurors:

> ...Marcia would just get too frustrated. I'm sitting right in front of her and I'm watching all her sighs and that to me was a sigh of weakness. You're here to do a job and if something is bothering you, don't let them see you sweat. And Darden, too. You know, I wouldn't know what was happening when we weren't there, but he would be doing his jingle thing with his keys and his legs jiggled when things got tense. It made me think, well, if your case is so strong, why are you so frustrated?[40]

If one watches the videotapes of Darden's closing statements to the jury, one can see that he has a tendency to look down and mumble when he addresses the jury. If we look at the list of winner traits for voice and body language, we see that this is opposite to most of them. To have eye contact with somebody is like having a conversation with people. You feel like you are being addressed, and since the eyes are the mirror for the soul, we can usually not lie and look people in the eyes at the same time! The voice of truth is loud and clear, like the voice Moses heard on the mountain. As one juror states, "I sort of felt that Chris was a little down. Maybe he was playing down. I don't know. He did not have that upbeat mentality. I thought he was very moody. He never could look you in the eye, either. Because when I would look at him some days, his eyes would sort of look the other way. I have a problem with people who can't look me in the eye."[41]

Several jurors stated after the trial that they sometimes had a hard time hearing what the prosecution said, because they were mumbling, but that they never had any difficulty hearing what the defense said.

The combination of the verbal and nonverbal communication is very important, because we view the ability to speak well as the best indicator of that one thinks right, and that it reflects a good and trust-worthy soul. This is why truth has its own strength, because it is easier to say what one views as the truth, then it is to fabricate a lie.

8. RECIPIENT AWARENESS

Nor should we speak as if from the intellect, after the manner of present-day orators, but from moral purpose.

Aristotle

From a rhetorical perspective good reasoning involves an appropriate mix of *logos*, *ethos*, and *pathos*. As previously mentioned, logos means a logical argumentation. Ethos means the trust and value that the communicator holds, and pathos means the emotions that your utterance stirs. You cannot in the same categorical way claim that factual reasoning as a matter of course is good reasoning. Reasoning may just as well fail by being too factual than by not being factual enough. We cannot expect to solve all questions, such as religious, moral, and ethical issues, on the sole basis of factual arguments. We always need to take into account the sender and the recipient as individuals. In rhetoric they do not fade away as individuals of secondary importance to universal truth, for rhetoric builds on a relativistic basis. Within rhetoric, the answer is not given in advance as it is with a mathematical paradigm. It is not pure relativism, but a truth we must find together within a certain defined area. Depending on the subject matter, the scope for this may vary.

Because we, within rhetoric, always find a speaker/writer and a audience that exists as individuals with unique backgrounds and personalities, the sender's morals, goodwill, and the emotions that occur are always indispensable elements in rhetorical reasoning. As recipients we must be able to trust that the sender speaks the truth based on what the sender himself holds to be true. As senders we must be able to arouse our recipient's interest, sympathy, and trust. These are factors we cannot dispense with when acting in practice. It is therefore unfortunate that the mathematical paradigm, due to its great success in the natural sciences, has gained ground as a model in areas where it does not belong.

The prosecution's mistaken view of the logical, mathematical paradigm as the only "true and correct" method of reasoning led them to concentrate almost exclusively on entirely logical reasoning. What is unfortunate about this way of thinking is that, by doing so, you easily lose contact with your recipient and at the same time you are under the illusion that you, as an individual and as the carrier of the message, are unimportant. This way of thought is reflected in Christopher Darden's statements to the jury that he was only the messenger of the "truth" was implied. This personal disassociation was attacked by Cochran since he wished to portray them as incriminated individuals. As Cochran said, "Mr. Darden said something very interesting today,... He said, 'I'm just the messenger'. How often [have you] heard that?... 'Don't blame me. I'm just doing my job.' Darden wasn't just *any* messenger,... He's a prosecutor with all the power of the State of California in this case. We are not going to let them get their way! We are not going to turn the Constitution on its head in this case."

In the Simpson case, we see how the prosecution, due to their conviction of the correctness of a mathematical, logical presentation of the case, lose their recipient's confidence. They do this by neglecting the ethos aspect of the argument, which in this case means neglecting the image, morals, and goodwill held by them, the police, and other witnesses involved.

Ultimately, for a fitting response to be a satisfying one, it must intersect with the values, ethics, and personal commitments of both speaker and audience.

The quotation below from Hank M. Goldberg, a member of the prosecution team, illustrates how strictly bound the prosecution was to the logic-deductive method which measures everything according to the principles of a mathematical paradigm.

> Often people ask me whether the Simpson case is an example of a rich person's being able to buy his way out of a

> criminal conviction. This notion stems from the perception that wealthy clients are able to purchase exceptionally talented, high-priced lawyers who can win an acquittal or skillfully negotiate more lenient punishment. It also stems from the misperception that public defenders, who represent the poor, are ineffective lawyers. This is far from the truth. Imagine that Simpson had lost all his money before the murders. I am absolutely certain that if he had been represented by the Los Angeles County Public Defender's Office, he would have been assigned a defense team with substantially more experience litigating homicides than Simpson's "dream team." They would probably have presented a more coherent, technically more proficient defense. Of course, the result would have been the same. The speed of the verdict indicated that the jurors not only ignored the prosecution's evidence and arguments but ignored those of the defense as well.[42]

Here Goldberg says that the better one is at making a "correct" procedure in a murder case, the better one is at convincing the jury of the reasonableness of one's opinion and thereby win the case. This illustrates his complete confidence in a predominantly logical reasoning based on the principles of the mathematical paradigm as the only correct way to reason.

Goldberg also claims in this quotation that the jury had decided on a verdict in advance, that they were unresponsive to arguments. There is no evidence in support of this. The jury was actually interested in assessing the quality of the evidence.

The only element that the jury wished to have specified before returning their verdict was some details concerning the time aspect. That is to say, where was Simpson at the time of the murders and had he had the time to commit the murders? The reason why the jurors were interested in the time aspect was that it was the only concrete piece of evidence that had not been collected by the police, the incriminated and untrustworthy institution.

The testimonies concerning the time aspect had been given by, among other people, Nicole Simpson's neighbors and a young man who had a temporary address with Simpson (Kato Kaelin). And, not least, by a limousine driver who picked up Simpson and drove him to the airport. These people had no direct connection to the police or any other public authority and therefore were not included in the conspiracy theory. Apart from Kato Kaelin, they could not be accused of having any personal financial or commercial interests in the case either. Kato Kaelin was accused by the defense of trying to boost his acting career, that he tried to gain publicity by testifying in court.

The limousine driver's testimony was especially important since he testified that he saw a black man the height and size of Simpson go into Simpson's house shortly after the murders had been committed. When the limousine driver first rang the doorbell, there was no answer. Not until the driver had waited a while and had seen a black man go into the house did Simpson answer the doorbell. Simpson claimed that he had overslept when he answered the doorbell.

This may be highly incriminating testimony, but it is still hard to convict a man of murder based solely on that. Therefore, we cannot infer that the jurors lacked the will to convict Simpson and take into consideration the evidence produced. They had simply lost confidence in most of the evidence.

Darden also tried to take advantage of his background knowledge of his audience, and not just appeal to logic, as seen in the following statement:

> The N-word evidence would issue a test, it will give them the test and the test will be whose side are you on? The side of the white prosecutors and the white policemen or on the side of the black defendant and his very prominent and black lawyer? That is what it is going to do. Either you are with the man or you are with the brothers. That is what it does.

From this quote we see that Darden tried to put himself in the jury's place, and address them on their own terms when it came to the racial issue. We can see that the prosecution was aware of what was happening, and that they were desperately trying to stop it. But they were defenseless because they were unaware of the rhetorical strategies that were at work. They were therefore not able to address the reasons why it was happening.

It was not enough to be able to state what is happening, it doesn't necessarily change what is being done. You have to be able to treat the injury. In this case it meant that the police's ethos needed some protection and reinforcement. The prosecution needed to protect the ethos of the institution that provided their evidence. In other words, it was the ethos foundation of the prosecution's argumentation that needed mending. If the jurors had already been convinced by the defense, and therefore did not share Darden's opinion, this statement was not going to make them change their opinion. This is a good example of vote gathering argumentation that sounds really good to the ones who already share your opinion, but it does not slide any votes in your direction.

We can see how the lack of rhetorical training in law school puts lawyers at a disadvantage in court. I do not mean that there is one right way to argue in court, but that there are components that have to be part of a lawyer's argumentation, in order for the argumentation to have durability.

Good rhetoricians may seem to have totally different approaches to winning a case, but the basic structure of their argumentation is the same. The approaches are merely different emphases on the same bone structure. Some tell a magnificent and sincere story, others point out the inconsistencies and the common sense aspects. These are the places where they put their emphasis, but that doesn't mean that they don't have the rest of the bone structure in place to hold up their argumentation. One therefore doesn't have to learn how to argue exactly as certain top trial lawyers do. One just has to know the basic structure of tenable argumentation and then phrase it and emphasize it in one's own unique way.

JOHNNIE COCHRAN'S RECIPIENT AWARENESS

In the course of the trial, Johnnie Cochran displayed an exceptional awareness of his recipient. His entire argumentation, presentation technique, and stylistic means were aimed at the jurors' common base of experience and memories. He was successful in using the transcendence tactic since a prerequisite of this technique was that the recipient sensed a point of agreement between "the manipulating object" and the new context. In this case the manipulated object would be the murders and the evidence pointing towards O.J. Simpson, and the new context would be a police conspiracy and possible drug-related crime, as the defense mentioned.

With his background knowledge, Cochran was able to find new themes and a new context which were acceptable to his recipients. A rhetorician may have to change an audience's opinion in one respect; but he can succeed only insofar as he yields to that audience's opinions in other respects. Some of their opinions are needed to support the fulcrum by which he would move other opinions.[43]

As an Afro-American, Cochran was able to play on many strings of collective memories such as the miscarriages of justice, racism, and the enormities committed against blacks by their white countrymen. He was also able to address these black Americans in a language they understood, language influenced by Christian metaphors and formulated and presented in a gospel way. In Cochran's speech there were strong reminiscences of black ministers' preaching style, a style which is full of metaphors, rhythm, ring, and repetition. It is a solemn, emotional style that in the original meaning of the words puts black against white. Cochran did use many allusions to the Bible, an area in which he found joint knowledge within the predominantly black jury. With the Bible in hand this ethical crusade was deeply rooted in the underlying meaning of what had happened and thereby legitimized the transformation of a murder case into a conspiracy. A conspiracy not only on the part of the police, but also on the part of evil itself, symbolized by Hitler. The purpose of the conspiracy was here expanded to include not only the miscarriage of justice against O.J. Simpson but the crushing of the very basis of American society: freedom and equality. The jurors were the selected few who could prevent this from happening: "Maybe this is one of the reasons we are all gathered together this day, ... Maybe this is why you were selected. There is something in your background, your character, that helps you understand this is wrong! Maybe you are the right people at the right time at the right place to say, no more, we are not going to have this!"

Cochran ended his argumentation by urging the jurors not to take part in this conspiracy, that this had been a search for truth: "Don't be part of this continuing cover-up...Do the right thing, remembering that if it doesn't fit, you must acquit. That if these messengers have lied to you, you can't trust their message, that this has been a search for truth."

In his speech Cochran also used Islamic metaphors. This is interesting when seen in connection with the fact that five million black Americans are Muslims. Cochran used a style that is similar to that of Louis Farrakhan the leader of the black Muslims. As Cochran said: "... the twins of deception. Fuhrman and Vannatter, twins of deception who bring you a message that you cannot trust, that you cannot trust!"

Here Cochran succeeded in making Fuhrman and Vannatter, two of the police investigators, appear as synonymous with the devil while at the same time throwing suspicion on white people and relying on the organization "Nation of Islam." Cochran echoed the style of Malcolm X and Louis Farrakhan. The term "twins of deception" was intended to invoke the devil. In the jargon of the Nation of Islam, "devil" meant white. Vannatter and Fuhrman were twin devils of deception. White devils.[44]

In addition, Cochran used a style and wording which led back to Martin Luther King. This made it possible for Cochran to indirectly link the case against O.J. Simpson to black people's struggle for civil rights, a battle that was also, to a great extent, won in court. In that connection Cochran quoted, among others, the famous early civil rights orator, Frederick Douglas: "... all Americans must share common citizenship, equal rights, and a common destiny. We haven't reached this goal yet ... But in this great country of ours, maybe a jury such as this can." By employing this method, Cochran was using the well-known trick of making people stick together against an outer enemy. Account cannot be taken to less urgent aspects, such as the conflict between rich and poor, oppression of women and wife battering, or the fact that O.J. actually had divorced his black wife and mother of his children for a white woman. All these aspects cannot be taken into account as we are here dealing with an attack on black Americans' basic existence and civil rights.

When Cochran mentioned figures of history such as Abraham Lincoln and Frederick Douglas, it produced a patriotic mood and was thereby a factor in making the audience stick together for a grand idealistic goal.

To base your argumentation on idol argumentation, as Cochran did, is to build your argumentation on a particular kind of authority. One advocates the imitation of a person that serves as an ideal within a certain endeavor. With the movement of Christianity into western civilization the imitation of the ideal person became very popular, with Christ as the exemplum par excellence. Today we mostly see it in commercials where sports heroes and actors recommend certain products.

We here again see that Cochran used a form of argumentation that was able to create consensus with his audience that was used to the Christian rhetoric.

Where our immediate sympathies lie, in a case of violence, often depends on whether we view ourselves as potential victims of violence or as potential victims of police assault. Persuasion in turn involves communication by the signs of consubstantiality, the appeal of *identification*. That is to say, our immediate sympathies are with the party with whom we identify, since, it makes us think "It could have been me." We look at the world from this person's viewpoint as if we had been in the same position. It is an unconscious decoding of the world based on our own person. The more we fear that it might happen to us, and the less capable we are of abstracting from our own person, the stronger the identification effect will be.

Johnnie Cochran did indeed understand how to play on the fear and disillusion that many blacks feel towards the police and law enforcement in general. Johnnie Cochran had a distinct focus, which was to discredit the police and other authorities, such as the prosecution and the forensic laboratory. Cochran said: "... things will come to you and you will be able to reveal people who come to you in uniforms and high positions who lie and are corrupt." Attention must instead be turned away from the specific details and towards the underlying deeper meaning of things. From being about a specific case it turned into a universal fight between good and evil as seen from this quotation: "There's something about good versus evil ... There's something about truth. The truth crushed to earth will rise again. You can always count on that."

The police, personified by Mark Fuhrman and Phillip Vannatter, are made into the evil itself: "the devils of deception." By contrast, Johnnie Cochran makes himself the guardian of good and a patriotic advocate of freedom, equality, and justice.

Cochran's speech may seem very thin in arguing facts and details. Other lawyers on the defense team did that; Barry Scheck argued the credibility of the DNA evidence. This technique of dividing up the assignments has been used since ancient Greece. Like Cicero, Johnny Cochran comes in at the end and ties up the loose ends, in a very emotional speech. Or as the reverend Brown from the Third Baptist Church in San Francisco phrased it: "...[Cochran's] closing argument for the defense, an argument both passionate and Ciceronian, echoed the great Roman orator's most imaginative assertion. For example, in defending Marcus Caellus Rufus in 56 BC, Cicero's primary strategy was to suggest a conspiracy by the prosecution because he had so little to defend his client with."[45]

A way of turning the benefit of a lot of evidence around is directly or indirectly, to claim, that *the validity of the entire evidence rests on the strength of the weakest point.* In other words, the strength of your argument is not stronger than your weakest argument. Indirectly it can not be said any clearer than Cochran's: "If you lie in small things, you also lie in big things." This is the common sense basis of this kind of argumentation. But the defense team was not satisfied with just saying it indirectly, since they wanted to be sure that their message went through. Therefore they set out to find a way where they could make it seem like it was the words of Judge Ito, and the law. Santa Clara University law professor and member of the defense team, Gerald Uelmen, said:

> ...we knew we could count on Judge Ito giving the standard CALJIC instruction on circumstantial evidence, and that became the foundation of our entire final argument. This instruction informs the jury in a case based on circumstantial evidence, as the Simpson case was, that if the evidence is susceptible of two reasonable interpretations, *one* pointing to guilt, the other pointing to innocence, the jury must acquit,

> because the defendant must be given the benefit of the doubt. It also says that, before the jury can convict, the proved circumstances must not only be consistent with the theory that the defendant is guilty, but they must be irreconcilable with any other conclusion.[46]

This sentence can actually be quite difficult to understand, because so much abstract information is crammed into a couple of sentences. This is unfortunately more the norm than the exception in legal discourse. This is due to the goal that seems to be to take all circumstances into consideration within one sentence.

An important consequence of this is that it becomes easier to confuse people. Here the defense spins on the word "one." and turns it into: *if the jury members have one doubt about any of the evidence, it means that the defendant must be acquitted.* Or as the jury members stated after the trial in a question and answer session: "The law states that all you need is one reasonable doubt. We had several reasonable doubts, plus the questions we had that never got answered. We went through all the exhibits and the evidence. We did all of that before we reached a verdict."[47] "...because we had no direct evidence and had to go on circumstantial evidence, I had no alternative at that time but to think he was not guilty. And it is important to remember that a not guilty verdict requires just one thing that can create reasonable doubt."[48]

> How can you explain away O.J.'s blood at the murder scene, found hours before his blood sample was taken?
>
> We can't explain it away. I don't think anybody has really tried to explain it away. Me, personally, I have not tried to explain it away at all. That was not one of the issues and that was definitely not the reasonable doubt we based our decision on."[49] [Other jury members stated, that they thought the blood samples had deteriorated too much.]

Not adequately countered, this in itself could be the stab of death for the prosecution. A common trait amongst successful trial lawyers is that they are able to transform abstract wording into straightforward and unambiguous language. A good example of this is Vincent

Bugliosi reformulating the concept of reasonable doubt:

> Finally, it dawned on me that the word "beyond" was not only a needless appendage, but much more important, in the term "beyond a reasonable doubt," it is misleading to the jury because it is not used in its principal sense of "further" or "more than." If it were, the prosecution would have to prove there is *more* than a reasonable doubt of a defendant's guilt, when obviously, they have to prove just the opposite that there is *less than* a reasonable doubt. Instead, "beyond" is used in its secondary sense of "to thc exclusion of." In my cases thereafter, after explaining to the jury the true sense in which the word "beyond" is used, I would say this to the jury: "The prosecution, then, has the burden of proving the guilt of this defendant to the exclusion of all reasonable doubt. With this in mind, we can completely eliminate the word 'beyond' from the term 'beyond a reasonable doubt' and come up with this [which I'd also write on the blackboard]: 'If you do not have a reasonable doubt of the guilt of this defendant, convict. If you do have a reasonable doubt, acquit.' We have eliminated the word 'beyond' from the term 'beyond a reasonable doubt' and we still have a very accurate definition and statement of the doctrine of reasonable doubt."[50]

When one uses overloaded sentences it is almost impossible for the jury members to remember what has been said. Contrary to that, Cochran comes in with sound bites and a speaking style that the jury is used to hearing. We can now see that it is not the judge's instructions that the jury members remember, but Cochran's explanations such as when he dealt with the difference between direct and circumstantial evidence. As stated by a jury member:

> "I remember, when Johnnie Cochran dropped his pen on the floor during opening arguments to show how deceiving circumstantial evidence can be," says Carrie. "They had a box down there and he said, 'Where did the pen fall?' This was how he was building his case to say circumstantial evidence wasn't foolproof. You weren't sure where it went, but you knew it

dropped. Where did the pen go? You could hear it, but you weren't sure whether it hit the floor or the box."[51]

This led Cochran on to claiming that you can not convict on circumstantial evidence, that you in fact needed direct evidence to be able to convict Simpson. Circumstantial evidence is the abstract label that is put upon all kinds of evidence except eyewitness statements.

Cochran not only knows where black American's fears lay; he is also a master at playing on these fears. We see the nature of two of these fears in this quote:

> For most black people, when Simpson was arrested, there was a sense of great danger for us as a people. We didn't quite know what form it would take, but we were worried that the message would go through, once again, that black men are animalistic and violent. Another of our fears: No matter how successful we are, we can be brought down....And I should say that while there were places where people cheered the verdict, I think a much more common reaction among black folk was one of relief.[52]

We can see how Cochran utilized this fear by stating to the blacks on the jury in closing argument that if the judicial system could be so cavalier with the life of a rich and accepted celebrity who is black, whose money enabled him to prove the existence of substantial police incompetence and police misconduct that directly related to the credibility of the police evidence, just imagine the lack of concern for the average black without the good fortune to have his police encounter videotaped. Or as Cochran said: "For some time it has been open season on African-American males...If it can happen to Michael Jackson or O.J., it can happen to any of us."

Cochran knew that Mark Fuhrman was the weak link; therefore Cochran started and ended his speech with Fuhrman. He knew that those sections of his speech were the sections his audience was going to remember the best. He had several opportunities to do that, since his closing statement was divided over two days. This was almost like being able to give two closing speeches, since most people can only comprehend about twenty minutes of a speech or lecture, unless something extraordinary happens. The last part of a speech will also be easier for people to remember. The fact that Cochran was given the opportunity of two beginnings and two endings to his closing statement gave him the opportunity to address the jury members with four slots of prime time instead of two. As an effective rhetorician Cochran used this time to stress his strongest point and, most importantly, the significance of this in connection to his main point. Cochran started out on his second day of his closing argument with: "Let's continue where we left off then, with this man Fuhrman. He's said some very interesting things."

> Cochran used this prime time to get into the issue of Mark Fuhrman in great detail:
>
> But what I find particularly troubling is that they all knew about Mark Fuhrman and they weren't going to tell you. They tried to ease him by. Of all the witnesses who've testified in this case, how many were taken up to the grand jury room where they have this pre-session to ask him all these questions....so they knew. Make no mistake about it. And so when they try and prepare him...get him ready and make him seem like a choirboy and make him come in here and raise his right hand as though he's going to tell you the truth and give you a true story here, they knew he was a liar and a racist....There's something about good versus evil. There's something about truth. That truth crushed to earth will rise again. You can always count on that.

The effectiveness of this technique lies very close to the effectiveness of getting the last word. The opportunity of getting the last word is not something that is only connected to closing and opening statement; these opportunities can be found all the way through a trial when advocates question their own witnesses and when they address their opponent's witnesses.

When one questions one's own witnesses it is one's own opinion that is supposed to be enhanced, so in a way one can say that the lawyer constantly holds the word, and that she doesn't take the word from anybody. She is entitled to lead the conversation, and the witness is willing to go along. Even so, the lawyer can by the way she goes about it give the audience the impression that it is she that in the end has the decisive statements in the case, and thereby contribute to a clearer opinion of what the important elements are. This she can do by spending a moment of her time on summing up what the witness has said, and present the statement so the main idea, or an important conclusion presents itself clearly and significantly, before she goes on to the next part of the questioning. This she can do, both when she at the end, wishes to be done with a witness, and during the questioning of the witness, when one goes from one point to another. In a way this is the same thing one does when one takes notes during a lecture.

There is no doubt that the strategy aimed at getting the last word is extremely important-- the lawyer sums up along the way during the discourse with her own witness, or that she does it by stopping a counter-witness, whichever way it seems to have a clearly positive effect.

So, in other words, when the witness is done talking, you sum up what the witness has said in a focused way. As for example:

- So in fact what Mr. Lange is saying here is ...

This technique can also be used with experts on the stand, after they have responded to your non-leading question and given their opinion as to how things happened, or as to how it happens to be. This could sound something like this:

- So what you are saying is, that it is your opinion that the light conditions were such that the plaintiff in this case should have been able to see my client perfectly clear and that they just pulled out in front of him, etc.

In a broader sense, getting the last word is also connected to rehabilitating witnesses on the stand. You not only recreate your witnesses' version of the story, and thereby your own version of the story, you also get the last say on how the events are to be interpreted.

In his closing statement Cochran also used repetitions and a technique known as a three-stage rocket. A three-stage rocket consists of three statements in an utterance. It can be three statements in favor of your point of view, or three statements against your opponent. A genuine and highly effective three-stage rocket is the kind where you build your opponent up in the first two statements, just to tear him or her down in the third statement, as for example:

> They want to give us more money.
> A secure life.
> And take away our freedom.

In this way you have made your audience immune to the points and arguments that your opponent is likely to bring forward. That is why this technique is often called "to vaccinate" your audience. Another variation of a three-stage rocket is this one, implied by Cochran. It both rhythms and ends on the same word. This helps tie the sentences together and seemingly gives them there own logic: "Mr. Simpson did not, could not, and would not commit the murders." These three-stage rockets and repetitions are factors in adding a very verbal touch to Cochran's speech. It is easy to remember the main messages as they, along with key words and maxims are repeated throughout the whole speech. Key words are words that carry the essence of your message. These techniques not only improved the jurors memory they also drew a red thread throughout Cochran's closing statement which blended together the speech to an overall unit of understanding. At the same time, the focus of the speech was kept clear to the jurors all through the speech.

This example illustrates Cochran's use of repetitions. This particular kind of repetition is called an anaphor. In an anaphor you keep repeating the first part of your statement:

> Now, thank heaven, Judge Ito took us on a jury view. You've seen this house. You've seen this carpet. If he went in that house with bloody shoes, with bloody clothes, with his bloody hands as they say, where's the blood on the doorknob,

> where's the blood on the light switch, where's the blood on the banister, where's the blood on the carpet? That's like almost white carpet going up those stairs. Where is all that blood trail they've been banting about in this mountain of evidence?

In this quote we see that Cochran has combined his use of anaphors with the use of three. The use of three gives a wholeness to your statement, as if you have taken everything into consideration.

Key words and maxims catch on in one's mind and are difficult to forget. Maxims stick to our memory and, like proverbs, they demand their own simple and unsubtle interpretation of the events. Quotations and proverbs may be essential in the legal efforts to find acceptance.[53]

We here see an example of Cochran's use of proverbs: "...Truth forever on the scaffold, wrong forever on the thrown, yet that scaffold sways the future and beyond the dim unknown standeth God within the shadows, keeping watch above his own." Here Cochran was able to phrase his words so they not only made sense, but they stuck in the mind as sound bites and slogans. It is a more marked way of stating your arguments; it means that the jurors keep hearing his argumentation long after they have forgotten what exactly the others said. This is shown in the way the jurors remembered what Cochran said; "If it doesn't fit you must acquit," almost as a direct quote, and only were able to remember the general idea of what the other lawyers said. As one juror said after the trial, "In plain English, the glove didn't fit. I know O.J. didn't do it."

Maxims are of great assistance to speakers, first, because an audience is pleased if an orator, speaking generally, hits upon the opinions that they specially hold. The maxim is a statement of the general; accordingly, the hearers are pleased to hear stated in general terms the opinion that they have already specially formed.[54] This example illustrates Cochran's very picturesque use of *maxims*: "There's something about good versus evil... There's something about truth. The truth crushed to earth will rise again. You can always count on that."

This use of maxims makes it possible for Cochran to gain a profile as a man of high moral and ethical standards. In other words, it gives Cochran the possibility of strengthening his ethos. Cochran needs to strengthen his ethos to support his allegation that Simpson is innocent. Aristotle writes on this aspect of a successful use of maxims: "...[A maxim] makes speeches ethical. Speeches have this character, in which the moral purpose is clear and this is the effect of all maxims, because he who employs them in a general manner declares his moral preferences; if then the maxims are good, they show the speaker also to be a man of good character."[55]

Moreover, Cochran asked a lot of *rhetorical questions* and does not mind starting a rhetorical conversation. This is seen in the following example where Cochran tries to refute the importance of a witness who saw a black man with a knit cap go into Simpson's house shortly after the murders had been committed. He places the knit cap on his head and states to the jury in his closing argument:

> You have seen me for a year. If I put this knit cap on, who am I? I'm still Johnnie Cochran with a knit cap. And if you looked at O.J. Simpson over there — and he has a rather large head — O.J. Simpson in a knit cap from two blocks away is still O.J. Simpson. It's no disguise. It's no disguise. It makes no sense. It doesn't fit. If it doesn't fit, you must acquit.

As previously stated a rhetorical question is a question you pose to your audience as part of your speech. The difference between an ordinary question and a rhetorical question is that the audience, when faced with a rhetorical question, is only supposed to answer the question within their own mind. A rhetorical conversation is when the speaker not only poses a question, but also proceeds to answer it.

Rhetorical questions attempt to get the listeners involved in the subject, as if it were a regular conversation. The listeners feel that they take part in what is said. It makes them think about the aspects of the issue that the speaker wants them to focus on.

The rhetorical questions and answers create a very direct, intense, and intimate tone, which gives an honest touch to the speech. In this way thoughts are diverted away from the specific rhetorical situation in which a biased party tries to convince the jury of the veracity of his version of the case to a more personal informal conversation. By so doing, it is possible to avoid some of the filters through which your statements would otherwise have to pass through in the juror's minds.

In order to get around the filters, Cochran says in his closing argument that he is going to have a conversation with the jury. In other words, he is not going to tell them his version of the story, but they are going to find the truth together as partners in a conversation. In order to achieve this effect, Cochran uses rhetorical questions. As is seen below:

> And so Fuhrman, Fuhrman wants to take all black people now and burn them or bomb them. That is genocidal racism. Is that ethnic purity? What is that? We are paying this man's salary to espouse these views? Do you think he only told Kathleen Bell, whom he just had met? Do you think he talked to his partners about it? Do you think his commanders knew about it? Do you think everybody knew about it and turned their heads? Nobody did anything about it.

We here see the brilliant way that Cochran was able to use Fuhrman to incriminate the rest of the police department and the public prosecutors. He used what is called *alliteration*, where he starts every sentence with the same words, "Do you think." He then changes the breadth of the question in order to expand the accusation. In this way the first three words holds the four sentences together, so the expanded statements are not felt to be a jump in reasoning, but a natural consequence.

He then ended his statement with: "Nobody did anything about it." In this statement he tried to bring the rhetorical situation to maturity. This means that the rhetorical situation was begging to be answered by the jury members in their verdict. As Cochran said earlier: "Stop this cover-up. Stop this cover-up. If you don't stop it, then who? Do you think the police department is going to stop it? Do you think the DA's office is going to stop it? Do you think we can stop it by ourselves? It has to be stopped by you."

Cochran's use of three stage rockets and the figure three in his rattling off and interpretations of options, etc., served to simplify reality and minimize the audience's options. As can be seen here:

"This is not a case for the timid or the weak of heart... This is not a case for the naive. This is a case for courageous citizens who believe in the Constitution."

In that sense you may say that this technique performs the same function as the *Socratic black/white dialectic*. In that technique the audience is directed, through conversation, towards a certain conclusion on the pretext that there are only two choices to the questions asked, one of which in reality is unacceptable. (see figures of thought in chapter 12)

Lists of three provide speakers with a way of underlining or giving progressively more emphasis to the point being made, and doing so in such a way as to give the impression that all possibilities have been covered and there is nothing else to be said on the matter. That three-part lists have an air of definite completeness about them is supported by the way speakers in ordinary conversation also routinely treat shared items as utterance-completion points.[56]

In other words, Cochran not only used the language elegantly, but he also, in an argumentative sense, had a highly effective use of the language. This alone does not determine the outcome of the case, but it does add the last drop to an already filled glass.

Like Cochran, the Roman orator Cicero would mainly appeal to ethos and the immediate emotions. With Cicero, eloquent use of the language and effective character assassinations, enabled him to slander and diminish his opponent, and thereby destroy his opponent's credibility. Like Cochran, Cicero would both directly accuse his opponents of being bad persons, and hint at them being immoral. One time Cicero insinuated that his female opponent was sexually involved with her younger brother. Another time he accused his opponent of having killed his own son from a previous marriage, because he wanted to marry a wealthy woman that did not want to marry anybody that already had children.

It is worth noticing that Cicero's allegations, like Cochran's, were not directly connected with the current issue being judged, but served as a overall discrediting of the opponent. In both cases they were able to demonize their opponent.

9. IDENTIFICATION AND PERSUASION

...whenever it is preferable that the audience should feel afraid, it is necessary to make them think they are likely to suffer, by reminding them that others greater than they have suffered, and showing that their equals are suffering or have suffered, and that at the hands of those from whom they did not expect it, in such a manner and at times when they did not think it likely.

Aristotle

Johnny Cochran said to the predominantly black jury members: "If it can happen to Michael Jackson and O.J. Simpson, it can happen to any of us" meaning any black American. Cochran thereby appeals to the jury member's fears. This can also be seen in his frequent use of the words "it is frightening" in his closing speech to the jury members.

If we are only able to understand the surrounding world based on ourselves, we may say that we can only understand "the other" if we are able to find similarities between the other and ourselves. If we are unable to do that, there will be no understanding of the other, and thus no acceptance either.

By understanding our recipient, we are able to know which basic opinions to ground our argumentation on when we wish to change our audience's opinions in other respects. Since people understand their surroundings based on themselves, it is not possible to change all or several of a person's opinions at one time. A foundation is required in order to achieve identification, and thus persuasion. The rhetorician may have to change an audience's opinion in one respect; but he can succeed only insofar as he yields to that audience's opinions in other respects. Some of their opinions are needed to support the fulcrum by which he would move other's opinions. Consequently, we must use some of our recipient's opinions in one area to change his opinions in others. This can be done by using ideas and images that identify the speaker's cause with the kind of conduct and opinions that the audience finds admirable.

By making use of the audience's own imagination, it is to a far greater extent possible to convince the audience than if we only advance arguments that do not involve the audience's imagination or ability to form conceptions. In this sense it is possible to create an imagined world more real than reality. In a way this is not so odd, as reality may be more-or-less accidental, whereas our ideas are often organized according to some common patterns and convictions.

Our sympathy towards an interpretation of our surroundings, which we have been a part in reaching, is closely linked to us. An audience is more sympathetic to a conclusion which they have been a part in drawing, than to a message the sender has pinned out for them. By so doing the audience feels as though they were not merely receiving, but were themselves creatively participating in the speaker's assertion. In such cases, the audience is exalted by the assertion as they have the feeling of collaborating in the assertion.

Ultimately, the audience's personal commitment is what forms the basis of their sympathy towards the sender's message. They do not fully understand a particular thing when they have not participated in creating it, even though they are "only" participating in their thoughts. It is especially in their thoughts that the language is alive, the languages, which they have created themselves by projecting their person out on to their surroundings.

The feeling one can generate in the audience of being an active participant and not simply a passive listener may be obtained in many ways and on many levels. One way of letting the listener become active in the listening and comprehending process is if one lets the listener draw his own conclusions instead of spelling out the points. At the same time it gives the receivers a feeling of having reach the conclusions themselves. This, as mentioned, gives a total other commitment to the conclusion reached.

When winding up a speech in praise of someone, we must make the hearer believe that he shares in the praise. This could be either personally, or through his family, profession, or in some other way. This method of activating the listener is interesting in the sense that it is very similar to the method used by Cochran in his closing statement in the Simpson case. He upgraded the jurors to become active agents for a better future without racism or public abuse of power. They were made the selected few that were to save the future of humanity. A profoundly religious, biblical motif, a topos, which is well connected to Cochran's frequent use of the Bible as a frame of reference. Not only is he able to make them accept his interpretation of the events by basing it on their convictions in other respects, he is able to make them active participants in the course of events. He is doing this both by making them draw their "own" conclusions, by the use of their imagination and ability to form conceptions, and by making them the selected few who can save us from oppression and extinction. That he makes them draw their "own" conclusions is seen from this example where Cochran shows a home video of Simpson with his and Nicole's two children at the end of the season dance that took place earlier on the night of the murders. To this Cochran says: "Let's look at this photograph for a minute, if you want to see how he looks while he is in this murderous rage ..."

Clark and Darden's logical production of evidence does not involve the jurors' imagination and ability to form conceptions to the same extent as Cochran's interpretation of the case does. Also, the jurors' opportunity for participating as active persons in the course of events is limited as regards the prosecution's interpretation of the case. It is restricted to ensuring that justice is served for two persons. This is an entirely legal judiciary appeal as opposed to Cochran's political appeal.

The prosecution could have involved the jurors a lot more in the course of events. They could have said that the jurors could send the message that rich people should not believe that they are above the law, and be entitled to treat the rest of us as they please, by buying their way out of punishment:

> Show these smart lawyers who only think about money that they can spare their efforts. We, ordinary people, are not just a bunch of ignoramuses they can drive around as they please.

The defense team tried to improve Simpson's ethos by creating a third person the jurors would like to identify with. This would counter the negative deeds, such as spousal abuse. This was a deliberate effort on the part of the defense team. As defense attorney Uelmen says: "...the recommendation of the entire team of lawyers was unanimous. It was not in O.J. Simpson's best interests to take the witness stand."[57]

They all knew that they had to keep Simpson quiet and Cochran speaking, if they were to succeed in having the jurors identify with Simpson. Creating this third ideal person would accomplish this. As Cochran states: "O.J. spoke frequently by telephone with Alan Dershowitz at Harvard. 'Whatever you do,' Alan told O.J. that night, 'make sure you keep Johnnie Cochran between you and that jury.'"[58]

By having the jurors see Simpson for a year without him saying anything, but instead having Cochran speak on his behalf, Simpson's looks and image went into a symbioses with Cochran's intelligence and eloquent behavior. In a sense they created a third person with the best traits of both.

One of the reasons for picking the jurors at random within the population is that they bring their different backgrounds and experiences with them into the deliberation room. A problem with the theme that the prosecution chose to focus on, spousal abuse, was that Judge Ito eliminated anyone that had had any experiences concerning spousal abuse from the jury.[59] You were then left with people that could only shake their heads at these kinds of scenarios, and wonder, why anybody would take that kind of abuse. In other words there was no understanding nor passion to drive them to look at the events from another angle than the racial conspiracy angle. A juror stated:

> We never had any type of abusive relationship. Just like anybody else, we had verbal arguments but nothing physical, so I cannot relate to that other than through people I knew who were in abusive relationships. Basically, I could not see myself even staying in a relationship like that. That's the

> reason why I can't understand why people think because you are black and from South Central that you can relate to these types of situations. I mean, that's not true at all.[60] ...I have never in my life seen that type of attitude from anybody. I've heard of people who accept that. They think, I've done something wrong so I guess he has the right to hit me. That type of stuff infuriates me. Nobody has the right to put his or her hands on anybody as far as I'm concerned. I can't relate to it and it makes me angry to think there are people out there who can relate to it. But if that's their choice, that's their choice.[61]

In a sense one can say that the combined wisdom that this jury had was stifled. This was done because they wanted to eliminate feelings from the decision process.

We want jurors to make decisions based upon logical reasoning, because the mathematical way of thinking is our ideal. The problem here is that we are *always* driven by emotions. Being angry that some people accept being abused by their spouse is also an emotion. By eliminating one set of emotions that may prejudice the defendant you replace them with another set of emotions that may prejudice the victim. The prosecution needed to be aware of that.

This emotional drive is not necessarily a bad thing. As Cicero said: "Emotions are what give human beings their wisdom."

JOHNNIE COCHRAN'S BACKGROUND

Johnnie Cochran is a black trial lawyer. Cochran specializes in civil rights and celebrity cases. His clientele consists primarily of people who claim to have been mistreated by the police, and celebrities who want his effective legal help.

Cochran has been working with black civil right cases since the 1950s. Fighting police abuse since the time when it was a lost cause, until the time when big rewards could be claimed. It is estimated that he has won about $40 million in awards against the Los Angeles police department, and earned about $15 million.

Besides having his own practice, he at one time was the third ranking person in the District Attorney's office. He led the investigations concerning police misconduct.

This not only made Cochran well known in the black community, but also highly esteemed. Johnny Cochran walked into this trial with a tremendous amount of "good" ethos, not least among the black community. As Cochran himself states: "America's African American communities are places where the vitality of oral history remains strong. Black women are the primary repository of their community's collective memory. In Los Angeles, that means they recall not only the lives of their immediate families and neighbors but also the outcome of legal cases that stand as landmarks in their community..."[62] It is likely that the predominately black female jury was aware of the ethos Cochran brought with him to the Simpson trial.

If we take a look at how Cochran acquired his rhetorical skills, we see that Cochran learned to speak and address an assembly in church. Through helping his father sell insurance he learned how to sell a subject to people. As Cochran states: "I was still quite active in our church as a Sunday school leader and as a speaker at the church youth programs."[63] On top of that it looks like Cochran has some solid knowledge of rhetoric, as can be seen from the quotes below:

> From the start. I went after Smith with every rhetorical weapon I could muster. It was crucial that the jurors see him for what he was, and, with that foremost in my mind, I described his conduct in the resonant language of the time. Melvin Smith, I told them, was "lower than a snake," an "Uncle Tom" who had fomented trouble for others to ingratiate himself with the police.[64]

> My dear father...was so eloquent his classmates dubbed him "Demosthenes," has several times quoted to me the Greek orator's famous aphorism: "There will be justice in Athens when those who are not injured are as outraged as those who are."[65]

It is not difficult to imagine that the lawyers that were up against Cochran in the Simpson case would have a difficult time, especially if they did not have any rhetorical training.

Presumably, Cochran, in his capacity as a defense lawyer over many years in criminal law, has a long experience in the available strategies when you have a case where the evidence suggests the accused's guilt. We must assume that Cochran, from time to time, has found himself in a position in which he was to defend a client where all indicators pointed at his client's guilt.

Often the behavior of defense lawyers in criminal law is far more flamboyant than that of lawyers in other fields of the legal system. The flamboyant behavior is probably intended to distract attention from what the case is really about. In this respect we may look at the civil legal system where the appeals of logical and long-term emotions are more preeminent than the pathos appeal, such as anger and joy. By behaving flamboyantly, emphasis is put on ethos and pathos to compensate for the lack of logos.

As a black American, Cochran carries with him the entire Afro-American gospel preaching style. This makes him able to speak to the black jurors in a style that strikes some chords. Cochran's reference "It just doesn't fit" often repeated by him while addressing the jury is taken right out of a commonly used refrain in American gospel style. The words could instead be "*It just doesn't look right.*" This phrase was used in a sermon I heard when I attended a service at a local black church. The sermon went something like this:

> I know that you were just talking, but being a married man and coming home at 3 o'clock at night from a girlfriend's house. *It just doesn't look right*. I know that your alarm clock didn't work this morning, but coming 15 minutes late to work. *It just doesn't look right*. I know that you would never do drugs, but hanging out with people that do. *It just doesn't look right.*"[66]

Moreover, Cochran's social and racial background has given him first-hand knowledge of how poor black Americans think and reason.

He knows the anger and frustrations felt by many black Americans from decades of oppression, and he is therefore able to choose the right topics that may arouse strong feelings towards things, other than the murder itself.

You persuade a man only insofar as you can talk his language by speech, gestures, tonality, order, image, attitude, and idea by identifying your ways with his. You can only persuade people of the correctness of your point of view if they are able to identify with you. They must feel that you have something in common, since we understand the world based on ourselves. In other words, we project ourselves into the world in order to understand it.[67] Evidence which we find in our language when we look at the creation of metaphors such as:

The head and mouth of a river
The heart of a nation
The back of a mountain
Mother earth
Foothills

We project parts of ourselves out onto our surroundings to be able to understand them. Since we basically only understand ourselves, we have to understand our surroundings through ourselves. Therefore we only understand what we have created ourselves. Metaphors are our own creations that enable us to understand our surroundings.

Generally we attach greater confidence to what is said by persons whom we see as being at the same level as ourselves, than to what we are told by authorities. We are more easily persuaded by those that are likeminded in our close or closest group than by authorities. For that reason alone Cochran with his background gained in his argumentation to the jurors. Cochran sought to intensify this effect, as we will see later, by making his opponent appear as a superior authority.

10. FROM THE PAST TO THE FUTURE FROM LEGAL SPEECH TO POLITICAL SPEECH

Examples are most suitable for deliberative speakers, for it is by examination of the past that we divine and judge the future. Enthymemes are most suitable for forensic speakers, because the past, by reason of its obscurity, above all lends itself to the investigation of causes and to demonstrative proof.

Aristotle

In rhetoric you divide speeches into three different categories, a legal speech that deals mainly with the issues of the past, a speech to the occasion that deals mainly with the present, and a political speeches that has to do with issues of the future.

The reason why these three kinds of speeches are divided into past, present and future is that we in legal issues judge events and deeds committed in the past. In speeches to the occasion we deal with present issues, such as the mourning of lost ones, or the celebration of an occasion such as a wedding. And in a political speech we deal with laws and actions of the future. Illustrated it would look like this:

Speeches	**Issues**	**Time**
Legal speech	Judging events	The past
Speech to the occasion	Mourning or Celebration	The present
Political speech	Future Laws and Actions	The future

The defense in the O.J. Simpson case opens the trial with a mix of legal and political forms of appeal. As the trial proceeds, they put more and more emphasis on the political form of appeal and end in Cochran's closing statement with an almost entirely political appeal to the jurors. Cochran, together with the rest of the defense, manages to change the discourse timewise. He changes the discourse from being a legal discourse in which we are to judge actions in the past, to a political discourse in which our decisions are of importance to the future.

That Cochran changes the speech situation from being a legal speech into being a political speech is one of the reasons why he is successful in using the deterrent Hitler. In his closing speech Cochran talks about how nobody took Hitler seriously either. In other words, this racially motivated conspiracy could evolve into another holocaust, if it is not taken serious in the beginning, and something is done about it.

By transforming the speech situation into being political, Cochran got the opportunity to expand the consequences of the case to affect not only the parties directly involved, but also the jury members as individuals. He not only elevates the importance of the jurors, but he also gets reasoning for his arguments in order to make them look beyond the individual case away from the facts and on to the further and universal consequences of their verdict. As one commentator stated:

> We were left arguing about whether the system was corrupt and who was responsible for it; whether Fuhrman is in the same league as Adolf Hitler; whether Cochran was wrong to be relying on bodyguards from the Nation of Islam; whether Los Angeles Police Chief Willie L. Williams was getting off easy because he is black. Everything except who murdered Nicole Simpson and Ronald Goldman.[68]

Throughout the entire trial the prosecution uses a completely legal form of appeal in their reasoning. Therefore, they are not in a position to answer the political accusations that are generally made against the police and the public authorities. At the same time, they are not able to turn the speech situation into a legal speech again, the main purpose of which is to decide on an action in the past. This makes it impossible for them to claim the consequences of an "unjust" sentence to be as far-reaching as Cochran's version that both frightens the jurors with the possible consequences and promises them a better future. In the entirely legal speech the prosecution has no possibility of promising the jurors anything which can be compared to what Cochran's political interpretation offers.

The sentence did actually have extensive consequences though not those that Cochran pleaded. I will revert to those consequences in more detail under the heading "Long-term Effects for the Parties Involved."

We are now going to see how Cochran transformed his closing statement from a legal speech into a political appeal by attacking the police.

> **A good efficient, competent, noncorrupt police department will carefully set about the business of investigating homicides. They won't rush to judgment. They won't be bound by an obsession to win at all costs. They will set about trying to apprehend the killer or killers and trying to protect the innocent from suspicion.**

Here Cochran sets up the standards that the police are to be judged by. He is also implying that the police have been doing the opposite.

> **But your verdict in this case will go far beyound the walls of department 103 because your verdict talks about justice in America and it talks about the police and whether they're above the law and it looks at the police perhaps as though they haven't been looked at very recently. Remember, I told you this is not for the naive, the faint of heart or the timid.**
> **So it seems to us that the evidence shows that professional police work took a backseat right at the beginning.**

Cochran is here expanding the verdict into something more than convicting a double killer. It is now about justice in general, and police misconduct. Cochran is here indirectly labeling the jury members as naive cowards if they do not rise to the challenge and acquit Simpson.

> **You saw Lange for about seven or eight days. Lange is different. He made mistakes. He has misstatements as you're going to see, but he was different. Remember that one day — and I'll tell you how you can characterize and understand he's different. It's very interesting. He's been on the stand for seven or eight days. One day he came in, he was a little different. He was a little more testy. And I asked him, I said, "Detective Lange, there's an article in the paper today"**
>
> ***Ms. Clark*: Objection, your honor.**
>
> ***The Court*: Overruled. It's in the record.**
>
> ***Mr. Cochran*: "There's an article in the paper today where Mr. Darden said that you're being too nice in answering my questions. Are you going to be tougher now? You know about that, don't you?". "No, Mr. Cochran. I'm just telling you the way it is regardless. "No matter how you asked this man a question or what anybody would want him to say, he seemed to try to answer the best he could. Now, we don't always agree with everything he did, but it was refreshing to have somebody like that who wouldn't be told by these prosecutors or anybody else what to say or what to do even when he's criticized in the paper. That was Lange.**

Cochran is making sure that he doesn't discredit all the police officers, since it seems more credible when one doesn't trash everybody. In an ironic way Lange is here used to trash the other police officers further by comparing them with him. Cochran is portraying Lange as honest, but he is still making sure that he is presented as dumb. In this way he still fits into the framing and incompetence theory. Lange is filling the roll of a dumb but honest kind of person.

By referring to the newspaper article, Cochran is able to tell the jury members that Darden has criticized Lange and the police in the media. This serves two purposes. First, it further erodes Darden's ethos foundation by criticizing the police. Second, it makes Darden seem manipulative. In the broader perspective this helps support Cochran's conspiracy theory, and his claim, that it was a rush to judgement.

> **...Riske ... said — and his candor was refreshing. "Have you had any training in crime scenes?" He said they kind of glossed over that at the academy. Remember he said that. I could have fallen over when he said that. They glossed over training in crime scenes at the academy. And, boy, was that ever more true. The first officer on the scene told us that. We knew that right early on, didn't we? It's nothing we made up.**
> **It's not about being anti?police. You saw the police you could believe and you now know the ones you can't believe. And anybody, anybody who believes that all police are perfect, that they don't lie, that they don't have the same biases and racism that the rest of society has, then they're living in a dream world. So this is not for the faint of heart. This is not for the timid. As I said, this is for the courageous who understand what the Constitution is all about.**

Cochran here starts out backing his incompetence claim, and ends up backing his framing theory. It is easier for him to claim police misconduct, when he gradually builds up to it by first talking about incompetence. Cochran again ends up with telling the jury members that they are naive cowards if they do not acquit Simpson. To this purpose Cochran uses a three-stage rocket, starting out with two negative statements and ending with a positive statement:

> This is not for the faint of heart.
> This is not for the timid.
> This is for the courageous

This is the way you would build up your own argumentation using a three stage rocket. If you wanted to tear down your opponent's argumentation, you would start out with two positive statements building your opponent up, only to tear it down with a negative statement in the end:

The prosecution wants you to have faith in the police - (Even though they have made countless mistakes)
They want you to believe in the evidence - (Even though most of the evidence is gathered by a racist)
And they want you to convict an innocent man - (Who has done absolutely nothing wrong)

The strangest thing about this blood. He can't explain why he carries it out there. It gets even stranger, doesn't it, because supposedly after the blood is carried out to O.J. Simpson's residence, Vannatter gives the blood to Fung, according to what we heard, but Fung then uses some kind of a trash bag, a black trash bag and gives it to Mazzola, but he doesn't tell her that it's blood. Isn't that bizarre? Remember the video when Mazzola is walking along carrying it almost bumping into the hedges and the shrubbery? The most bizarre thing you have seen. She doesn't even know it. And then talk about cover?ups, Mazzola is asked, "Well, do you see — did you see when Vannatter gave the blood to Fung?" And she says, "No. I had sat down on the couch and I was closing my eyes on Mr. Simpson's couch at that moment. I wasn't looking at that moment." It sounds like a cover?up to you, always looking the other way, not looking, doesn't want to be involved, covering for somebody. It's bizarre, absolutely bizarre and it's untrue. It doesn't fit.

So Vannatter, the man who carries the blood, starts lying in this case from the very, very beginning, trying to cover up for this rush to judgment. Those are words. That's rhetoric. Let me prove it for you. He tells us — and this is a board — the board is entitled "Vannatter's big lies," the man who carried the blood. He tells us that O.J. Simpson is not a suspect. That's the biggest lie we've heard probably in this entire trial. O.J. Simpson is not a

suspect. They handcuff him within 30 to 45 seconds of the time he gets back here. He lies about that. Weitzman sees about getting him uncuffed and they take him downtown.

Cochran has now progressed in his argumentation. He has carried the audience along with him, and he now feels that he is able to talk mostly about police conspiracy. Vannatter and Fuhrman are the main guys. Fuhrman is out to get Simpson and Vannatter actively participates in the conspiracy. Linguistically Cochran does this by building his statement up gradually:

1) The strangest
2) Even stranger
3) Isn't that bizarre
4) The most bizarre
5) It's absolutely bizarre

In this way Cochran's conclusion comes naturally.

Then they bring in commander Bushey, otherwise a good man, get him involved in this.

Again Cochran makes sure that not everybody within the police looks bad, in order to be able to make the bad guys look really bad.

Something interesting happened in this case. In 1985, Mark Fuhrman responded to a call on Rockingham. Mark Fuhrman is a lying, purging, genocidal racist, and from that moment on, any time he could get O.J. Simpson, he would do it. That's when it started, in '85.

Cochran here comes up with a reason why Fuhrman would go after Simpson. We see here how Cochran has eased his way into addressing Fuhrman, by first addressing the incompetent police officers, then the bad (Vannatter), and now the really bad police officer. By doing it this way, it makes him seem less preposterous.

But Vannatter comes in, says, "Yes, Fuhrman told me

about the thumps on the wall," contrary to what Fuhrman had said. So these are the lies of the co? lead detective in this case. If you cannot trust the messenger, you can't trust the message that they're trying to give you. You can't trust the message. So this man who starts to lie from the very, very beginning.

Let me have just a second. We covered the lies and the things that he did. And then they rope in commander Bushey, try to back him up by saying, "Well, I ordered them to do this. It's a direct order to do this." Isn't that interesting? Let's think about this. You look at those logs and see how many police officers came out to Bundy and Rockingham. Maybe more than 30. You think that of those number of officers, that maybe one of them, maybe one of the patrol officers could have went to give him notice? It took all four detectives, all four LAPD experienced detectives to leave the bodies. They had to notify the coroner. They didn't have a criminalist to go over to notify O.J. Simpson.

Cochran is putting forth reasoning for his framing and incompetence theory. We see Cochran using key words to make his speech stand out, and rhetorical questions to address the jury. By using rhetorical questions Cochran tries to engage the jury members in his speech.

So they're worried about dead bodies and people being in that house and saving lives? Who goes in first? Arnelle Simpson goes in first. These big, brave police officers, and the young lady just walks in there first. They don't go upstairs looking. They just want to be inside that house and make her leave to give Fuhrman a chance to start what he's doing, strolling around the premises and doing what he's doing there.

This reasoning is in support of Cochran's police misconduct and framing theory. Cochran only insinuates what Fuhrman might be doing on Simpson's premises. This is because it is too early to say it straight out, since he has not yet carried the jurors far enough towards his point of view. If he spells out his framing theory too early, he risks having the jury bulk at his claim. We again see Cochran addressing the jury directly by using rhetorical questions.

> **Then we come to detective Phillips, a nice man. But even he makes misstatements in this situation. Now, he knows Fuhrman probably better than anybody because he's the one who calls Fuhrman. He's the one that works with Fuhrman. Fuhrman in the culture of LAPD has been promoted. We have heard that in '85, when he goes out to this incident, he's a patrol officer. Now he's a detective, moving up in the ranks, working with Phillips.**

Cochran again makes sure that not all the police officers look equally bad, at the same time as he makes sure that he has something on every policeman involved. In Phillips case it is his close work relation with Fuhrman, the rotten apple. It is necessary for Cochran to have something incriminating on every police officer involved, since they are backing each other's testimony.

> **And who would know Mark Fuhrman better in this case, his lack of credibility, his lying, racist views than Ron Phillips, his supervisor, who apparently chose to look the other way. And I am sure he is as embarrassed as anybody else by this disgrace, Fuhrman. So it's important at the outset that we understand the role of Phillips as we understand the role of Vannatter. He was the one allegedly given this order by Bushey to go over and give the death notification. He didn't comply with it until much later. And presumably the reason they were going to go over was to give the notice to Mr. Simpson and Fuhrman was going because he was needed.**

Here Cochran further clarifies Phillips' shortcomings. Cochran comes as far as he possibly can to telling Phillips that he should be ashamed. By belittling and shaming Phillips, Cochran takes another stab at the police ethos.

Now, can you imagine this? Fuhrman with his views, genocidal views, was going to go over to give notice to O.J. Simpson, to help O.J. Simpson in his time of need. Can you imagine that? He's going over there to help him, help him with his kids. That is ludicrous.

So from Riske to Bushey, you've seen and are seeing part of this code of silence, this cover?up, the cover?up that Laura McKinny talks about. The male officers get together to cover up for each other, don't tell the truth, hide, turn their head, cover. You can't trust this evidence. You can't trust the messenger. You can't trust the message.

Cochran here puts forth reasoning for the conspiracy theory. To this aim Cochran uses irony, rhetorical questions, and repetitions of key words. Cochran forms his key words in three-part utterances that start with an "anaphor." This form strengthens and maximizes the effect.

When Fuhrman gets on the witness stand and says, "I haven't used this 'N' word for 10 years," You think Phillips knows he's lying? Some of you probably knew he was lying. It took those tapes to make those of you who didn't believe these kind of things exist to take place.

Didn't he have an obligation to come forward under those circumstances? For — if Fuhrman speaks so candidly to this lady that he met in a restaurant in west L.A., you think he talks like that to the guys on the force? She talked about he said those words in police administration, police procedures. That's the way he talks. That's the way he is. Nobody came forward to reveal this. We revealed it for you.

Here Cochran again makes sure that he has incriminated Phillips and the police officers in general by the use of Fuhrman. On top of that, Cochran makes sure that he, along with the rest of the defense team, gains the credit.

This whole thing about the police and what they've done in this case is extremely painful to us and I think to all right-thinking citizens because you see, we live in Los Angeles and we love this place. But all we want is a good and honest police force where people are treated fairly no matter what part of the city they're in. That's all you want. So in talking to you about this, understand, there is no personal pride. But I told you when we started, this is not for the weak or the faint of heart.

Cochran again puts up the standards that the police are to be measured up against. Cochran lets the jurors know that they are weak if they do not acquit Simpson. Cochran dos this by talking about emotions and morals.

And then even Tom Lange, personal favorite of mine — but in this instance, he made more mistakes than anything else. Human foibles and seems to be quite different than some of the others.

Cochran is now getting ready to set up Lange's character. He is a kind-hearted but dumb kind of person.

Remember he told us how he took these tennis shoes that O.J. Simpson told him he was wearing? I said, "What did you do with those tennis shoes?" He said, "Well, I took the tennis shoes and I put them in the trunk of my car and was going to take them home for the night because it was too late to book them." Then we looked at this video, and the tennis shoes he got, remember, he put the tennis shoes in the front seat with him. Maybe he stopped halfway up on the road, on the freeway and put them in the trunk. But that's not what he did then.

Cochran is here building up his characterization of Lange as dumb by implying that he can't give correct testimony.

Then he was part of the group who says O.J. was not a suspect, turned his head perhaps. Maybe that's his partner. But you notice, he wasn't involved in this whole debacle with these Fiato brothers and agent Wachs. He wasn't involved. He's smarter. He didn't let that happen. You know, it's interesting because it's his case. That's his case that they're working on. You didn't see him come running in here trying to cover for anybody. He didn't do that, to his credit.

Cochran is here making sure that he is not totally trashing Lange, because he needs him as a contrast to Fuhrman and Vannatter.

Then we come, before we end the day, to detective Mark Fuhrman. This man is an unspeakable disgrace. He's been unmasked for the whole world for what he is, and that's hopefully positive. His misdeeds go far beyond this case because he speaks of [a] culture that's not tolerable in America.

Now Cochran can finally concentrate on Fuhrman, now that he has characterized the other policemen in order to contrast Fuhrman. But he has still discredited them enough, to be able to dismiss their testimony. Cochran comes out with a marker that is intended to reassure the jury, that he is soon done. This gives a tired audience hope and renewed strength to hang on.

But let's talk about this case. People worry about, this is not the case of Mark Fuhrman. Well, it's not the case of Mark Fuhrman. Mark Fuhrman is not in custody. He's not — that's the man who they're trying to put away with witnesses like this, a corrupt police officer who is a liar and a perjurer.

You know, they were talking yesterday in their argument about, "Well, gee, you think he would commit a felony?" What do you think it was when he was asked the questions by F. Lee Bailey so well put? And we'll talk about that at the very end, about whether he ever used

the "N" word in 10 years and he swore to tell the truth and he lied and others knew he lied. But what I find particularly troubling is that they all knew about Mark Fuhrman and they weren't going to tell you. They tried to ease him by.

Here Cochran briefly addresses the issue that he has changed the focus of the case. Since this is his weak point, he quickly goes on to discredit his opponent by the use of Mark Fuhrman. We again see Cochran use rhetorical questions in order to give his speech a direct and informal tone.

And so when they try to prepare him, talk to him and get him ready and make him seem like a choir boy and make him come in here and raise his right hand as though he's going to tell you the truth and give you a true story here, they knew he was a liar and a racist. There's something about good versus evil. There's something about truth. The truth crushed to earth will rise again. You can always count on that.

Cochran elaborates further on his strong point. The opponent's association with Fuhrman. Cochran ends his thought pattern with a maxim aimed at elevating his statements up to a higher level, from where he can focus the jury members upon the overall perspective. Cochran here uses God as an authority figure above the law. The framing theory and the overall perspective are what opens the door for the political appeal.

...He's the one who says the Bronco was parked askew and he sees some spot on the door. He makes all of the discoveries. He's got to be the big man because he's had it in for O.J. because of his views since '85. This is the man, he's the guy who climbs over the fence. He's the guy who goes in and talks to Kato Kaelin while the other detectives are talking to the family. He's the guy who's shining a light in Kato Kaelin's eyes. He's the guy looking at shoes and looking for suspects. He's the guy who's

doing these things. He's the guy who says, "I don't tell anybody about the thumps on the wall." He's the guy who's off this case who's supposedly there to help this man, our client, O.J. Simpson, who then goes out all by himself, all by himself. Now, he's worried about bodies or suspects or whatever. He doesn't even take out his gun. He goes around the side of the house, and lo and behold, he claims he finds this glove and he says the glove is still moist and sticky.

Now, under their theory, at 10:40, 10:45, that glove is dropped. How many hours is that? It's now after 6:00 o'clock. So what is that? Seven and a half hours. The testimony about drying time around here, no dew point that night. Why would it be moist and sticky unless he brought it over there and planted it there to try to make this case? And there is a Caucasian hair on that glove.

This man cannot be trusted. He is sinful to the prosecution, and for them to say he's not important is untrue and you will not fall for it, because as guardians of justice here, we can't let it happen.

Now that Cochran has opened the door to the political appeal, he is able to go full-fledged into the conspiracy theory. It is worth noticing that Cochran uses the effective technique of repeating important words or sentences in order for them not to get lost on the jury. Cochran ends up merging himself and the rest of the defense team with the jury going from you to we. They are now the guardians of justice.

In perspective, we talked about a police department who from the very beginning was more interested in themselves and their image, and that carried through. We talked about socks that appeared all of a sudden that weren't there, socks where evidence was planted on them. We talked about police officers who lie with immunity, where the oath doesn't mean anything to them. We talked about messengers where you couldn't trust the message. We talked about gloves that didn't fit, a knit cap that

wouldn't make any difference, a prosecution scenario that is unbelievable and unreasonable. In short, we talked about reasonable doubt.

Cochran is now summarizing his claims, and drawing his conclusion. Cochran uses the word "we" in order to tie strings of connection between him and the jury members. He uses the words: "We talked about" to tie his summation together. Cochran mentions why they can't trust the evidence, and frames it in a key word form: "messengers where you couldn't trust the message." He then ends up summing their entire effort up in one sentence: "We talked about reasonable doubt."

And he [Vannatter] said something really interesting. It was really preposterous when you think about it. He said, "Mr. Shapiro, Mr. O.J. Simpson was no more a suspect than you were." Now, who in here believed that? Did he really think he was going to come back in here and we were going to believe that that O.J. Simpson was no more a suspect than Robert Shapiro? That is what he told you. Big lies. You can't trust him. You can't believe anything he says because it goes to the core of this case. When you are lying at the beginning, you will be lying at the end.

The book of Luke talks about that. Talks about if you are untruthful in small things, you should be disbelieved in big things. There is no question about that. We have known that all along.

Now Cochran is making sure that he has discredited Vannatter enough to be able to tie him together with Fuhrman as the devil in disguise. In order to give his speech credit and reach a frame of reference with his audience, Cochran uses maxims and sayings that are deeply rooted in the Bible.

So this man with his big lies — and then we have Fuhrman coming right on the heels and the two of them need to be paired together because they are twins of

deception. Fuhrman and Vannatter, twins of deception who bring you a message that you cannot trust, that you cannot trust.

We here see Cochran pairing Fuhrman and Vannatter together as the twins of deception. Cochran is repeating his main message and appealing to the jury by using biblical terms. How focused Cochran's speech is towards his specific audience can be seen by Cochran's use of the word: "twin devils of deception," which not only is a biblical term, but also, in the slang of The Nation Of Islam, means: "white devils."

Vannatter, the man who carried the blood; Fuhrman, the man who found the glove.

Cochran is making sure that the audience understands Vannatter's and Fuhrman's roll in the conspiracy. This is also exactly why they had to be character assassinated.

Why did they then all try to cover for this man Fuhrman? Why would this man who is not only Los Angeles' worst nightmare, but America's worse nightmare, why would they all turn their heads and try to cover for them? Why would you do that if you are sworn to uphold the law? There is something about corruption. There is something about a rotten apple that will ultimately infect the entire barrel, because if the others don't have the courage that we have asked you to have in this case, people sit sadly by.

Cochran is here providing reasoning for the rest of the police officers participation in the conspiracy. He is also indirectly telling the jury that they are no better then the incriminated police department if they do not acquit Simpson. Cochran again uses repetitions to stress his main message, and rhetorical questions to address the jury.

We live in a society where many people are apathetic, they don't want to get involved, and that is why all of us,

to a person, in this courtroom, have thanked you from the bottom of our hearts.

Because you know what? You haven't been apathetic. You are the ones who made a commitment, a commitment toward justice, and it is a painful commitment, but you've got to see it through. Your commitment, your courage, is much greater than these police officers. This man could have been off the force long ago if they had done their job, but they didn't do their job. People looked the other way. People didn't have the courage.

One of the things that has made this country so great is people's willingness to stand up and say that is wrong. I'm not going to be part of it. I'm not going to be part of the cover?up. That is what I'm asking you to do. Stop this cover?up. Stop this cover? up. If you don't stop it, then who? Do you think the police Department is going to stop it? Do you think the D.A.'s office is going to stop it? Do you think we can stop it by ourselves? <u>It has to be stopped by you.</u>

Now Cochran has gone totally over to the political appeal, were he urges the jury to change the future through their verdict. This is not what one could call an appeal to jury nullification, because Cochran also claims that his client is innocent. Cochran builds up his statement by using a string of rhetorical questions. In this way he is able to talk directly to the jury. The climax is when he tells the jurors that it is up to them to stop police misconduct.

I hope that during this phase of it I have demonstrated to you that this really is a case about a rush to judgment, an obsession to win, at all costs, a willingness to distort, twist, theorize in any fashion to try to get you to vote guilty in this case where it is not warranted, that these metaphors about an ocean of evidence or a mountain of evidence is little more than a tiny, tiny stream, if at all, that points equally toward innocence, that any mountain has long ago been reduced to little more than a molehill under an avalanche of lies and complexity and

conspiracy.

Here Cochran summarizes his reasoning, and tries to change his opponent's metaphors so they support his position.

> **But <u>you and I, fighting for freedom and ideals and for justice for all</u>, must continue to fight to expose hate and genocidal racism and these tendencies. <u>We then become the guardians of the Constitution</u>, as I told you yesterday, for if we as the people don't continue to hold a mirror up to the face of America and say this is what you promised, this is what you delivered, if you don't speak out, if you don't stand up, if you don't do what's right, this kind of conduct will continue on forever and we will never have an ideal society, one that lives out the true meaning of the creed of the Constitution or of life, liberty and justice for all.**

Cochran is again carrying forth his political appeal. Since it is near the end of his speech, Cochran wants to end on a high and idealistic note. This only has a positive effect if the jury is already taken by one's argumentation. Otherwise it can have the opposite effect. We here see that Cochran is pairing himself and the jury members. They are now together fighting for noble things and guarding the Constitution. Cochran is telling the jury members that they, through their verdict, can give us all a better future. This elevates the jurors, and gives them a sense of importance - Who wouldn't like to fill out this role?

> **Don't be part of this continuing cover?up. Do the right thing remembering that if it doesn't fit, <u>you must acquit</u>, that if <u>these messengers have lied to you, you can't trust their message</u>, that this has been a search for truth. That no matter how bad it looks, if truth is out there on a scaffold and wrong is in here on the throne, when that scaffold sways the future and beyond the dim unknown standeth the same God for all people keeping watch above his own. <u>He watches all of us and he will watch you in your decision</u>.**

Cochran ends his closing statement telling the jury members that they will be part of the conspiracy if they do not acquit Simpson. And for that, they will be held accountable to God.

If we look at the argumentation model, we can see that "the will of God" is the ultimate and most fundamental back-up of any warrant that this presumable deeply religious audience has. In a sense, Cochran hereby ends up securing the bases of his entire argumentation.

If we put Cochran's argumentation in to the argumentation model, it would look like this:

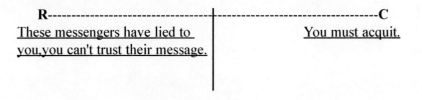

R--**C**

These messengers have lied to you,you can't trust their message.

You must acquit.

W

You can't convict people when you are not sure that they are guilty.

B

This is the will of God.

In this case, Cochran chose not to mention the warrant, but goes right to the back-up. Cochran chose this back-up because he knows that this will go well with his religious audience. In another case, the back-up might have been the Constitution.

11. CHARACTER ASSASSINATION

Let us then define making mild as the quieting and appeasing of anger. If then men are angry with those who slight them, and slight is voluntary, it is evident that they are mild ... towards those who admit and are sorry for a slight; for finding as it were satisfaction in the pain the offenders feel at what they have done, men cease to be angry.
Aristotle

Mark Fuhrman and Christopher Darden were too cornerstones that stood in the way of the defense winning their case. They stood in the way, and had to be eliminated. Fuhrman because of the evidence he had collected, and Darden because of the tactic chosen to eliminate Fuhrman. Since they could not just take them out back and shoot them, the next best thing was a character assassination.

The so-called race card had been chosen to discredit Fuhrman's ethos. Without ethos we have no foundation to build our relationship with other people. We are therefore, in a social sense, eliminated.

They assassinated Fuhrman's character by crucifying him for the mistakes made by the police department, and the sins committed by the white race. Fuhrman was even betrayed by his own because they were afraid.

Fuhrman was let down to the extent that his own lawyer dumped him and went public with how disgusted he was with him. His own union denied helping him with the cost of fighting the allegations of perjury. This forced him to plead no contest to a felony.

Because of the decision to use the race card to eliminate Fuhrman, Darden stood in the way of a black and white interpretation of the case. Darden's mere presence contradicted a racially motivated cover-up. Therefore Darden had to be turned into an Uncle Tom, a useable fool in the hands of evil players. To understand this fully we have to look at the theory of character assassination, or as it is called, "*ad hominum argumentation.*" In Latin, this means going for the man, not the ball, so to speak.

Ad hominem arguments can be a decent tool to use, especially when you have to take often-contradictory expert statements into consideration. When this happens you are left with having to judge the person's character, sincerity, and judgment.

There are three different groups of incriminating arguments used to throw suspicion on one's opponent[69]:

1) **the coup argument**
2) **the henchman argument**
3) **the errand boy argument**

In the coup argument, the debater accuses the opponent of *personally* having an evil intent, a hidden agenda so to speak, that is the real reason for his engagement in the current debate. Since the opponent is attributed a personal hidden motive, this kind of argument is always distinctly aggressive. A good example of this was the allegations put forward about Fuhrman. It basically said that Fuhrman planted the glove because he is a racist who wanted to frame Simpson. In this way Fuhrman was given a hidden agenda and an evil intent.

In the henchman argument, the debater doesn't accuse the opponent directly, but claims that he is *a tool* for evil players. Here the debater also claims that there is a *direct connection* between the evil powers and the current debate. Evil powers have been influencing the case and have been able to manipulate the opponent. Henchman arguments contain a direct or indirect accusation that the opponent is dumb or naive. If this is made explicit, the henchman argument is clearly aggressive. The indirect form of the argument can be aggressive, but the debater can also phrase it as a kind of excuse for the opponent. Since one views him as led astray, one will not question his sincerity. Even in the cases where this is well meant, the argument will often be perceived as disparaging.

The arguments put forward against Christopher Darden are a good example of this kind of ad hominum argumentation. Darden was suppose to be an Uncle Tom who let the evil players manipulate him and use him in their evil conspiracy.

In the coup and henchman arguments the debater rejects the opponent's claim because it springs from an evil intent.

In the errand boy argument, the debater accuses his opponent of running somebody else's errand. Since this arguments is a part of a refutation strategy, they are often used by debaters who wish to defend the status quo.

The debater also claims that evil players have an interest in how things turn out. But he doesn't attack the opponent's own integrity. Nor does he claim that the hidden players have manipulated the opponent directly or even had anything to do with the current debate. In the errand boy argument, the debater, on the other hand criticizes the opponent for *benefiting other interests than the ones he is aiming at.* He, in other words, is claiming that the person is unknowingly making himself into an errand boy of evil interests! This means that the argumentation goes from the issue of *motive* to *consequences*, since the debater does not so much reveal an evil intent, as she warns against evil consequences of accepting the opposite view. The errand boy argument therefore stresses the contradictory element of the opponent's argumentation. The more the attack has this trait, the less it can be viewed as an ad hominum argumentation. It doesn't have to be aggressive, even though it often has aggressive undertones because the debater insinuates that the opponent is "a useful fool."

Judge Ito is a good example of a person in this trial that has often been characterized in this way, that he was a useful fool for the defense team, being way too lenient and star struck.

Cochran used the coup argument against Fuhrman, and the conspiracy argument against Darden. Cochran is defending his client's freedom, and therefore wants to maintain the status quo.

The determination of whether this is a manipulating trick or a decent argumentation tool mainly depends on whether there is something to the accusations. It cannot in itself be indecent to warn against evil intentions unless one denies that people are driven by other motives then those they are claiming. The problem with these kinds of arguments about hidden motives is that it usually is as impossible to document that a person has wicked motives, as it is to clear oneself of the suspicion. This means that the attack can be used as a feint maneuver that can seem a little too obvious on a critical audience, if it is not well documented. The allegations, even if they are without any foundation, can be an effective countermove in situations where one is fighting an uphill battle. It is this everpresent possibility of abuse that makes many view arguments that throw suspicion on the opponent's motives as improper argumentation. People are on guard, and rightfully so, to a debater's use of these kinds of arguments.

As Fuhrman says: "Since you can't prove a negative, it's almost impossible to convince people that you aren't a racist. Therefore, the charge often sticks. Even for those who refute it, the stigma remains."[70]

The henchman argument is by definition less aggressive than the coup argument, because it doesn't contain a direct personal accusation against the opponent. On the other hand it can be used in an insinuating way that can be more indecent than the straightforward apparently aggressive attack. Since the henchman argument always plays on fear, it is nonobjective in the sense that it plays upon strong emotions. However, in the same way as in the coup argument, one cannot claim that conspiracies do not exist, and where there is a well-grounded suspicion, it should be legitimate to warn against it.

The errand boy argument is the least genuine of the three types of ad hominum arguments, and the aggressive element can be quite minor. The more clearly it aims at the consequences of the opponent's position, and contradictory to the opponent's declaration of good intents versus the independent evil group's interests, the more matter-of-fact it is. Even though it plays on fear, this kind of argument cannot be said to play on the emotions to such an extent that it can displace other relevant considerations, in the way that the coup and henchman arguments can.

Ad hominum argumentation can be extremely effective, especially if it is not adequately countered. In this case, ad hominum argumentation made it possible to turn a trial of one person into the trial of another.

It was therefore necessary to be aware of these tactics and how to counter them. As Bill Hodgman, former assistant district attorney in Los Angeles County said; "It's a real tragedy that we have a mountain of evidence to convict O.J. Simpson, and he walks free. Meanwhile, Mark Fuhrman, with an almost total absence of evidence against him, is convicted."[71]

In this instance, the prosecution team needed to defend both Fuhrman and Darden's ethos, since one was being used to get to the other. In Darden's case a counterattack upon Cochran's ethos would probably have been the most effective tactic. This would have given the prosecution a chance to defend Darden's ethos, while at the same time, the focus was not kept upon the defense teams' slurring of his ethos. That defense could have sounded something like this:

> Ladies and gentleman of the jury. Before I address the issues we are faced with today, I would like to address the issue concerning my competent and sincere colleague Christopher Darden. Mr. Cochran has for quit some time tried to attack my colleague's motives and ethics, and tried to discredit him in your eyes. To that I can only say that either Mr. Cochran is desperate or he is without shame.
>
> Money is the core issue of what is going on in this case. Ask Mr. Cochran, he should know better than any one of us, that rich people can buy their way out of anything from child molesting to murder. As the Bible says, "It is wrong to sentence the poor and let the rich go free. Whoever says to the truly guilty you are innocent, people will curse him and nations denounce him."

Even though this would probably cause some objections, it would get through, if it were put forth with enough strength and indignation.

That it was a deliberate character assassination of Darden is seen by the fact that Cochran was blaming Darden for acts that he had not done. A witness said that he heard two voices at the time of the murders, presumably one that sounded like the voice of a black man. This witness also said that he afterwards saw a white vehicle that looked like a Bronco drive away from the crime scene. Cochran blamed Darden for saying that you could hear that it was a black person's voice.

Darden, who is black himself, was accused by Cochran of being racist, because he asked a witness on the stand if it was correct that he at the time of the murders had heard two voices, one of them sounding like the voice of a black man. This was presumably a reference to the man's tone of voice and possibly his use of the language. As any other ethnic minority or subculture, parts of the black population use completely different words and expressions than the rest of the population. This comment made Cochran object and claim that it was a racist statement.[72] Cochran's claim also served the purpose of changing the agenda, when one of the defense team's own witnesses was blowing up in his face. As Cochran said:

> [Mr. Darden's] remarks this morning are perhaps the most incredible remarks I've heard in a court of law in the thirty-two years I have been practicing law. His remarks are demeaning to African Americans as a group. I want...to apologize to African Americans across this country.... It is demeaning to our jurors to say that African Americans who have lived under oppression for two-hundred-plus years in this country cannot work within the mainstream, cannot hear these offensive words.... I am ashamed that Mr. Darden would allow himself to become an apologist for this man.

In this way Cochran succeeded in shifting the focus away from the two voices and the Bronco. It would have been desirable if Darden had asked Cochran whether he thinks being black is so terrible that it is a problem that you could tell from a man's voice that he was of Afro-American origin.

The most important thing you can do in a situation like this is to hang on to the agenda by refusing to let your opponent steal the agenda. In order to be able to do this, it is necessary to be on the offensive, exposing your opponent's techniques and attacking his or her ethics. At the same time you need to keep coming back to the issue that your opponent is trying to avoid. If you merely try to defend your own actions it will enable your opponent to score points.

When it came to Fuhrman, a massive boost of his ethos was necessary. This could be done successfully by providing black people that could vouch that he was a good person. "*Vir bonus*," as the old rhetoricians would call it, the foundation for a whole person. In order to rehabilitate Fuhrman, this had to be combined with a time and content aspect:

It was ten years ago. He was in a life crisis, and he had not acquired the friendship of African Americans, that he has today, and so on.

This then had to be combined with a view of him as a human being that makes mistakes. This could then have been rounded off with a 1999 Clinton-style plea of forgiveness.

The boost of Fuhrman's ethos shouldn't have been hard to accomplish, since there were black witnesses willing to come forward to testify on Fuhrman's behalf. As Fuhrman himself points out:

> Ed Palmer, a black police sergeant, said, "There have been times I have worked with people [and] you wonder about them. I never wondered with him. I knew he was aggressive. I knew he was a little arrogant. But I never got racism at all. If he were that way, and as much a racist as the tapes indicated, then it would have come out somewhere, and somebody would have spoken up."[73]
>
> Danette Myers is a black district attorney and very close friend of mine. She was ready, at the drop of a hat, to do anything for me. ...Danette knew me personally and professionally. She became close to my wife, played with my kids, and visited my home. We shared stories, secrets, and lunches.

> We tried cases together, and once in a while I'd protect her from the irate family or friends of a suspect she had put away. She is still my good friend. In one of her few statements to the press, Danette said; "Mark saw a lot of negative stuff, and maybe it got to him. But the person I know isn't a racist."
>
> Patricia Foy is a black woman, the victim of a robbery, who chased the white man who had just robbed her. I solved the case by catching the man who did it and told her, "You were incredibly brave, but incredibly foolish to chase him. You could have ended up dead." When interviewed on CNN by Art Harris, Patricia said, "He's not a racist. They're just trying to hang something on him so they can cover up for the defense, that's all they're doing."
>
> Carlton Brown, a black detective whom I trained and worked with in West Los Angeles Robbery, also stood up for me. He told *Parade* magazine, "I never heard Mark refer to anybody in racist terms. I'd absolutely count on Mark to save my life."
>
> Carlton was one of the guys I played basketball with early every Monday, Wednesday, and Friday morning. One time, Mark Brown, a black news anchor from Channel 7, showed up at the gym with a camera crew. Mark was a nice guy, so we allowed him to film the game.[74]

Here it could have been good to have been able to show the video of Fuhrman playing basketball with his black colleagues, and simply ask: Is this what you call a hard core racist? A man obsessed with framing black people?

Another incident that would have been good to bring up was the incident where Fuhrman cleared a black man of the charges of murdering a white man. Then the prosecution could have asked the jury, why would Fuhrman, an alleged racist that is bent on framing black people, work so hard at freeing a black man? A black man charged with killing a white man. A black man that everybody else thought was guilty.

In other words, one had to take seriously that it now was Fuhrman and not Simpson that was put on trial. By acknowledging the situation it enables one to quickly mend the damage and turn the agenda back in one's own favor.

Mark Fuhrman's plea of forgiveness could have sounded something like this:

Marcia Clark: Mark Fuhrman is not a saint. He is a human being. He has done some dumb things in his life, including trying to impress a young attractive screenwriter with compulsive and derogatory language while creating a screenplay.

These statements can really not be excused, as many other things we have done in our life. This is why God, in his almighty wisdom, has given us forgiveness. For this Mark himself has to come up and ask for your forgiveness. Not for his police work. Because he is one of the best detectives I have seen, but for being inadequate as a human being.

Mark Fuhrman: I want you to now, that this is one of the hardest things I have had to do in my entire life. But I guess this is the price I have to pay for being so crude and stupid.

I did a "man thing" and tried to impress a young female theater writer with crude language and wild stories. I got greedy and thought that I could earn a little extra money if this screenplay took off. I didn't admit to something I said years earlier. I would like to think that I forgot. But maybe I was too embarrassed or felt too much pressure.

On this I guess that I can only ask for your forgiveness for my shortcomings.

One thing I will not ask for forgiveness for, or in any way excuse, is my police work. I have always been good at my work, and I take pride in it. I thank you for being fair, and listening to me.

A good example of what effect this could have had on the jury is illustrated by a letter addressed to Fuhrman:

I watched your interview with Diane Sawyer of ABC

Primetime. I just wanted to drop you a note to let you know that I was impressed with your thoughtfulness and integrity. It takes a man of strong character to admit his wrongs, ask for forgiveness, and to move on to a better place of being. I applaud this most manly of acts and do forgive you for your error. Hopefully, this will lead to your recovery.

You see, I am a black man. The courage it took for you to face me (all other black men and women), should not go unnoticed nor unacknowledged. It is also a form of courage on my part to pardon you, but what else can a man do? You lead the way, in this instance, I'll follow your lead.

God bless you, and may you find peace in your life.

Move on. You've done your duty. Peace.[75]

The prosecution states that they could not press Fuhrman to testify or make him come up and make a plea of forgiveness. But they certainly didn't encourage him either. It is not hard to understand why Fuhrman didn't want to go on the stand again. As Clark states in her book:

By now, we were no longer speaking to him. We remained in suspense until nearly the last minute--would he invoke the Fifth Amendment? I had mixed feelings about this. Part of me wanted him to speak out--to admit he'd lied about the racial slurs, and to reassert the truth that he'd never planted evidence. The other part of me just wanted him out of my life.[76]

Or as Fuhrman himself explains:

I took the Fifth because I had no choice. The prosecution had abandoned me, and I was left twisting in the wind.[77]

"Have Marcia call me," I said every time I talked to Ron. "I'll fall on my sword. I'll go back on the stand for as long as it takes. I'm willing to do whatever they want. But I needed to talk to them first. I need to know what to do."

Ron relayed the message, but I never heard from Marcia,

> Chris, or anyone from the district attorney's office. I would have done anything the district attorney's office asked me to. But they wouldn't talk to me. Their star witness was tarnished.[78]
>
> Despite the fact that these investigators had uncovered so much evidence, the prosecution never used it against the people who were attacking me. If they had introduced even some of the evidence, and argued that the tapes were only the record of a fictional screenplay, we could have fought back and I would not have taken the Fifth. If you want to win, you've got to play the game. But the prosecution only played dead.[79]

This is a man that would have had everything to gain by being given a chance to exonerate and rehabilitate himself on the stand. It should not have been impossible to have persuaded him to do that. It is likely that the prosecution could have gotten Fuhrman to testify and come though with a plea for forgiveness, if they had not stabbed him in the back, and if they had made it clear for him that it was in his own best interest, that this was his only chance to survive socially.

One can wonder way the prosecution chose not to defend Fuhrman. But if we look at a quote from a book written by Hank Goldberg, one of the lawyers on the prosecution team, we see that this could seem like a logical thing to do:

> ...Chris was in an untenable position as a cross-examiner. He knew that her previous take on the tapes was contradictory to her current testimony. He also had love letters McKinny had written to Mark, contradicting her claim that they were not romantically involved. However, any false move on cross-examination could open the floodgates for the excluded portions of the tapes to come crashing down on our heads. If Chris impeached McKinny with the quote from North Carolina or otherwise suggested that Fuhrman was attempting to create a work of fiction, the judge might rule

> that the defense should be able to put in other uses of the "N" word so that the jury could determine whether they reflected Mark's true feelings. Similarly, any effort to rehabilitate Fuhrman by calling character witnesses would have opened the floodgates to the tapes. Nor would it have been wise for Chris to have been seen as rushing to the defense of Fuhrman.[80]

This is a seemingly logical way of thinking, if one is not aware of basic rhetorical theory that everything, even logic based evidence, needs a credible ethos to support it. When we do not educate lawyers in rhetoric, fundamental flaws like this will occur, and we will be extremely vulnerable, even when it seems like we have truth on our side.

As Cicero said: "*Wisdom without eloquence does too little for the good of states.*"

In order not to miss out on a vital form of appeal in a legal case, this can be used as a check list:

A case consists of *three* aspects:

1. A provider of the evidence (police and witnesses)
2. The evidence
3. The issue at hand

The *provider* of the evidence has to come with the *ethos foundation*
The *evidence* has to bring the *logos foundation*
The *issue* at hand has to provide the *pathos*

The reason why the issue has to provide the pathos is that the issue at hand has to be of some kind of interest to the audience.

If we look at the three forms of appeal ethos, logos, and pathos in connection with what makes up a legal case, it looks like this:

What a case consists of	Forms of appeal
Provider of the evidence	Ethos
The evidence in itself	Logos
The issue at hand	Pathos

If the provider of our evidence, the evidence, and the issue don't posses these three traits, there is something vitally wrong with our case.

So how can we use this? Well, if we see that the issue has to posses pathos, this means that we have to make our issue relevant for our audience. The jurors need to be convinced that what a person is accused of really is a crime, or that a person deserves compensation. They need to feel in their gut what the consequences would be for this person if they were denied compensation. And so on.

The lawyer that has to deliver the evidence (logos) to the audience, has to posses ethos and pathos, in order for all three forms of appeal to be present in the delivery to the jury.

So if a lawyer's presentation of his evidence to the jury doesn't contain his own credibility and a appeal to emotions, there is something lacking in his presentation, which will weaken his case.

12. RHETORICAL FIGURES OF SPEECH

One should even make use of common and frequently quoted maxims, if they are useful; for because they are common, they seem to be true, since all as it were acknowledge them as such.

Aristotle

A speech can be divided into word figures and thought figures. It is a word figure when work has been put into the build-up, fine-tuning, and flow of the language. A thought figure is the contents and thought pattern used to build up the speech.

I am going to mention some figures of speech that can be effective in an argumentative speech. There are many figures of speech, but some of these are more appropriate in fiction or poetry. This is because too much rhythm and ring is not always appropriate in an argumentative speech. I have chosen examples within the legal setting, These figures of speech can, of course, be used in any argumentation or persuasive setting such as teaching or preaching;

Alliteration

Alliteration is a figure of speech where either the words following each other in a sentence start with the same letter or vowel, or the beginning words in following sentences start with the same letter or vowel. Such as: "This case is about murder, money, and manipulation." This example is also an assonance.

Assonance

You have an assonance when different accented syllables strike a common tone. This can have a very onomatopoetic effect. The assonance can, as seen above, often be combined with the alliteration.

This was also the case when Barry Scheck was able to turn his description of the evidence presented against Simpson into a combined assonance/alliteration. The defense argued that the evidence was contaminated, deteriorated, or planted. Scheck was able to rephrase this into the evidence was <u>contaminated</u>, <u>compromised</u>, and <u>corrupted</u>.

The benefit of these two figures of speech is that the words cling to your brain and carry their own logic by the way they fit together smoothly.

Anaphor

It is an anaphor when several sentences begin with the same word or group of words. This still applies even though they speak to different issues. For example:

> We are gathered here today to find the truth.
> We are gathered here today to get justice.
> We are gathered here today to prevent it from happening again.

Or as Scheck said in his closing speech:

> And <u>it's so easy to do that</u> and not be aware of it, and <u>it's so easy to do that</u> when you're in a hurry, and <u>it's so easy to do that</u> when you're only out of training for six months and you're in a tough position, and <u>it's so easy to do that</u> and not really be aware of it, <u>so easy</u> to make that kind of mistake when you really haven't had the training, <u>so easy</u> to do it when you're handling 21 samples that morning in one day, something that an experienced technician like Gary Sims tells you it takes days to do, <u>so easy</u> to make that mistake and cross contaminate these samples. <u>So easy</u>.

Epifor

In the figure of speech called an epifor one does not, as in the anaphor, repeat the same first word or words, but instead returns continuously to the same word or group of words in the end of the sentence. For example:

> Big corporations only take one thing serious -- money.
> Insurance companies only calculate one thing -- money.
> If you want to show them that they were wrong, and prevent this from happening again, you have to speak a language that they understand - money.

In this passage of Cochran's closing speech we see how he first uses a whole string of anaphors, and then ends with three epifors:

> Gee, why would all these police officers set up O.J. Simpson? Why would they do that? I'll answer that question for you. They believed he was guilty. They wanted to win. They didn't want to lose another big case. That's why. They believed he was guilty. These actions roll from what their belief was. But they can't make that judgment. The prosecutors can't make that judgment. Nobody but you can make that judgment.

Complexion

Complexion is the figure of speech that combines the two previous figures of speech, the anaphor and the epifor. Thereby the sentences start in the same way and end in the same way:

> There is no doubt that the nurse behaved recklessly and carelessly.
> There is no doubt that the doctor behaved recklessly and carelessly.
> There is no doubt that my client has suffered greatly as a result of their reckless and careless behavior.

Or as Barry Scheck stated in his closing statement to the jury members:

> You must distrust it. You have to distrust it. You cannot render a verdict in this case beyond a reasonable doubt on

> this kind of evidence. Because if you do, no one is safe, no one.

Play on Words

Here in this figure of speech we can repeat the same word without offending good taste. In this way it even makes the speech more eloquent:

> If we in life don't want to take risks, we risk that the risks are being taken for us.
> If we in life just want to be secure, we can be sure of one thing, that our security is being based on other people's risk taking.

Antithesis

It is an antithesis when the speech is constructed by concepts that create a contrast effect, for example:

> We are here today to make sure that unfair actions only lead to fair judgments. That unlawful acts to get ahead only put you legally behind.

Rhetorical Questions

A rhetorical question is a part of speech that is formulated as a question to the audience, for example:

> Can we let somebody get away with committing murder?
> Can we let somebody pay their way out of committing murder?
> Can one be allowed to commit murder because one has a skillful advocate?

A rhetorical answer is correspondingly an answer given to one's audience that is built in as a part of the speech. As for example:

> Ladies and gentlemen, you can get away with committing murder if you are rich, have a skillful lawyer, and the opponent doesn't know how to approach the situation.

If you ask and answer the question it is called a rhetorical conversation. For example:

Is it possible to get away with committing murder? - Absolutely.
Can you pay your way out of committing murder? - Without a doubt.
Can you be allowed to commit murder because you have a skillful lawyer? Certainly.
Dear jury members, don't let them seduce you.
Don't reward lack of morals and greed.
Don't let an evil act committed by a vain person stand unpunished.

The Enthymem

The enthymem is a figure of speech that uses two contrary statements to establish easily and briefly that one of them is true. This statement could have been used in the Simpson trial:

> Simpson cannot both be given lenient treatment by the police, by them looking the other way when Simpson batters his wife, and then claim that the police are trying to frame him because they have racial biases against him.

Or as Barry Scheck said in his closing statement:

> How can you just assume you're doing everything right when we can prove they're doing everything wrong?

This is a sophisticated statement. Scheck is addressing the jury members directly and at the same time he is referring to the prosecution as the ones they can't assume are doing things in the right way. In this way Scheck makes the statement personal, at the same time as he addresses his opponent's actions.

Colon and Link

A colon in a speech is a short unit that in itself doesn't contain the whole meaning, since it is not a complete sentence, as in this example:

> Not only did you dismiss my client's legitimate request for compensation...
>
> This unit is called a colon; thereafter it is matched by another colon:
>
> you hired experts to disagree with my client's position....

This figure can contain two colon, but the most pleasing and well-rounded figure is the one that consists of three cola, like this:

> Not only did you dismiss my client's legitimate request for compensation, you hired experts to disagree with my client's position, and you lied under oath.

Or as Cochran said in his closing speech:

> They don't have the courage. Nobody has the courage. [It's] a bunch of people running around with no courage to do what's right.

A link in a speech is when the single word is stated separately in a split up stream of words, as Cochran states in his closing statement:

> So when we talked about this evidence being <u>compromised, contaminated</u> and <u>corrupted</u>, some people didn't believe that. Have we proved that? Have we proved that it was <u>compromised, contaminated, corrupted</u>, and yes, even something more sinister? I think we did.

Or one could say:

When the police act like prosecution, judge, and jury, to whom should we plead our case?

The difference in strength between the colon and the link is that the first one hits slower and with larger intervals, where the latter hits close and often. These two figures of speech either slow down, or increases the pace of the speech.

Hypofora

A hypofora is a figure of speech where you ask your opponent what can be said in their defense. You simply question what can be said in their defense, or against you. Thereafter you add what should be said or shouldn't be said, and what would be your strong point, or the most revealing points of your opponent's argumentation. For example, the prosecution could have said:

> One can ask if the collected blood from the murder scene, Simpson's house, driveway, and car was planted, since it has been claimed that some of the blood from Simpson's blood sample is missing.
> Well, first of all, there is probably not any missing blood, since the assumption that there was blood missing from the blood vial is built upon the statements from a nurse that gave an estimate of how much blood he drew from Simpson. This nurse has, after further consideration, realized that his first estimate was incorrect, and therefore there isn't any blood missing.
> Secondly, it is unlikely that the amount of blood that we are talking about here could have been spread out over such a large area. They claim that some of the blood found at Simpson's estate and driveway came from his injury to his hand.
> One can speculate about at what point the blood drops stopped being planted, and the bleeding from the hand started.
> Now why is the defense clinging to such a weak theory? To this there is only one simple and straightforward answer. It is the only way they can explain their client's blood at the scene

> of the murders.

Or as Cochran said in his closing statement:

> Gee, why would all these police officers set up O.J. Simpson? Why would they do that? I'll answer that question for you. They believed he was guilty. They wanted to win. They didn't want to lose another big case. That's why. They believed he was guilty. These actions roll from what their belief was. But they can't make that judgment. The prosecutors can't make that judgment. Nobody but you can make that judgment.

In this figure you can, in question format, put forward what should have been done, and then state that this has not been done. It is easy to outrage your audience due to the extent of the act, as is seen here:

> Shouldn't the head detective have stayed at the original crime scene? Instead he went off to notify Simpson about the death of his ex-wife.
> Weren't the police suppose to have obtained a search warrant before they entered Simpson's estate? They didn't do that.
> Shouldn't the police have adequately concealed and protected the crime scene? The Bronco was left in the street unprotected for hours, while it was used as a coffee table by the news crews.
> Ought the forensic expert not collect every blood drop from the crime scenes? Mr. Fung only collected every fifth blood drop.

This is a figure of the same type as when you relate a hypofora to your own person, in this way:

> But what should I have done? Denied giving blood? There was no reason for that, since I had nothing to hide. If I had denied giving blood, that's when it would really have looked weird. Should I then have demanded that the blood was

> drawn on a hospital, and not at the police station? But how could I, even in that situation, be sure that they didn't get a hold of my blood?

With a hypofora of this type one creates the impression that it wouldn't have been better to do anything else than what was actually done, since the hypofora seemingly takes all issues into consideration, it is very closely related to the Socratic black and white dialectic. The hypofora is in monologue form what the Socratic black and white dialectic is in a dialog. This means that the hypofora, though traditionally placed under the category figures of speech, also can be seen as a figure of thought.

Demarcation

A demarcation is a figure of speech that summarizes some qualities briefly and thoroughly in this way:

> Ladies and gentlemen, the evidence of spousal abuse alone shows that there is a 35 to 50 percent chance that Simpson is the one that killed his wife.
>
> The fact that the blood samples provides a positive match means that they could not have deteriorated. The fact that there was so much DNA evidence pointing to Simpson shows that it could not have been caused by mere cross-contamination.
>
> The fact that much of the blood was collected before Simpson gave a blood sample, let alone before Vannatter returned to the crime scene, shows that the blood was not planted.

This figure is useful because it in a brief and clear way puts forth and explains the issues in a clear and overviewable way. This gives the impression that it couldn't have been said better with more or fewer words.

Crossing

It is called a crossing when one briefly outlines what has been said, and then in the same way with a few words states what is to come. This could be:

> We have just looked at the statistics showing that if a woman is murdered, and she was battered by her husband, ex-husband or boyfriend there is a 35 to 50 percent chance that he is the one who did it. We are now going to combine this with the actual evidence we have against Simpson.

This figure of speech is good for two things: It reminds the audience of what the speaker has said, and it prepares them for what is to come.

The Correction

In a correction one takes away the word one has just said, and replaces it with one that seems more suitable. In this quote we see a correction where the word mystical is replaced with the word parental:

> Cochran's stature in L.A.'s black legal community was such that the relatively inexperienced Darden was, perhaps understandably, intimidated by his mere presence (and the older man would use this against the younger man time and again during the course of the trial). Cochran's hold over Darden bordered on the mystical or, more precisely, the parental. This often led the prosecutor to behave like an adolescent, appearing alternately to disdain and beseech his elder. When Cochran spoke in court, Darden would often hunch over in his seat, hold his head in his hands, puff his cheeks, and pout theatrically.[82]

This figure of speech makes an impression upon the audience. When you use an ordinary word, it is merely looked upon as being mentioned. However, after the speaker's own correction of what is said, it is as if the issue has gotten a special reference all by itself. But wouldn't it be better, at least when one is writing, to use the most appropriate word right away? This is not always the best approach. If the ordinary use of the first word doesn't give the statement the weight it deserves, the correction technique puts more focus on the issue. If one has used the "correct" word from the beginning, one cannot stress the meaning one wants to convey in the same way. Neither the issue nor the elegance would be noticed.

Passing Over

Passing over is used when you say that you will not mention, do not nor will say what you are actually saying. This tactic could have been applied by the defense team when they wanted to make the jury aware that Vannatter lived in Simi Valley, an area that is almost entirely white and has a reputation for being prejudice towards blacks. This is, among other things, the area where the first Rodney King jury was from. Cochran did in fact mention to the jurors that Vannatter lived there:

> Do you think that Fuhrman is alone in his racist views upon blacks? What about Vannatter, the carrier of the blood? Do you think that he knew about Fuhrman? Do you think that he wasn't a part of the good old boys? We won't even get into that Vannatter lives in Simi Valley, and has done so for the last 20 years.

> Or as Fuhrman says in his book:

> If a racist is someone obsessed with race, whose perception is clouded by the color of a person's skin, and who sees himself as a member of a racial group first and a human being second, then Chris Darden could be called a racist. But I won't.[83]

This figure of speech is useful if:

1. One either has an advantage of reminding the audience secretly about something that is not fitting to say openly to just anybody, or

2. If what one wants to say is too long and drawn out or,
3. If what one is hinting at would be to improper to say straight out or,
4. If it cannot be recounted clearly or,
5. If it can easily be attacked.

Then it is more beneficial to have spread a hidden suspicion than to have stated something clearly that can be countered.

Reduplication

Reduplication is a repetition of one or more words in order to create amplification. It can also be used as a plea for forgiveness. Cochran's repetition of the word "frightening" was an example of the amplification technique:

> You cannot believe these people. You can't trust the message. You can't trust the messengers. It is frightening. It is quite frightening and it is not enough for the prosecutors now to step up and say, oh let's just back off. The point I was trying to make, they didn't understand. That it's not just using the "N" word, forget that, we knew he was lying about that, forget that. It's about the lengths to which he would go to get somebody, black and also white if they're associated with black. It's pretty frightening, it's not just African Americans, it's white people who would associate or go out with a black man or marry one.

Or as Scheck's said in his closing statement:

> But you know, there is a very, very interesting point that you might have missed in Dr. Rieders' testimony.

> Well, you know, it is their burden. It is their burden after all.

Repetition of the same word makes an impression upon the audience, and is able to damage the opponent further in the same area.

Interpretation

Interpretation returns to the same word without repeating it. This is done by connecting the first word to another word with the same meaning, seen in this quote from Cochran's speech:

> You're the ones in war. You're the ones who are on the front line.

Or, Cochran, again:

> I want to tell you about what is troubling, what is frightening, what is chilling about that Kathleen Bell letter.

The audience cannot avoid being affected when the seriousness of the first statement is repeated in a new way. This figure of speech was also used by Scheck in his closing statement in his attempt to strengthen the credibility of his own experts:

> Because he is experienced, he is knowledgeable, he is learned.

Elimination

Elimination is when you first state a group of reasons why something could happen or not happen, and thereafter eliminate them one by one, until there is only one left, the one that confirms your theory. This can be done in this way:

> Ladies and Gentlemen. With the DNA evidence pointing to Simpson as the killer, we are faced with only four possible scenarios:
>
> 1. Either somebody planted the blood.
> 2. The blood deteriorated.
> 3. It has been cross-contaminated, or,
> 4. Simpson murdered the two people.
>
> Vannatter, who collected Simpson's blood, was not able to make it back to the crime scene before Fung had collected most of the blood evidence. Therefore the blood could not

have been planted.

If the blood were deteriorated, the blood samples would have been indecisive, not a positive match with Simpson's DNA. Therefore the blood could not have deteriorated.

Cross-contamination at the crime scene would not have affected the socks and glove found at Simpson's estate, nor inside the locked bronco. Therefore, the DNA match cannot be explained away by the possible effects of cross-contamination.

This leaves us with only one explanation of this event. Simpson killed these people. Not only is this the most straightforward explanation, it is also the only possible explanation.

This figure of speech mostly supports production of evidence concerning the actual events. Contrary to most other figures, you cannot just use elimination when you feel like it. You can only use elimination when the nature of the problem allows it.

Antithesis

The figure of speech called an antithesis brings contrasts together. It can either be a word figure (page 160) or a thought figure depending upon whether it brings contrasting words or thoughts together. As a word figure it could look like this:

They can't live together, and they can't live apart.

The antithesis as a thought figure was used by Cochran in his closing statement as follows:

Fuhrman wants to take all black people out and burn them or bomb them. That's genocidal racism. Is that ethnic purity? What is that? What is that? We're paying this man's salary to espouse these views.

Aposiopesis

When you start out saying something, and then you don't finish what you started to imply, it is called an aposiopesis. An example is found in this statement used by Cochran:

> So when we talked about this evidence being compromised, contaminated, and corrupted, some people didn't believe that. Have we proved that? Have we proved that it was compromised, contaminated, corrupted, and yes, even something more sinister?

Here a suspicion without words becomes more threatening than a detailed explanation would have been. This figure of speech can also be used in the same way as the "passing over," where you state a claim that, if it was said directly, could be viewed as too low, drawn out, or easy to attack. This can be seen from Scheck's use of this figure of speech in his closing statement:

> Again Martz, he — he is — he has a bachelor's degree, he had some trouble with PI, I don't want to belittle that, but he didn't even — there are some disturbing parts of his testimony, let's face it.

Permission

It is called a permission when the speaker in the middle of his speech shows that he turns over and entrusts the whole case to another person's decision. As Christopher Darden said in his closing speech in the Simpson case:

> Whatever you do, the decision is yours, and I'm glad it's not mine.

Even though this figure can be used in different circumstances, it is especially suited to evoke pity.

Dubitation

Dubitation is when the speaker seemingly asks what he should choose to say among two or more possibilities. It could be said in this way:

> Now why would Simpson think that he could get away with committing these murders? I do not know if I should say that it was due to his outrageous vanity or his staggering naiveté.

Or as a reader of *Time* magazine commented concerning Barry Scheck and his Innocence Project:

> Through his own arguments [concerning DNA], we are left with two possible conclusions: either Scheck is freeing potentially guilty people through the Innocence Project, or he successfully defended a double murderer he knew to be guilty. I don't know whether to laud this man or deplore him.[84]

This figure can both enhance the effect of one's statement, and make one seem more credible.

Figures of Thought

The Metaphor

In the metaphor two well-known items are merged and thereby create or explain a third item or concept. Metaphors are connected to the way we come up with new ideas. New ideas are created like a metaphor, where you take some well-known components and put them together in a new way. Metaphors can be shown to exhibit on a small scale some of the processes of thought which appear to operate on a large scale in all creative thought.[81]

A predominate metaphor in this case was the prosecutions description of their evidence as "a mountain of evidence." To counter this, the defense came out with a further development of this metaphor that turned it into a "molehill." It was important for the defense team to counter the prosecution's metaphor, since the winning metaphor shapes our view upon the world. A metaphor is like a miniature story that makes you see the event from a certain perspective. While a good story shapes our belief on a overall level, the metaphor shapes our way of thinking on a concrete level.

Metaphors shape our view of our surroundings, as it redefines our way of looking at things. The way we chose to address something influences our way of thinking about it. This is the basis for political correctness.

You can basically counter any metaphor if you put a little effort into it. We are here going to see how Cochran countered Clark saying that all the pieces of the puzzle pointed at Simpson. Clark was illustrating this by putting a piece of a puzzle down for each piece of evidence she was presenting. In the end the puzzle showed a picture of Simpson:

> ...the prosecution had a puzzle, and it was interesting how they did this puzzle, technology is wonderful and you saw they kept under this puzzle putting on pieces and that sort of thing. And so we thought about that. I thought about this puzzle, thought about what it meant in this particular case.
>
> I got a call from a very, very wise, wise, wise lady who reminded me that if you ever have gone to the store and bought a puzzle, when you buy a puzzle, on the outside of the box of the puzzle there is a picture, so you know what the puzzle looks like when it is finished. Well, in this case the prosecution took a photograph or picture of O.J. Simpson first, then they took the pieces apart.
>
> If they really wanted to talk about reasonable doubt, you don't jump to conclusions at the beginning. You don't rush to judgment and then be concerned about an obsession to win. What you do is you take the pieces and put them together and then you come to the conclusion. They have got it all backward.

The prosecution team can of course counter this by saying that they did not go out and buy themselves a puzzle, but that they merely assembled the pieces that they found.

There are two ways to counter ones opponent's use of metaphors:

1. Create a new and overruling metaphor
2. Build onto the opponent's metaphor.

Socratic Black and White Dialectic

Socratic black and white dialectic, received its name from Socrates, one of the first known users of this technique. Socrates would carry on a dialogue with his opponents putting questions to them that seemingly only had two answers, one of which was totally unacceptable. By this question and answer technique, you steer your opponents in a direction that in the end will force them to agree with you.

This technique can be exemplified by another trial lawyer, Gerry Spence.

As Spence says, on the issue of whether a lawyer should defend a man he knows is guilty:

> *Spence*: Let's suppose we both know the defendant is guilty and we have the power of justice in our hands. Should we simply take the man out and hang him?
>
> *Person*: Well, no.
>
> *Spence*: What should we do, then? Give him a trial?
>
> *Person*: Yes, of course.
>
> *Spence*: We should give him a trial and *then* hang him, right?
>
> *Person*: No answer.
>
> *Spence*: If we give him a trial, should it be a fair trial?
>
> *Person*: Well, yes, of course.
>
> *Spence*: If it should be a fair trial, should we provide him with an attorney?
>
> *Person*: Yes.

> *Spence*: But the attorney knows that his client is guilty. Knowing of his client's guilt, should the attorney try to lose the case? That is knowing he is guilty, would it be permissible for the attorney to intentionally throw the case?
>
> *Person*: Well, no. That would be dishonest.
>
> *Spence*: Suppose then that the attorney, knowing his client is guilty, uses his best efforts to make sure that the prosecution proves the state's case against his client with honest and proper evidence. Should he do that?
>
> *Person*: Yes, of course. That's his job.
>
> *Spence*: And after he's done his job, suppose the jury finds there is a reasonable doubt, and the jury acquits a guilty man. What then?
>
> *Person*: No answer.
>
> *Spence*: Should we blame the defense attorney for doing his job? Or should we blame the prosecutor for failing his?[85]

The possible, indecency in this argumentation technique lies in the fact that most issues contain more options than two. The Socratic black and white dialectic is a very powerful argumentation tool, since it provides a seemingly logic and overall worldview. And you often have to be very quick to detect the flaws in what is said.

In this case one can wonder what Spence means by:

> Making sure that the prosecution proves the state's case against his client with honest and proper evidence.

Since Spence points out that the lawyer knows that his client is guilty, Spence's presumption seems to be that there is a difference between guilt and legal guilt an interesting ethical presumption.

In regards to Spence saying:

> Knowing of his client's guilt, should the attorney try to lose the case? That is knowing he is guilty, would it be permissible for the attorney to intentionally throw the case?

Knowing that his client is guilty, it may not be permissible for the lawyer to throw the case, but one can argue that it may not be permissible for the lawyer to argue that his client is innocent either.[86]

Distribution

The figure of speech known as distribution occurs when certain roles are distributed among several things or persons. An example of this technique could have been said like this:

> Vannatter carried the blood. Fuhrman planted the blood, and the rest of the police department cooperated with these two twin devils of deception by initiating a code of silence.

Or as Cochran said in his closing statement:

> They made a judgment. Everything else after that was going to point toward O.J. Simpson. They didn't want to look at anybody else. Mr. Darden asked who did this crime. That's their job as the police, we've been hampered, they turned down our offers for help. But that's the prosecution's job. The judge says we don't have that job, the law says that. We'd love to help do that. Who do you think wants to find these murderers more than Mr. Simpson? But that's not our job. It's their job...

This figure of thought is very rich in contents, since it combines a lot of events in a short form. By giving each issue its part, this figure distinctly divides several things.

To Underestimate

It is an underestimation when you says that you, or the one that you are defending, has an advantage due to nature, fate or hard work, and then diminishes and tones it down in your speech in order for it not to be seen as bragging. This can be done in this way:

> Why would Mr. Simpson kill Nicole because he couldn't get her? He had a beautiful girlfriend and access to beautiful women all over the world. Simpson had wealth and fame that gave him access to whatever a man could wish for. In spite of this Simpson never forgot where he came from and always remained loyal to the community.

Or another example of underestimation could look like this:

I have been blessed with winning some big awards and have to date never lost a case, though I have always had to work hard at presenting my cases and arguments in the best possible way.

I bless the Lord for my fortune, and put faith in the ways he leads me.

If he had said, "I am among the very best" then he could easily seem to be bragging, even if it was true. In this way you can both avoid envy and receive praise or recognition.

When using your common sense to avoid envy, you should also, as a speaker, use your reflection, so it doesn't create distance between you and your audience.

Detailed Description

Detailed description is the name of the figure that in a powerful way gives a clear overview and clear account of an event. This technique could have been applied by the prosecution when addressing the consequences of Nicole Brown's death for her two children:

> And so how are things different for Justin and Sidney? Instead of long talks that they would enjoy with their mother, instead they write a letter to their mother on Mother's Day and bury it at her grave. Instead of getting hugs every day from their mother, they look at photographs. Instead of happy

> thoughts when they think of their mother, they get sad because they miss her. Instead of looking at her mother's eyes, Sidney looks at this ceramic portrait that she made of her mother, that is the most valuable possession she has in her room.
> Justin has a nervous stomach because his mother is not there. Unfortunately, the ceramic bust and the photographs that they pull out and look at every several weeks are not a replacement for the loss of their mother. This is what Simpson has done to his children. Not only did he beat Nicole up during her pregnancy, and accuse her of not losing weight fast enough after she had given birth he killed their mother, the most valuable and irreplaceable person a child can ever have.

This technique was used by Cochran in his closing speech when he addressed the relevance and importance of Fuhrman's derogatory statements.

> The point I was trying to make, they didn't understand. That it's not just using the "N" word, forget that, we knew he was lying about that, forget that. It's about the lengths to which he would go to get somebody, black and also white if they're associated with black. It's pretty frightening, it's not just African Americans, it's white people who would associate or go out with a black man or marry one. You're free in America to love whomever you want. So it infects all of us, doesn't it? This one rotten apple and yet they cover for him.

In both these examples an issue is addressed both in a clear and overviewable way, at the same time as the speaker is able to get into specific details. In this way it is possible both to prove one's point and at the same time keep it simple. These figures can evoke anger, indignation or pity when all the consequences of an act or event are gathered and presented briefly in a clear speech.

Dividing

A dividing splits a problem into two alternatives. It then presents a conclusion that covers both. This example shows how this technique could have been applied in this case:

> To charge Simpson within a week after the murders had been committed, without even considering any other suspect, shows that the police were either incompetent or biased against my client. Therefore, we cannot put our trust in the police.

Or a more general example:

> Why should I blame you now? If you are a decent human being, you have not deserved blame, and if you are not a decent human being, it will not affect you anyway.

Accumulation

When the subjects that are found throughout the whole speech are gathered in one place in order for the speech to become either serious, more poignant or more accusing, it is called an accumulation. The extent and density of an accumulation can be anywhere from several paragraphs to a single sentence. Barry Scheck's statement concerning the evidence against Simpson is an example of this.

> The prosecution's mountain of evidence has turned into a molehill that is contaminated, compromised, and corrupted.

If the prosecution had applied this technique when dealing with the spousal abuse issue it could have sounded like this.

> Simpson meets Nicole when she is 17 years old. He dates her, and marries her a few years later. He starts beating her a year after they meet each other, and continues to abuse her, both physically and psychologically until she is 35 years old. At this time she tries to get away from him for good. He therefore decides to kill her to achieve the final control.

An accumulation is useful in cases where suspicions are insignificant and weak when they are mentioned in a scattered fashion, but gain strength when they are gathered in one place. This seems to make the case obvious and not just suspicious. This can be done in this way:

> Dear jury members, try to imagine a person that has no alibi, and has given several suggestions to where he was and what he was doing when the murders were committed
>
> This person has a history of violence towards the murdered person.
>
> He runs away from the police when about to be taken into custody, carrying with him a large amount of money, a passport, a disguise kit and a loaded gun.
>
> Try and imagine a person that says he has dreams of killing the victim.
>
> Try to imagine a victim that had stated to several people that she was afraid of being killed by this person.
>
> Try to imagine a victim that a week before she is killed had called a battered woman's hotline and said that she was afraid for her life because her ex-husband was stalking her.
>
> Try to imagine a person that has several explanations of how he got a scar-producing injury to his hand, at the time of the murders.
>
> Try and imagine a person that runs around bleeding excessively in his own house, driveway and car the day of the murders, a man that is seen driving away from the scene of the murders at the time the murders were committed.
>
> Try and imagine a person whose blood is all over the crime scene. And that has blood from the victims inside his car.
>
> Ladies and gentlemen. You know that there is something called reasonable doubt. May I suggest to you that there is also something called unreasonable doubt?

It is a powerful figure, and in cases with controversial questions concerning the actual events it is almost always necessary. This thought figure is also often used in other areas of communication dealing with controversial questions.

To Dwell at the Same Point

To dwell at the same point means that, for quite some time, you stay with, or several times returns to, your strongest point the one that the whole case is dependent upon. There are great advantages to using this figure, and it is to a high degree the characteristic trait of a skilled speaker. This is because you do not let the audience get a chance to focus their attention on anything but your strongest argumentation. As Cochran said in his closing statement while quoting a letter from Laura McKinney:

> ...Officer Fuhrman said that when he sees a nigger, as he called it, driving with a white woman he would pull them over. I asked, what if he didn't have a reason? And he said that he would find one. I looked at the two Marines to see if they knew he was joking. But it became obvious to me that he was very serious. Now, let me just stop at this point. Let's back it up a minute, Mr. Harris. Pull it back down please. If he sees an African American with a white woman he would stop them. If he didn't have a reason, he'd find one, or make up one. This man will lie to set you up. That's what he's saying there. He will do anything to set you up because of the hatred he has in his heart.

Then Cochran goes on to use this thought figure to further stress the fears that are especially harbored by black Americans and other minority groups:

> A racist is somebody who has power over you, who can do something to you. People could have views but keep them to themselves. But when they have power over you, that's when racism becomes insidious. That's what we're talking about here. He has power. A police officer in the street. A patrol officer is the single most powerful figure in the criminal justice system. He can take your life. Unlike the Supreme Court, you don't have to go through all these appeals, he can do it right there and justify it and that's why, that's why this has to be rooted out in the LAPD and everyplace else.

Vaccination

To vaccinate one's audience is to mention and refute the counter-arguments before your opponent has time to state them. This could be done in this way:

> Ladies and gentlemen, the defense team is going to tell you that their client is being framed, and that every single witness is lying or concealing information. They are going to do this, because it is the only defense a guilty man has.

This is a strong and expedient persuasion method. By getting a small part of the "disease" the audience is made "immune" against the opponent's reasoning. The vaccination technique is a powerful argumentation tool that effectively limits your opponent's means of counter reasoning. Like in chess, you can corner your opponents so no matter what move they decide to make, they lose.

An interesting variation of the vaccination technique is when one doesn't so much vaccinate against a certain argument, as vaccinate against a certain argumentation technique or preferred theme or favorite subject of one's opponent. To deprive an old horse of its ways can often throw it off course. A good example of this technique is when Bugliosi in his book suggested how he would make it difficult for Cochran to use his favorite theme, and usual tactics:

> Incidentally, near the end of my opening argument, I might have left a Bible and a copy of the U.S. Constitution on the lectern, telling the jury: "Mr. Cochran talks about the Bible and the Constitution in all of his cases, and if he decides to do so in this case as well, I just want to help my colleague out." If, when Cochran got up, he started quoting from the Bible and Constitution, he'd look a little foolish, and if he didn't, he'd have to do without a lot of the emotional underpinnings of his argument.[87]

One can in other words vaccinate against both the form and contents of an argument that one's opponent may employ. Here it is most important to vaccinate against one's weakest points. This of course has the effect of vaccinating against one's opponent's strongest points. The vaccination technique can be carried further than just vaccinating against ones opponent's counter-argumentation. It can be used to vaccinate against the jury member's own thoughts. Bugliosi has another good example concerning that:

> ...the prosecutor has to make the assumption that defense counsel, as incompetent as he may be, is at least going to see and argue, however poorly, the main weaknesses in the prosecution's case. The dilemma arises when defense counsel doesn't see one or more of these weaknesses in the prosecution's case, particularly the more subtle ones. As a general but not ironclad rule I find a way in rebuttal to raise and discuss these issues myself. Why? Because a jury consists of people with hundreds of years of collective human experience, and even though defense counsel never spotted a particular weakness, chances are at least one of the jurors will have. And if just one juror sees it, all twelve learn about it as soon as he brings it up during deliberations. And if the jury is talking about a weakness in my case back in the jury room, I want to have been heard on the issue.[88]

This is the same thing one has to do when writing an article, since one does not have the audience's counter-reasoning available to respond to. This variation of the vaccination technique not only insures that one is heard, even though one is not present, it also places a great deal of elegance and sophistication onto one's argumentation.

Excuse

Here you start out your sentence or speech by excusing yourself. You often see this figure of speech used in the beginning of a person's speech. It is:

> I am not a speaker but....

Or as Darden says:

> We are just doing our job.

> You also see it used when somebody wants to say something good about himself:

I may not have received very high grades in school, but I have been extremely successful in life.

Or:

> As a man I may not be the right one to talk to you about how a woman feels, but I hope you will bear with me, when I tell you how this has affected my client, as a human being, as well as a woman.

It is here used as a way to say something positive about yourself or somebody else, without seeming like you are bragging. It also makes you seem more credible, because it makes your statement look more realistic.

By looking at both the rhetorical figures of speech and thought, the interaction between form and contents shines through. What we say, and how we say it influences the other, just as mind and body affect each other.

An important aspect of getting support for your point of view is how you start out addressing your audience. The legal community has found out that you do not just start out presenting the evidence to a jury. That there is more to it than that. It has become very fashionable to start out telling a story. The reason this can be effective is that many times it satisfies the two things that you need to achieve in the beginning of a speech or text:

1. Create interest for what you are saying.
2. Achieve good will for yourself and your case.

It is important to be aware that this is what you are trying to achieve, because there are other ways of addressing an audience that satisfy these demands that may be more effective in a specific case.

You can tell many different kinds of stories not all of which will have the intended result. It can be a very precise story, which doesn't necessarily mean that it is a very interesting story. If you don't know why you are suppose to do something, it is a little hard to focus on the key issues. Therefore we are going to look at two other ways of beginning a speech:

In Medis Res

In this technique, you start out addressing the main issue straight on without any introduction. Marcia Clark could have begun her closing statement by saying:

When Simpson was told, "Mr. Simpson, I am sorry to have to inform you that your ex-wife is dead", what was Simpson's response?

Did he ask how it happened?

Did he ask when or where it happened?

Did he even ask what happened?

Nor did he try to call back later to find out what had happened.

Was this because Simpson didn't have access to a phone on his way back from Chicago? No, he was on the phone several times talking to his lawyer. Now *why* would this be the first person Simpson called, without even knowing what had happened?

There is only one reason Simpson would not ask any of these questions. O.J. Simpson *already knew* what had happened to his ex-wife. And this is why we are here today, ...

In a moderated way, this technique can also be applied in the opening statement. As long as you make sure to preface all your statements with, "During this trial we are going to show that...". In this way, one can say almost anything in an opening statement.

Suspense

In this way of addressing the audience, they are kept in suspense as to where you are heading, and how you are going to connect it to the issue at hand:

We all want to be our own God, but few of us has the caliber for that! When we get into a crisis, we understand the

> Christian language right away. The Christian message of love and compassion helps us to find our own true self, so God can accept us, as he himself has created us. God knows what you have done, Mr. Simpson, and it is from him that you have to seek forgiveness. God knows what is right every time. God does not keep a check and balance book. Two wrongs do not make a right. This is not a rich man's civil rights case. This is a rich man's murder case. Have you ever heard about a rich man's civil rights case?

In this way you can get your audience interested and listening to what you now are going to say. This is because they are intrigued by why you are saying this things, and how you are going to tie it onto the issue at hand. This could then have been tied onto the issue of Simpson's guilt in this way:

> We have presented evidence of Simpson's guilt that is so strong that it can only be countered by claming that Simpson was framed, and that is exactly what they have done. But no matter what happens, someday we all have to answer to a higher authority, and what will *you* say? This man killed two people, and if it hadn't been for all his money, he would have been behind bars by now. Now let's start at the beginning and lets look at the evidence and why it isn't a case of framing or people covering up for each other. And lets look at why the defense team used the arguments that they did. ...

We have focused mostly on Johnnie Cochran until now. We will now look at a lawyer, Barry Scheck, whose importance in the Simpson case has been overlooked, partly because he is not as flamboyant as Cochran. But never-the-less, he is probably the one man that the Simpson defense team could not have done without.

13. BARRY SCHECK

Another method consists in counter-attacking the accuser; for it would be absurd to believe the words of one who is himself unworthy of belief.

Aristotle

Barry Scheck was the attorney who along with Cochran, presented the defense's closing statement. Because Scheck was not as colorful as Cochran, his importance in the Simpson case has not been entirely acknowledged. There is no doubt that this was a team effort, and that all the hand-picked lawyers and consultants contributed with important elements in the trial. But if one had to pick one person on the defense team that the defense could not have done without, it would be Barry Scheck.

Barry Scheck is important in that he was the one that provided the logos foundation for Cochran's speech, which mainly focused on ethos and pathos. In other words, Scheck provided the reasoning for Cochran's emotional appeal.

Laying the foundation for Cochran, Scheck gave his speech shortly before Cochran. In a civil case, one could say that Scheck took care of the liability issue, while Cochran focused on the damages.

Barry Scheck himself is an effective rhetorician, though his style differs from Cochran's. But this is just a difference in style. Like any good rhetorician, he knows the basics of what effective argumentation contains. We see how he uses many of the same techniques as Cochran:

> Barry Scheck came up with some colorful alliteration to describe our route: We would argue the "mountain" of evidence was a molehill that was "contaminated, compromised, and corrupted."[89]

We see that Scheck, like Cochran is good at using metaphors, and skillfully applies alliterations and the use of three.

Scheck is faced with the task of countering all the evidence put forth against Simpson. Therefore, Scheck's argumentation is a good example of what can be labeled "the battle amongst the experts." In such situations the outcome of a case does not necessarily depend on the strength of the evidence, but on the way you are able to present it. When things get too complicated, and it is hard to know what to believe, people use common sense. But unfortunately, a simple and common sense interpretation of the events can also be the result of manipulation.

Achieving this effect becomes a lot easier if one side is fully aware of that their audience is trying to seek refuge and understanding in common sense, and the other side is not.

Because Scheck is so important, we are going to go through his closing speech and see exactly how he is able to counter the prosecution's evidence and create the foundation for Cochran's statements. This is not Scheck's entire speech, since his closing statement lasted for several hours, but it is most of the main points presented in the chronological order Scheck chose in his speech.

Barry Scheck's argumentation

Scheck starts out stating the defense's overall argumentation, which he shapes into three issues to strengthen his claim.

> **Mr. Scheck: The <u>integrity of this system</u> is at stake. You cannot convict when the core of the prosecution's case is built on <u>perjurious testimony of police officers, unreliable forensic evidence and manufactured evidence</u>. It is a cancer at the heart of this case and that is what this evidence shows.**

Here he employs the metaphor "a cancer at the heart of this case." This is not an overused metaphor, so it is still capable of creating a vivid picture in the minds of the jurors. It is furthermore an issue to which most people can relate. Something that has to be rooted out, or it will spread and eventually kill or infect the entire entity. This can be a person, case, or police department. In this way Scheck is also changing the focus from the case to the system.

> **When you go through it patiently, when you go through it carefully, when you go through it scientifically, logically, that is what the evidence shows, and you cannot convict on that evidence.**

The use of three runs through Scheck's entire speech. By just stating scientifically and logically right after each other we can see how Scheck keeps his statement within a three-part utterances. We also see that Scheck by using the words patiently and carefully, uses a "interpretation" to state the same thing in a variant way.

> **So in the words of Dr. Lee, something is wrong. Something is terribly wrong with the evidence in this case. You cannot trust it, it lacks integrity, it cannot be a basis for a verdict of beyond a reasonable doubt.**

Here Scheck turns the words of one of his experts into a key word that he uses throughout his entire case. This key word not only collects strength from an authority figure, but it supports Scheck's appeal to common sense. These key words the defense team also uses to tie their statements and speeches to the jurors together into one collective unit. They do that by using the same key phrases and metaphors when they address the jury.

> **As you recall, it shows the evidence from Bundy, the evidence from Rockingham and the Bronco, the evidence from Mr. Simpson itself passes through the Los Angeles police department, the messengers that Mr. Cochran was talking about, the lab, criminalists, coroner's office, and then it is tested by the FBI, the Department of Justice and Cellmark.**

Here Scheck reminds the jury that almost all the evidence passed through the LAPD, "the incriminated institution that no longer can be trusted." Scheck is, in other words, making sure that the ethos foundation for the prosecution's argumentation is cut off, leaving the prosecution's argumentation groundless. Scheck doesn't need to question the FBI and the other laboratories, because they didn't get the evidence before it had gone through the LAPD.

> **If it is <u>contaminated, compromised or corrupted</u> here, it doesn't matter what the results are by these other testing agencies, because if it happens within that black hole of LAPD, it doesn't matter how many times you test it.**

Here the three-part utterance that summarized the defense claim is turned into three key words. These three key words are furthermore turned into an alliteration, where the words start with the same two letters. This helps to tie them together. They become easier to remember as a sound bite and they create a coherent way of understanding the events.

> **So you ask the question how did the Los Angeles police department, how does any laboratory become <u>a black hole that impairs the integrity of the evidence</u>?...**
>
> **Any laboratory has to have three things: You have to have <u>rules and training</u>, you have to have what is known as quality assurance and you have to have chain of custody, security of the evidence.**

Here Scheck again employs the metaphor "a black hole" to validate the claim that all the evidence that went through the LAPD laboratory is worthless. The statement is shaped as a question. This not only engages the jurors in Scheck's reasoning, but also passes over the issue *if* the LAPD is "a black hole," as if there no longer is any question about this. In other words this way of phrasing your sentences lends credibility to itself.

If we look at the words, rules, and training, we see a good example of how you can turn something into a three-part utterance even though, in reality, it consists of more elements.

> **Well, what have we heard about rules and training at the Los Angeles police department laboratory? Well, this laboratory is run without a set of rules. That everyone knows. They don't even have a manual. Think about that. That is extraordinary. And then they have this draft manual and it is ignored by the criminalists, Fung and Mazzola. They don't know what is in the draft manual, what procedures there are.**

Here Scheck comes forth with arguments to support his claim that the LAPD criminalists are incompetent. Scheck is now providing the logos foundation for the defense teams' claim that Simpson is innocent.

> **And then the laboratory director, Michele Kestler, well, she was the acting laboratory director. Actually <u>one of the real problems here is at the time of this case the head of the laboratory was a police officer, not a scientist</u>, but Michele Kestler, she had that draft manual on her desk for four years going through it.**

Here Scheck stresses the connection of the LAPD laboratory and the police department itself. He hereby makes it totally clear that it is the police department that they are dealing with.

> **And <u>she says, well, some of this is no good and they didn't get around to it</u>, so that is how you become a black hole.**
>
> **The testimony is clear in this case they did not give their criminalists training in state of the art techniques, in particular[and]of great relevance here, there was no DNA training for the evidence collectors.**

Here Scheck is verifying his one claim of incompetence by seemingly getting the head of the LAPD laboratory to admit to sloppiness and that things were not running the way they should.

What is going on here? There is a failure to document how you collect the evidence, a fundamental duty as DR. Lee showed you, remember, with that chart, [the]fundamental duty of the criminalists to document the evidence. In other words, where it was picked up, how it was picked up, when it was picked up.

This is a further founding of the incompetence claim, and a hint at possible alterations and manufacturing of evidence.

There was no serious supervision of these people. That is just clear. You saw it. This lab was not inspected. This lab is not accredited. This lab is not subjected, certainly the DNA, to external blind proficiency testing which you know, which you know, is what you need.

Here the argumentation is taken further towards a founding of the alteration that supports the evidence and framing theory.

We further see how Scheck is using a "reduplication," where he repeats the words "which you know." He does this in order to commit the jurors to accept his claim, that outside control of the work of the police laboratory is a necessity.

Now, this is critical. Chain of custody and security. There is absolutely nothing more fundamental to preserving integrity of forensic evidence than a chain of custody, than having security. You have to know what you are picking up. You have to be able to document it, otherwise bad things can happen and nobody can trace it.

In this case they did not count the swatches when they collected them. They did not count the swatches when they got back to the laboratory and put them in the tubes for drying. They did not count the swatches when they took them out of the tubes and put them in the bindles.

The general claim of incompetence and sloppiness is now connected to specific pieces of evidence in the Simpson case. Again

Scheck phrases his claims in three-part utterances.

> **We don't know how many swatches they started with. They didn't book the evidence in this case for three days. They kept it in the least secure facility, the evidence processing room, for three days, without being able to track the items.**
>
> **The lead homicide detective in this case, and we have talked about it a little and we will talk about it some more, is walking around with an unsealed blood vial for three hours. It is unheard of. The other lead detective in this case is taking shoes home right out of — this could be critical evidence. The shoes that they suspect he was wearing that night, taking it home.**

Scheck is further founding his claim of sloppiness and the opportunity to plant evidence by the police. It is vital for the prosecution to restore the credibility of their witnesses, the police, otherwise the foundation for their argumentation is gone, since their case rests on the evidence provided by the police. In this situation where Scheck claims that the lead detective walks around with Simpson's blood vial, or as he otherwise claims, goes on a three hour coffee break, Clark needed to defend the lead detective. She could have responded that he spent most of this time interrogating Simpson at the police station, and the rest of the time driving back to Simpson's estate to deliver the blood vial to the forensic pathologist. Further, Clark could have gone from the defensive to the offensive. This is generally a better place to be as a prosecutor. She could have claimed that the fact that no evidence was found on the shoes that the detective had taken custody of was proof that the police weren't just trying to frame Simpson by planting evidence. Here was the perfect opportunity to ask: Why wouldn't the police have taken advantage of that? As Scheck so skillfully has shown us, there is always an opportunity to interpret single events in one's own favor.

> **Now, you know, it was amazing, when Mr. Fung testified, the extent to which, you know, they have lost all tract of the rules. At one point I asked him, well, it would have**

been all right if they took the blood home and he said sure you could put it in the refrigerator overnight. Do you remember that answer? I mean, there is no sense of what has to be done in order to give you reliable evidence. None.

Think about the Bronco. They finished doing the collection in the Bronco and then it is abandoned literally for two months. There is a box supposed to check off, give special care if you are going to check it for biological evidence, not checked off. It is sent to Viertel's. It is abandoned for two months. There are no records of who went in and out of that car. There was a theft. Everybody was around in there. And then on august 26th they are collecting evidence from it.

And then finally, and this is — could we have the next board. This is a critical point that I think demonstrates all you need to know about security and chain of custody in this laboratory, the missing lens, the missing lens. Now, this is very important evidence. This is the envelope that is found at the crime scene with the prescription glasses. If you are investigating a case, you are very concerned about this.

...now, we can tell, as Dr. Lee pointed out, on this lens there are smears of blood, trace evidence. There could have been fingerprints from the perpetrator who was going into that envelope. On June 22nd Dr. Baden and Dr. Wolf got an opportunity just to look, just to look at the evidence, not touch or examine or test, just to look, and they saw two lens there, made a note of them. February 16th, think about it, that is the first time we got a chance to inspect and just even handle the evidence. You are already sitting here February 16th. <u>There is something wrong</u>. When we look at it, that lens is gone. There is no report, no record, no investigation of its disappearance. Nobody comes in and tells you what happened. Now, that tells you a lot. Did somebody take this from the laboratory as a souvenir? Did somebody walk off with this? How can that be? This is critical evidence in a case? How

can that be? It just vanished down this black hole?

We now see Scheck further securing his claim of incompetence and sloppiness. "There is something wrong" is a keyword that runs through Scheck's speech, making sure that this general idea is always held up in front of the jury, tying the speech together, and clinging to the jurors minds long after Scheck stops talking.

> **They have all the evidence items in boxes, like the sock and the blood drops, and they will put them in the serology freezer and they are in a box there and then somebody will hit the computer and they can go in and then they can take any item they want out of that box. It is not tracked by specific items. There is no good security in this system. There is plenty of access if you want to tamper with evidence if you are authorized personnel, if you are a lead detective, if you are somebody there. It can happen.**

Now Scheck goes on to secure his claim of evidence tampering. Throughout Scheck's speech, he talks about *them* and *us*. In this way Scheck tries to create strings between himself and the jury, at the same time as he tries to cut the connection between the jury and the prosecution.

> **You know, science is not better than the methods employed and the people who employ it. DNA is a sophisticated technology. It is a wonderful technology. But there is a right way to do it and a wrong way to do it. The issue in this case is not is DNA good or bad DNA technology. The issue is right or wrong. So Miss Clark gets up here and tells you, well, Dr. Lee said DNA is okay, therefore the DNA evidence in this case is okay. That is ridiculous.**

Scheck says straight out what he has been implying all the time that the people who provided the evidence, the police, are not trustworthy, and that the evidence therefore is not worth anything. This is how Scheck gets around the DNA evidence, and this is why Marcia

Clark's efforts and argumentation fell on unfertile ground. We can see why it was far more important for Clark to defend the police than the DNA technology. It is not her logos, but her ethos foundation that needed to be strengthened.

> **Dr. Lee writes the manual and in that manual they say you don't put these swatches in plastic bags because you put wet blood swatches in plastic bags, you are going to degrade all the DNA in them.**

Here Scheck is founding his claim that the evidence had degenerated.

> **And you can have the most sophisticated technology in the world and if you don't apply it correctly, you can't trust the results.**

Again a direct attack on the prosecution's ethos.

> **I fully anticipate that most of the matters I am going to address to you she has been planning to address in her rebuttal summation because she certainly didn't address them in her closing argument, did she. You can't just say sloppy criminalist, sloppy coroner, big deal. She said DNA — insult to your intelligence, frankly — DNA is used to identify the war dead therefore accept all the evidence in this case.**

Scheck is addressing Clark's almost sole concern for the evidence itself, to the extent of further trashing the police, in order to spend as much time as possible on the evidence. In order to be as effective as possible, Scheck doesn't just let Clark slit her own throat; he helps her along the way.

> **They argue that the defense has to prove exactly how, exactly where, exactly when tampering occurred with any of this evidence. That is not our burden. That is not our burden. They have to prove that this wasn't tampered**

with beyond a reasonable doubt. When people tamper with evidence they try to do is with some stealth, they try to cover their tracks, and as Mr. Cochran pointed out, <u>it wouldn't take more than two bad police officers to do this and a lot of people would look the other way</u>.

Scheck, in a subtle way, turns the burden of proof around from the police and prosecution having to prove their accusations, to the them having to prove their innocence. Scheck can do that because he pretends still to be the defending party, when in reality he has turned into the accuser. The police have to prove their innocence, the defense doesn't have to prove their allegations of framing and tampering.

This contradiction of course should be exposed to the jury members by the prosecution. This would provide the prosecution the perfect opportunity to get into the offensive again, and attack their opponent's morals and ethics.

In this paragraph we also see the defense mix framing with passivity. This is an advantage because framing, or should we say evil intent, is more comprehensive in its severity, and therefore more difficult to prove, than to prove passivity and incompetence. This means that the defense team is able to take the route of least resistance whenever possible.

"Each fact which is essential to complete a set of circumstances necessary to establish the defendant's guilt must be proven beyond a reasonable doubt." Each essential fact. That is what is special about a circumstantial evidence case. For each essential fact they have to prove it beyond a reasonable doubt. If they fail, <u>if there is a reasonable doubt about an essential fact, you must acquit.</u> Those are the rules.

Scheck succeeds in turning another fundamental legal aspect around that is, if one piece of evidence is dismissed, the entire load of evidence has to be dismissed. The general practice is that if one thing showed, with 100 percent certainty, that the defendant is guilty, then he is convicted. As we have seen from the jurors' statements after the trial, the defense succeeded in convincing the jurors that they needed just one reasonable doubt about one piece of evidence to acquit the defendant. Since it is easier to find a flaw in a lot of material than in a few items, and because there was so much evidence against Simpson, this in one step took the defense team from an disadvantaged situation, to an advantaged situation.

> **Now, we don't have to prove anything and we don't have the burden of proof here and <u>I'm going to confront each and every one of these essential pieces of evidence in this case and raise a reasonable doubt about it, more than a reasonable doubt, many reasonable doubts. But if they fail in one of their essential facts, you have to acquit.</u>**

In order to confuse the issue, Scheck mixes up his claim that you only have to have one reasonable doubt concerning one piece of evidence in order to acquit the defendant, with saying that he is going to provide one reasonable doubt about every piece of evidence. Here Scheck spins the confusion around the word "one."

> **We are going to go through the sock — <u>another reason I put this up here is that you will know when I'm getting close to done and you can follow along</u>. The socks, the stains on the back gate, the missing blood, the hair and fiber, the evidence of struggle at Bundy, the testimony of Dr. Baden and Dr. Lee, the Bronco, the Rockingham glove. <u>That is what we will be discussing this morning</u>.**

To display a list, that your audience can follow along with and see how far you have come is a good way to keep people's attention. It keeps people awake, gives them an overview of your argumentation and a sense that this speech is progressing and ultimately has an end. This helps prevent the audience from drifting off in the middle of your speech.

Scheck knows that the key to a successful speech, where the audience *understands*, *notices*, and *remembers* what you say to them, is to first say what you *want to say*, then to *say it*, and then end up pointing out what you *have said*.

> **You have children; I have children. Did you ever see them go out to play in dirt like that closed?in area at Bundy, get into some kind of ruckus? Socks come back, they are filthy. It would have to be here if there is anything on them at all. Nothing. Nothing there.**

Scheck is using a common sense argument to which they can all relate. This is what Scheck is later going to refer to as weak circumstantial evidence, when applied by the prosecution.

> **If there were that stain on the sock, that big stain on the sock, they would have seen it. Gary Sims told you he was disturbed by it, that a trained criminalist should have seen it.**

Scheck is here supporting the foundation for his tampering and contamination theory.

> **Now we have evidence of the wet transfer going through surface 1, surface 3 through the little holes in the sock to surface 3. It is pretty simple. If there is a leg in those socks, you can't have the transfer. ...can't get it when the leg is in the sock.**

We here see a further support of the tampering and contamination theory.

> **Got into the house, took off the socks, left them there and then it is still wet. So if it is still wet when he takes off the socks, you get the transfer to surface 3. Well, there is a big problem with that. Then you should have seen something on the carpet if that is what happened. It doesn't make sense. It doesn't fit.**
>
> **Then the next explanation is on august 4th when Mr. Yamauchi did the pheno test taking the swab and brushing the stain to see if it were blood, that that somehow created wetness that transferred into the third surface. Or — well, Dr. Lee and Dr. MacDonell said that**

that doesn't make sense when you look at the stains because if that brushing had occurred you would see a diffusion and you don't see that kind of diffusion and that is not the way you do the test anyhow. Just touching it couldn't cause that kind of transfer through to surface 3. Highly improbable said the leading forensic scientists in America.

Scheck is building the foundation for the defense tampering and framing theory, turning some of the most damaging evidence against Simpson into evidence of Simpson's innocence. We here again see the use of the keywords "It doesn't make sense. It doesn't fit." This statement is imbedded in common sense.

The most likely and probable inference is the one that is <u>not for the timid or the faint of heart</u>. Somebody played with this evidence and <u>there is no doubt about it.</u> And you know why <u>there is no doubt</u> about it? Because <u>they got so upset</u> in the opening statement about the socks, about the back gate, so upset that they sent it to the FBI. And Mr. Harmon wrote them a letter saying <u>please refute</u> the defense theory that somebody tampered with this evidence. <u>Please refute it</u>. Those were the words. Not exactly an objective way of sending it out. Please test this for EDTA. <u>Please refute</u> what the defense has to say.

The sound bite "not for the timid or the faint of heart" is also used by Cochran, and thereby helps tie the defense team's speeches into one coherent unit.

In order for his message to stick and sink in the minds of the jurors, Scheck repeats the words that contains the main message in his statements.

They looked for blood on June 29th on a lab paper with reasonable light, three people with 25 years of experience, and they don't see it.

We again see Scheck's use of common sense to create the foundation for his framing theory. With a little bit of imagination, you can usually always find an angle from which to apply common sense, if the facts themselves are not to your advantage.

> **Is this coincidence, all these things with the sock, or is it corroboration? I say it is corroboration that something is wrong, something is terribly wrong with the most important pieces of evidence in this case. It is a cancer that is infecting the heart of this case.**

Scheck employs rhetorical conversation in order to engage his audience and seem more impartial. He is turning the two options that he is giving his audience "coincidence and corroboration" into an alliteration, where the words start with the same letters. This not only makes it easier to remember, but ties the two concepts together, so it is easier to jump from one to another. The cancer metaphor was one that the defense team's jury consultant suggested that Scheck use when he addressed the jury. She suggested that he should use it most in the beginning and in the end of his speech. This is because these are the two prime time slots, when your audience is the most likely to remember what you have said.

> **"A witness who is willfully false in one material part of his or her testimony is to be distrusted in others. You may reject the whole testimony of a witness who has willfully testified falsely as to a material point unless from all the evidence you believe the probability of truth favors his or her testimony in other particulars." Thank you. Now, yes, that applies to witnesses, but I would argue to you that by analogy it applies to the messengers who are bringing you this forensic evidence as well. Because let's just think about the socks. The LAPD officers and lab people who are responsible for the collection of this, for the chain of custody, for preserving the integrity of this evidence, are the same people that are bringing you everything else.**

Here Scheck is able to use the abstract jury instructions given by Judge Ito about Fuhrman's perjured statement against the entire police department. This is how he ties Fuhrman's statements that he hasn't used the word "nigger" in the last ten years together with his assertion that the jury should reject everything the police have been involved with. This is the fascinating and scary aspect of rhetoric that, as with any powerful tool, carries with it the ability to do immense good and profound evil. A good rhetorician, not accurately countered, can make almost everything seem credible.

> **Remember what Dr. Lee said about the socks? He said it is like eating a plate of spaghetti. Looking — bowl of spaghetti I think he said. You see a cockroach. Do you then take every strand of that bowl of spaghetti to look for more cockroaches or do you just throw it away and eat no more?**

The cockroach metaphor is a fresh and unused metaphor that can creep into our imaginations as a vivid picture. On a emotional level, it is the disgust against cockroaches in one's dinner that Scheck wants to transfer onto the police. If we buy into the analogy, Fuhrman's statements, and any other mistake made by the police department, would enable us to reject the entire case.

> **Well, just wait a second. Just think about what that means. If they manufactured evidence on the sock, how can you trust anything else? How in this country, in this democracy, can they come in — there is no doubt Fuhrman is a liar and a genocidal racist. There is no doubt about that. But there is really no doubt either that they played with this sock, is there? And if that can happen, that is a reasonable doubt for this case period, end of sentence, end of case.**

Here the socks are turned into evidence, not of Simpson's guilt, but of the police department's guilt. Because the prosecution has not protected Fuhrman, he has now gone from denying that he used a derogatory word to being a genocidal racist. This is then mixed with the evidence against the police. The so called, "planted socks." This comes out as a lethal cocktail against the prosecution.

In order to strengthen his emotional appeal to the jury, Scheck connects Fuhrman and the socks with a nationalistic appeal, aimed at evoking pride and indignation. By not ending his sentence, Scheck is able to tie his nationalistic appeal together with the demonization of Fuhrman, without the use of any reasoning.

It is a test of citizenship. Not in this country.

This further appeal to national pride is aimed at leveling the ground for Cochran's upcoming speech which aimed at higher ideals and broader perspectives.

> **The blood drops at Bundy were degraded and had extremely low DNA concentrations. 117 had enough for an RFLP test. It was 27 times as much as 47, the first blood drop, 45 times as much as 48, 270 times as much as 49, 51 times as much as 50, 11 times as much as 52. ...This supposedly had been out there from June 12th to July 3rd. ...There is no question sunlight degrades DNA. Moisture and bacteria degrade DNA. Why are these concentrations so much higher? ...These samples are not degraded. How can that be? Nothing.**
>
> **Now, there is something interesting here, too. The prosecution is now saying, well, it is on a different surface than the Bundy blood drops. Bundy blood drops are on cement. This is on a metal gate, painted metal gate. So there is something magical about this that will prevent it from degrading at all in over three weeks. ...Remember the blood on the handrail as you are leading up Bundy? Same kind of surface. Totally degraded. Remember the samples from the front gate? There was blood on the front gate. Gary Sims' testimony. No question about that, severely degraded, just like the other samples from Bundy. So those are the same kind of surfaces, so this explanation don't pass the laugh test.**

Here Scheck is founding his claim of evidence tampering. This is a piece of strong argumentation. Even with the prosecution's explanation of why the blood drops collected three weeks later were in better condition then the ones that were collected right away, you wonder why blood drops collected three weeks later would be in better condition than the ones that were collected right away. The prosecution could here claim that it was because the blood drops were not stored properly (placed in plastic folders), and had been kept for several hours in a hot trunk. The problem the prosecution then would run into is that they then would stress their own incompetents, and indirectly support the defense claim that the blood was deteriorated to the point where it couldn't be trusted anymore.

Scheck builds up his argumentation by saying:

> Magical degraded
> Totally degraded
> Severely degraded

This leads to his climax of ridicule he calls "The Laugh Test." This plays on the issue of testing, and indirectly pokes fun at all the testing that has taken place.

> **Now, there is another thing. They are going to say, well, you know, officer Riske, Phillips, I believe, Fuhrman, Rossi, that night when they were entering the premises, the back gate, they had their flashlights and they were looking up and down and they think they saw some blood on the back gate, so they all testified to it, so you know it is there. Well, first of all, we know — you have been there — that this gate was rusty. There were all kind of darknesses, imperfections. There were berries all over there. There is all kind of discolorations.**

This is Scheck's way of explaining away that the blood was seen upon the gate before any blood sample had been taken from Simpson. We here see that boldness and vigor can, by itself, lend credibility to an argumentation. If not picked out and focused on by the prosecution, weak spots in Scheck's argumentation can be covered up by the rest of his rattling.

If the jury doesn't buy this explanation, the defense has created a security net for themselves. In this instance it consists of two components.

1. Any evidence or testimony that comes from the police can not be trusted and has to be dismissed.
2. You only have to disregard one piece of evidence in the entire load of evidence, to be bound by law, to acquit the defendant.

This is another good example of Scheck speaking about them and us: "They are going to say, but we know..."

> **You recall how they did the collection, that they started, they put down a photo number, not the evidence item number, so they started on the walkway with 112 and they put down 112 and that was sample 47 and they collected that. Then they went and they put down no. 113 and that was sample 48 and they collected that. Then they went down and they put down 114 and that was sample 49 and they collected that. Then they put down 115 and that was sample 50 and now we are right by the back gate and they collected that. Now, this is what shows you there was no blood on the back gate. Because at that point what do they do? They go to the front gate. They walk all the way back to the front gate where the bloodstain patterns are, that is 116, and then they go back all the way to the end of the driveway and then get the last blood drop, no. 52, 11.**
>
> **Why did they go all the way back? I will tell you why. Because detective Lange had told Mr. Fung, as he testified, that there was blood on the back gate, and they looked, he heard reports of it, and they didn't see any blood on the back gate. So the only blood they saw on the gate was on the front gate, so they went back and collected 116.**
>
> **And you know what else shows you that? Could we have the picture? Where is it, Mr. Fung? They took no pictures of any blood on the back gate, 117. There is some discoloration there that may be consistent with 115, if it is**

blood at all, but there is no 116.
So there is no pictures either. Thank you.

Here Scheck is founding his claim that there initially wasn't any blood on the gate, but that it was planted there later by the police.

On a linguistic level Scheck uses a rhetorical question to make his statement seem more a matter of fact. By the way Scheck uses the words "they" and "we," he alienates the police and ties strings of identification between the jury and himself.

Let's look at the back gate. No documentation or photos on June 13th. Discovered on July 3rd. DNA concentration. EDTA. <u>Coincidence or corroboration that something is wrong, something is terribly wrong</u>. There is a cancer at the heart of this case. This is a reasonable doubt. You put this together with the sock, <u>how many cockroaches do you have to find in the bowl of spaghetti</u>. ...and remember the circumstantial evidence charge about whether if there is two plausible reasonable interpretations, you have to take the one that goes with innocence?

Scheck is summing up his main points before going onto a new issue. In this way he makes sure that his strong point is not lost in his lengthy argumentation. This is especially important, because it is an oral presentation, where his audience can not go back and review what he has said earlier, or catchup on a connection that they missed. In order to give his speech as much effect as possible, Scheck divides his long speech into many small speeches. This gives him many beginnings and endings in his speech, and thereby more prime time. It also wraps it together along the way, so it is easier for his audience to keep track of the different issues in his speech. This makes it easier for Scheck to bury weak reasoning in the text. If he can somehow get to his mini-conclusion, the weak links will easily be forgotten, since they do not stand out like the summations.

In order to infuse as much strength as possible into the summations, Scheck fills them up with maxims, keywords, and metaphors.

All the digital data he threw away. He came up with this

thing where he says he tests his own blood and he finds some level of EDTA in it but he threw away the documents about what he did. He put it in a test?tube for two weeks that has silicon in it, that has a red stopper in it that could be a source of EDTA. He doesn't go and test anybody else's blood.

Here Scheck is using reasoning and counterarguments for his claim that traces of EDT in the blood evidence shows that the blood came from the blood sample drawn from Simpson. EDT is just to prevent blood samples from clotting. The reasoning that Scheck is up against is the statement from the prosecution that the levels of EDT in the blood sample is much higher. Furthermore, their scientist drew some blood from himself in order to show that you can find traces of EDT in that too.

I would now like to talk about missing blood, and I think that we can talk about this in the following way: Access opportunity and the smoking gun, nurse Thano Peratis.

Here again we see that Scheck makes sure that he tells the audience *what* he is going to say, before he says it. In this way it is hard to miss the message, and easy to turn the audience's attention to what he wants them to focus on. This is again done through the use of the three-part utterance.

Now, detective Vannatter, the man who carried the blood, picked up blood from the coroner's office of Nicole Brown Simpson and Ronald Goldman, blood tubes that contained EDTA. Let's show them all.

Remember these? These are pictures of both sides of the tubes. Just pull them out. I think the point is made. One after another covered with blood. He got those from the lab. He carried those. Those tubes, the testimony is, have EDTA in them. He carried them on June 15th. Now, we do not have records. There are no records of the amounts that were initially put in those tubes or where he went, how long he went. No real evidence that we can

examine about that, but <u>he carried</u>. On the other hand, when we turn now to Mr. Simpson — that is enough.

Scheck is here basing his claim that Vannatter and Fuhrman could have manufactured and planted the evidence by themselves. Vannatter's main role in the conspiracy is to be the carrier of the blood. Scheck is making sure that this is not overlooked by the jurors, by repeating it several times in his argumentation. Fuhrman and Vannatter were the two police officers who had to be demonized in order for the conspiracy claim to be coherent. In order to do that, the defense team had to find a weak spot that would give them access to discredit the two police officers' ethos. In Fuhrman's case, it was his denial of using the word "nigger" and the racist statements on the Fuhrman tape. In Vannatter's case, it was his claim that they entered Simpson's property without a search warrant because they were afraid Simpson's life was in danger, since they saw blood drops in his car. Vannatter was denying that Simpson at this time was a suspect, claiming that there is a difference between a potential suspect and a actual witness. The defense team said that this statement was ridiculous, since everybody knows, that the husband, ex-husband or boyfriend is always the prime suspect.

This is the defense teams path to discredit Vannatter's ethos. But their foundation for discrediting Vannatter's ethos is not as strong as the one they have on Fuhrman. In order to strengthen their foundation, they have to try to amplify Vannatter's misdeed. This is done by calling it "Vannatter's big lie."

Detective Vannatter, as Mr. Cochran pointed out, was so upset about how this goes that when he was asked, well, when did you get the blood vial? <u>He said 3:30. Well, it was 2:30. We know that</u>. His testimony is, <u>he gets the vial of blood and he goes off and he has a cup of coffee and he is walking around Parker Center with a blood vial in an unsealed tube.</u>

And as you know, the rules are you are supposed to book it immediately. <u>You can book it in that building, Parker Center. You can walk — go a mile away</u>. Takes just a few minutes. And you book them at Piper Tech

where the SID lab is, and you buy a DR number, which is the number for the case, and the case starts. That is what the rules say. But that is not what they were doing.

As mentioned, it was very important for the prosecution to protect the ethos foundation for their case and make the jurors aware that Vannatter was not on a three-hour coffee break, but interrogating Simpson after the blood sample was taken. This is why Vannatter says he received the blood an hour later, when he was done with interrogating Simpson. It is also important to point out that Vannatter had to deliver the blood sample back to Fung, so the evidence could be booked under the same evidence number.

The defense knew that they had the prosecution cornered, because the prosecution had chosen not to introduce the interrogation of Simpson to the jury. Presumably, thought that their scientific evidence was worth more than the common sense arguments that could be drawn from the initial interrogation of Simpson. They knew that they had to focus their case in order to strengthen it, and they thought this was a good way to do it. It is important to be aware, that focusing does not necessarily mean that you cut away entire sections of your speech. Focusing can also be accomplished by summing up and using key words. The most effective way of focusing one's speech is to sum up and use keywords along the way, as we have seen Scheck do. You don't necessarily have to prune sections of your argumentation away in order to focus it.

It doesn't make sense. It doesn't fit. It is a serious problem, isn't it?

It has become fashionable to call every training session within the legal community a focus group. The word is out, you have to focus your speech, but rarely is anybody told how actually to do it.

In order to understand what true focusing means, we can look at this one sentence employed by Scheck in his closing speech. This is a sophisticated figure of speech. It is a combined anaphor and assonance, where the three sentences are tied together by the word "it." Scheck is strengthening his utterance by turning it into a three-part utterance. He is using the second word in his sentence to turn it in to a three-stage rocket, where the first two sentences state what it isn't, and the third states what it is. He then ends up turning his last sentence into a rhetorical question. This makes his statement seem less square, and engages his listeners in his thought process.

We also see how this one line is saturated with appeals to common sense. All this is achieved in one line consisting of fourteen words. Focusing does not necessarily have to do with how many issues you are addressing in your speech, but often has more to do with what weight and emphasis you put upon the different issues within your statement. This, as we have seen, can be done by current summations, repetitions, and the use of keywords and maxims.

> **And of course when she ultimately testified, poor Miss Mazzola had to go over and sit on the couch and close her eyes for twenty minutes, because she was tired and didn't see what went on in the foyer.**

Now Scheck is backing his reasoning that several of the people at the LAPD are turning their heads and keeping quiet about police misconduct. He is doing this by referring to Mazzola, the forensic scientist, Fung's, assistant. When asked about certain events, Mazzola said that she didn't know, because she was sitting on a couch closing her eyes for a minute. They also showed a video of Mazzola sitting on a couch closing her eyes.

In order for the prosecution to stay on the offensive, they needed to turn the whole argumentation around. In this case it could be done by claiming that the video film shows that Mazzola is telling the truth and therefore not trying to avoid answering any questions. This would then open up for an direct attack upon Scheck, where he could be accused of groundless slander of this young woman, all in order to achieve personal fame and gain. Mazzola's ethos needed to be defended by attacking Scheck's ethos. When we have an age difference, as in this case, it is best done by presenting Mazzola as young and vulnerable, and Scheck as wiser and more cynical person who takes advantage of people, who are not able to defend themselves. In this way the prosecution could have worked at demonizing Scheck.

What is going on? There is <u>something wrong</u>. It is not coincidence. There is <u>something wrong, terribly wrong.</u>

Here we see the repetition of the word "wrong" in order to cement it in the jurors minds. This repetition is aimed at the issue of reasonable doubt. In other words, he wants them to think that the evidence does not meet the burden of proof.

Let's face it, the Matheson explanations can't get around the 1.5 (cc. Blood) missing right away. There is 1.5 missing right away and toxicology proves it and they know it. So the only other way to explain the missing blood is Thano Peratis must have been mistaken. That is the only way.

Here Scheck is turning the argumentation around, from the only way they can explain Simpson's blood at the crime scene is that blood was missing from the blood vial, to the only way they can explain away the missing blood is that the nurse must have been mistaken. There is always a counter-argument to be made any argument can be turned around. This is why we should never leave out common sense argumentation, because it is often the determining factor for what the audience is going to believe.

From Thano Peratis. In the first clip, he was under oath. He said when he drew Mr. Simpson's blood, he looked at the syringe and that's how he knew it was between 7.9 and 8.1. No doubt about it, something he does all the time, routine, something people in this field would do and know. He looked at the syringe. Then, because he couldn't live with it, because 1.5 is missing — and they could have called Thano Peratis in their direct case and put him under oath — Mr. Goldberg goes out and does this statement, this strange bizarre statement in Mr. Peratis' home which they told you is unscripted or that is to say, <u>let's not say gave a script</u>, but <u>common sense tells you</u> that they spoke to this man before they went and did this videotape. And you could tell at parts, he literally said, "I don't

remember," because he was forgetting certain parts of what he — I guess what it was — what was planned to say.

Here Scheck makes sure that he is appealing directly to common sense. Scheck also uses the "passing over" technique to insinuate that the prosecution has manufactured the nurse's statement. It is necessary for him to say it indirectly since this is a serious accusation that Scheck doesn't have any facts to back it up with. This is an attack not only on the nurse's ethos, but also the prosecution's ethos, and is a strong support of the defense team's tampering and framing theory.

But let's get down to the substance. I mean, this is not under oath. It is the only testimony you've gotten in this case that is not under oath, which is fairly extraordinary. But you know what's even weirder? It's what he said. His position is this now. First of all, you can see the syringe and you can see the calibrations on the syringe. So now he's saying, "Well, the syringe was turned over and I didn't see the numbers." Well, that's pretty strange, but I think that <u>what's even more odd is that it is his position that he now realized that he goofed. How does he know?</u>

He says that he took one of these tubes — you know, these are items in evidence — and he looked at it, and he now remembers months later that when he drew Mr. Simpson's blood on June 13th, he can remember the level that the blood was in the vial. And based on his recollection of where the blood is in the vial, he then starts putting water into another test tube to get it up to that level, and then he says, well, that's 6.5. <u>Well, that's not worthy of belief, is it; that you can remember all these months later the exact level and that's how you come up with 6.5?</u> So not only is it not under oath and not only is it obviously a convenient recantation and appears to have been prepared, shall we say, to suit the prosecution's purposes <u>when things just didn't fit</u>, but the story is an absurdity. It is just an absurdity. It is not worthy of belief. It is a reasonable doubt in and of itself. Blood is missing.

Scheck is strengthening his claim that there is blood missing from the blood test taken from Simpson. He founds his argumentation in common sense and ties it together with the keywords "just didn't fit."

> **So let's review the bidding. Missing blood, access opportunity and Mr. Peratis, the smoking gun.**

Scheck never lets go of his opportunity to use mini-summations and headings as his speech progresses. By referring to Perats as the smoking gun, Scheck indirectly says that the issue of the nurse in itself is enough cause to dismiss the case. This fits well with Scheck saying that the jurors only need "one reasonable doubt" to dismiss the entire case.

> **Something is wrong, something is terribly wrong at the heart of this case?...If you can't trust the man who carried the blood, if you can't trust where this blood went—I mean, EDTA missing blood. Coincidence? Corroboration? Something is terribly wrong.**

Scheck is here delivering the foundation for Cochran saying: "If you can't trust the messenger, you cant trust the message."

Scheck not only uses a lot of keywords, metaphors and maxims at the end and the beginning of his speech, but also at his mini-summations, as they act as small conclusions with their own endings. It strengthens his conclusions and ties them to the overall reasoning.

> **Now, I'd like to move to the blood drops found at Bundy. And there are two aspects of examining this evidence. <u>The first</u> has to go to the integrity of the samples and <u>the second</u> one goes to the issue of cross?contamination.**

Scheck moves on to the next issue by telling his audience what he is going to tell them. Besides the number three, the number two is also a very effective number to use when you want to divide your reasoning. Number one has the strength of being the one and only truth. Number three seems like a lot, as if one has taken all issues into consideration, but it is still overviewable. Number three is rooted deep in our soul, with the Trinity, three wishes, the three challenges the hero in myths has to go through, and so on. Number two stands for the polarization in life: good and evil, heaven and earth, mom and dad, life and death.

In order to strengthen his speech, almost all of Scheck's utterances consist of one, two or three-part utterances.

> **I expect they'll come in and they'll say there's a swatch sandwich, they were all stuck together so they wouldn't dry. Nonsense. Use your common sense. How do you get wet transfers like this? Well, within three hours of the time that they were taken out and put in bundles, if somebody had switched swatches, you'd see wet transfer.**

Here Scheck is using the vaccination technique to secure his argumentation. In this way he weakens argumentation the prosecution could have come forward with, at the same time as he uses the technique to further attack and incriminate the police. In this way Scheck manages both to attack the prosecution and defend himself at the same time.

> **There was a cesspool of contamination in this laboratory. No mistake about it. Cesspool of contamination.**

Cesspool of contamination is the metaphor used to intensify and shorten Scheck's argumentation against the laboratory data. This is intended to support the contamination and framing claim. On a linguistic level the words "cesspool" and "contamination" create an alliteration that makes the statement stick in the juror's mind.

> **...Handling multiple swatches in a hurry, handling samples from both crime scenes at the same time, not changing gloves, not routinely between samples, not changing paper and washing down between samples, when you scrape the swatches out of the tubes creating aerosols, all these things create risk of cross?contamina-**

tion. All these things Gary Sims told you, their witness, were wrong.

But the single worse thing that was done, the cardinal rule of handling these samples in a DNA lab is the one in the upper right?hand corner, and that is handling Mr. Simpson's reference tube at the same time that you are processing the swatches and the glove. That is the biggest <u>no-no</u> that forensic labs have learned from bitter experience as we'll discuss in a minute.

Scheck is now creating the foundation for his incompetence and cross-contamination claim. Scheck is using baby language that, on an indirect level, says that this was such basic knowledge that even the newest lab technician would know not to do this.

All of a sudden, he said, "I remember now. I opened up the tube, and the blood spurted up through the chemwipe and it got on my gloves." Now, he was a little vague about what he did with the gloves. He doesn't remember whether he put them in a bio?hazard bag right in the evidence processing room or got out and went to the serology room and got rid of them there. But all of a sudden, we now know there was a spillage of blood there. Now, that is extraordinarily significant because there's plenty of high molecular weight DNA in the smallest drop if you get it on your gloves or if you don't change the gloves. And frankly, I think there's no reason to believe he did, to contaminate these samples that we know are degraded.

Here Scheck further pushes his incompetence and cross-contamination claim. This is one of Scheck's weak points, where it would be beneficiary for the prosecution to come in and state that in order for all five blood drops to have shown only Simpson's DNA, all the DNA in all the blood drops would have to have been totally deteriorated. At the same time cross-contamination would have to have occurred in all the blood samples, but not in any of the control tests designed to detect possible cross-contamination.

If you recall, the California association of crime lab directors gave a proficiency test where they used degraded samples in 1989. And in this test, they gave samples to Cellmark and to other labs, and they were false positives and Cellmark got two false positives, the first and the second time.

You remember what DR. Cotton told you about what they learned of that? When they did these tests, the second one in particular, the way that they got a false positive through cross?contamination is that they had a degraded sample. And the Cacad study is the only one where they're really sending these labs degraded samples just like here. It's a degraded sample. That creates a risk of cross?contamination, when you degrade out the initial DNA. And the only thing — you recall this. The only thing they could isolate is that they were handling the reference sample at the same time they were handling the degraded sample. And what was interesting about her testimony is, she testified that they had a witness in the room. In other words, when they were doing these proficiency tests, they were witnessed. Each transfer was witnessed by somebody standing right there. And all they could reconstruct, all they could reconstruct at the end was that they had made a mistake. ...so it happens. And it happened to a much better lab than LAPD and it happened when they were just beginning, just the way LAPD is just beginning here with far less trained personnel frankly.

Scheck is further expanding his cross-contamination claim with a related example. His use of concrete examples was a good way to strengthen his argumentation.

Here the repetition of the word "it happened", carries the entire meaning of Scheck's statement. Scheck takes it from "*it happens*" to "*it happened*" through the use of examples. In this way, Scheck takes it from being a theoretical possibility to this is what happened in the Simpson case. Scheck also *talks directly* to the jury. This catches the jury members' attention and makes what he says more relevant to them than if he had just been *talking about* the subject.

> **Now, if we look at the hair and fiber evidence as a whole, there are — and this is just weak association evidence. Nonetheless, there are powerful inferences consistent with innocence and these were put on slides that are in evidence. I would like to review them briefly with you. Both gloves, no hair consistent with Mr. Simpson on the Bundy glove, no hair consistent with Mr. Simpson on the Rockingham glove. That's the slide we put up.**
>
> **Do you know what we should have added to that slide? Very significant facts that I hope you don't forget. <u>There was an unidentified Caucasian hair on the Rockingham glove. Did they test mark Fuhrman? Did we get a hair example from him? Uh-uh.</u>**

Scheck ties his implications of cross-contamination in with his evidence alternation and framing theory. This is again done by asking why there isn't more evidence. Since it is hard to imagine a case with a larger amount of evidence, we can see that this kind of argumentation can be used in any case, as long as the evidence load is split into smaller sections.

Scheck has put himself back in an offensive position. This is again done by the use of Fuhrman, the personification of deception.

Later in his closing statement Scheck had to take his statement that they hadn't tested the hair of the police officers back. The defense had in fact demanded hair specimens from all the police officers present at the crime scene.

> **So very simply, he's saying that this is hair from the soft under belly of Kato the dog, the kind you would expect to be shed if he were lying on the ground there, not the kind that you get if the dog sort of passed you, all right, or comes up on you as you're — they're going to probably claim fleeing the crime scene or something. It's a soft hair. It's the kind you would find on the ground in the closed?in area. What does that mean? That means that Rockingham glove started at Bundy. Somebody took it**

somewhere else, and you know who that was.

It is an interesting theory about the soft belly hair on an Akita since an Akita is double coated, with a soft inner coat that surrounds the entire dog. Undisputed we see that it is not so much the correctness as the feasibility that counts. As was the case when Scheck implied that the hair on the glove could come from Fuhrman. Scheck probably got his theory from the saying, the soft underbelly of a dog.

This "cluster bomb" technique, where attacks and allegations are thrown out in numerous areas at once, is used to put the opponent off balance, so they lose their focus. By having the opponent run around trying to put out fires all over the place, one forces the opponent into a defensive position, a generally bad place to be as a criminal prosecutor due to the higher burden of proof. Especially in these situations it is of extreme importance to be able to coordinate your effort and responses according to an overall focus, to tie your seemingly scattered argumentation into your overall theme.

The socks. There's no fiber on the socks consistent with either glove. And these are cashmere gloves where cashmere would easily come out and get on your hands, transfer to the socks. No fiber consistent with Mr. Goldman's clothes. And we know there was hand?to?hand combat here. No fiber consistent with Nicole Brown Simpson's clothes. Nothing on those socks. Also, we should add, no soil on those socks, no trace, no berries, nothing. Pretty interesting, those socks. <u>Next one, please</u>.

As far as the hair is concerned, no hair from Mr. Goldman, no hair from Nicole Brown Simpson on those socks. <u>Next, please</u>.

As far as Bronco fiber is concerned, no Bronco fiber is found on either glove. No Bronco — no fiber consistent with Mr. Goldman's clothes is found. No fiber consistent with Nicole Brown Simpson's clothes is found. <u>Next</u>.

As far as hair, no hair consistent with Miss Nicole Brown Simpson. No hair consistent with Mr. Goldman on the Bronco. Okay. And I should add, you know, in the Bronco, what they did is not only they take out that carpet,

but they went in and they vacuumed it. They vacuumed it to get all the hair and trace. They vacuumed it.

Scheck is good at turning the issue around, as in this case where he asks why there isn't more hair and fiber evidence. This is the same tactic Cochran uses when he addresses the amount of blood found in Simpson's car, house, and so on. This argumentation is put forth in support of the evidence alteration and framing theme. Talking the entire load of evidence against Simpson into consideration, this is a pretty bold statement. This argument only takes hold because they look at the evidence in smaller segments, and not the entire load of evidence.

By saying: "Next one please," Scheck, on a conscious level, signals a slide change. On a subconscious level, by his intonation and posture he, signals to the jury that they don't need to waste anymore time on this "weak" evidence that has been totally discredited by him.

Now, Mr. Sims had said that he would expect that when you did fingernail scrapings, you would find — excuse me for just a second — he would expect that there would be skin under the nails. Now, he's a fine man and a fine forensic scientist. I have no quarrel with him, but he was admittedly testifying in an area outside of his expertise when he told you — he was saying that was his common sense understanding.

Here Scheck succeeds in turning the common sense aspect against the prosecution, when they use it. This clearly shows, that Scheck is aware that there is always a counterargument to be made. In this situation it helps, when you don't feel the guilt of double morals.

That Mr. Goldman was taken by surprise, dropped the envelope to the ground. So her theory is not that he kept that envelope in his hand as the struggle was continuing or that he would make the blood imprints on the envelope with his fingers. But somebody who's interested in that envelope, somebody appears to have opened up that enve-

lope and created a bloody smear on the one lens we have remaining. Somebody made the mirror image fold on that envelope. Somebody was looking in it for some reason who had been in a struggle and left a bloody imprint of fingers. <u>It's interesting, isn't it? And it is consistent with—well, it is inconsistent certainly with the prosecution theory of Mr. Simpson committing these crimes and consistent with others.</u>

Here Scheck is trying to support the theory, that somebody else committed the murders. The defense teams' suggestion was that it was a drug-related killing. Coming up with an alternative theory is a way to get out of the defensive position. To be put in a defensive position is especially damaging for the prosecution in a criminal case, since the burden of proof is higher.

Scheck is using an "aposiopesis," not completing his sentence. He can then tie the two conflicting theories together, without having to get into any facts. In this instance, where the alternative theory of who killed Brown and Goldman is pretty weak, a hint is more effective than to say it right out.

Why wasn't Mark Fuhrman eliminated? Why didn't they take examples from the police on this? Why?

But I think that a fair inference consistent with innocence, which you are under oath obliged to take. You must consider that Mr. Fuhrman was in the Bronco and the evidence is that a picture, 4:30, around 4:30 in the evening, he is pointing at that glove at Bundy, walking through a pool of blood. Now comes into that Bronco, the vicinity of that Bronco, the area of 5:00 in the morning, right, initially, then go out and does his circuitous little trip where he finds the glove and is alone for fifteen minutes around 5:15.

Scheck tries to further strengthen his framing theory by connecting Fuhrman to the evidence.

Now, if you have, as again Bodziak indicated, blood that

> **is caked on the inside of your shoe, even if loafers like Mr. Fuhrman in the inside heel area in your shoe, and then you walk through a wet area and then you step onto the carpet, you are going to get the same kind of pattern that was testified to for the prosecution side in terms of the fibers going into the shoes and getting out blood that would be consistent with the genotype of Nicole Brown Simpson that is found on the carpet of the Bronco.**

Now Scheck works further on his contamination theory, still making sure that Fuhrman is in the picture. In a sense, this exemplifies the defense team's mix of the contamination theory with the framing theory.

> **You know, Miss Clark was trying to say, well, this is how the blood got there. We know the Rockingham glove had a lot of blood, mostly from Mr. Goldman, some from Nicole Brown Simpson, and that was somehow placed on the side of the console, so that is why we get the little amount of Goldman's DNA that is on the console.**
>
> **That is their theory. Well, that is consistent with Mr. Fuhrman placing the glove in there. It is consistent with even Mr. Fuhrman having handled the glove and getting blood on his sleeve and just searching around the area for one of the other police officers and just getting a small smear of it with his sleeve on the console. That is consistent with this evidence.**

We again see the mix of the contamination theory with the framing theory. We even see the mix with in the implications of Fuhrman's actions and behavior.

> **That he is wearing these clothes that we've just been through the evidence of struggle. <u>If there is blood on pants, it is going to be on the seat. If there is blood from the struggle with Goldman, it should be there. We know there is no hair. There is no trace. There is no fibers from clothing. There is no berries</u>, there is nothing in that**

Bronco that would be consistent with somebody that had committed a violent double homicide that had been in a life and death struggle with Mr. Goldman.

Scheck again claims that there should have been more evidence. This means that only planting and cross-contamination would have produced so little evidence. The prosecution of course has to dispute this claim, and point out that there seldom has been a murder case with so much evidence. That actually is the reason the case dragged on for so long.

And haven't we shown you by credible, fair and reasonable evidence that this detective Fuhrman would have gone in that car? And by his own testimony and exposed lies from the prosecution's own witnesses, there is evidence he was there.

Those — those stains on the doorsill give you the lie, don't they? He was in that car and probably more than one of them was in that car.

Here Scheck tries to conclude that Fuhrman was in the car, by the use of ethos and logos argumentation. The logos argumentation is that Fuhrman was not able to see some of the stains from the outside of the car. The ethos argumentation is that you cannot trust what Fuhrman says, since he has been exposed as a liar. He has lied about using the word "nigger." Therefore, it is a given that he planted evidence. What Scheck is saying is: "We have shown you A, and B, and C, therefore D is also true."

Now, let's talk about the glove. The first point to be made about the glove is an integrity issue, and that is that you will recall that when Mr. Yamauchi opened up the reference tube in the morning and spilled out the blood, the first thing he did after that was this examination of the Rockingham glove, (indicating). And as you recall, he was putting his initials in, he was doing all these pheno testing, these <u>manipulations</u>, all in the wrist area of the glove and <u>manipulating</u> it.

<u>There is so little DNA in these few areas</u> here from the D1S80 tested, <u>minuscule nanogram amounts, very, very small</u>. Consistent with a <u>small</u> sample handling transfer from Mr. Yamauchi, and this alone I think can explain the <u>small</u> amount of DNA on the glove.

Now Scheck goes on to secure the contamination theory, when it has to do with the evidence found on the glove.

Scheck makes use of the two meanings of the word manipulation. This enables Scheck to say one thing to the jurors' conscious awareness, and another thing to their unconscious awareness. Scheck stresses the word small. There are very small amounts of DNA.; It almost doesn't exist any more.

So what I've tried to do in my remarks is review with you essential pieces, circumstantial evidence of the prosecution's case. And we don't have to do that. We don't have the burden of proof in this case.

Here Scheck turns the issue of having the burden of proof into the defense doesn't have to refute or address the evidence that is presented against Simpson.

All through Scheck's argumentation he takes pains to point out that they are dealing with so-called circumstantial evidence. Direct evidence is if somebody claims that they have seen Simpson commit the murders. Circumstantial evidence is where circumstances point to the defendant's guilt. This means that circumstantial evidence is all kinds of evidence except eyewitness statements. Throughout the defense teams entire argumentation they tried to diminish the importance of circumstantial evidence, and thereby weaken the prosecution's case. By constantly using the words direct and circumstantial evidence a person without a legal education can easily come to view direct evidence as worth more than circumstantial evidence, because the words indicates that direct evidence has a closer connection to the truth. But witness testimony is often one person's word against another's.

And each essential piece, I think it is fair to say, there is a

> **reasonable doubt and some, some of these are so profoundly disturbing in terms of the manufacturing of evidence in this case, that I'm sure you really can't abide it, not in this country, not in this democracy can we allow dishonest manufactured evidence to lie at the heart of a case like this.**

Now Scheck is getting ready to round up his closing speech, and is therefore trying to tie his speech together with Cochran's upcoming speech. He does this by stating that he has raised reasonable doubt about each piece of evidence. This has been the focus of Scheck's speech. To provide the logos foundation for Cochran's emotional appeal. Scheck is trying to strengthen his claim by appealing to nationalistic feelings.

> **Let's just talk a little bit about the criminalists and what you can view in terms of that evidence and how that affects on their credibility, because if you lie in small things, and some of these are not so small things, you lie in big things, and if you are trying to turn the other way and cover up real problems, real problems, serious problems, you can't abide it.**
>
> **Now, one I alluded to early, and I just think it goes to the heart of the hair and fiber evidence and so much in this case.**
>
> **And your common sense tells you they moved Mr. Goldman's body, they were traipsing around that crime scene, and we know the envelope was moved and the glove was moved and somebody put it back.**

Now Scheck goes in on an overall level and tries to incriminate and discredit the criminalists. Because we are now in the end of Scheck's speech, we see him employing more maxims and key words. The maxim, "If you lie in small things ..." is further applied by Cochran in his upcoming speech to the jury. This not only makes their speeches seem like one unit, it also makes the transition from Scheck to Cochran, logos to pathos, seem more gradual. It is worth noticing that this is a maxim from the Bible, a general reference point with the jury. We here again see the repetition of a word "problem" in order to amplify its effect. It is put into a three-part utterance that escalates from "real" to "serious." The gradual escalation of a claim is meant to bring your audience with you to the desired height of feelings. If one starts out with big words and a trembling voice, one can easily be seen as appalling, embarrassing, or humorous. This can also be seen as a warm-up for Cochran's more emotional speech.

We again see that Scheck makes sure explicitly to anchor his appeal in common sense. Scheck is able to turn the issue of the missing envelope into proof that the glove was moved. If we put Scheck's statements into the argumentation model it looks like this:

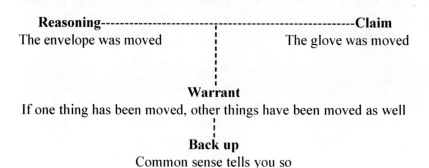

Reasoning--**Claim**
The envelope was moved — The glove was moved

Warrant
If one thing has been moved, other things have been moved as well

Back up
Common sense tells you so

By backing up his warrant, Scheck makes sure that he has reached a level upon which he shares a consensus with his audience. At the very beginning of this quote, Scheck starts out saying: "Let's just talk ..." By addressing the jury in this way Scheck makes it sound like he is having a conversation with the jury, and that they are together, him and the jury - together against the prosecution.

> **And how — I mean, they are covering this up. They are covering up how miserably this was handled and how the integrity of the evidence was compromised. It is as plain as day. It is an insult to your intelligence to say otherwise.**

Scheck strengthens the mix between incompetence and framing.

> **Well, why did you move the bodies? Why did you wait so long to bring the criminalists in? Why did you move the bodies before you collected the evidence? Because that is lunacy.**
>
> **And the answer was this is what you call a closed?in crime scene and in a closed?in crime scene where the evidence is close to the bodies, the first thing you do is move the bodies. That was a make?up. It was nonsense.**

Here Scheck employs a rhetorical conversation in order to refute the police's reasoning, and thereby strengthens the incompetence claim. It is worth noticing Scheck's use of the word make-up, which can easily be associated with the word cover-up. By having the jury reach this association/conclusion in their own minds, it becomes the jury members' "own" idea, and they are therefore much more likely to embrace it.

> **There is something wrong with the quality of testimony like this. There is something wrong when Miss Mazzola conveniently begins to close her eyes because the problem of carrying the blood vial out, sitting on the couch.**

Scheck is still working on the incrimination of the criminalists. Here the emphasis is put upon the framing theory. "There is something wrong" is here the key word that is being repeated.

> **So much of the essential facts in this case are just shot through with reasonable doubt. There is something wrong. There is something terribly wrong about this evidence. Somebody manufactured evidence in this case. There is missing blood. There are EDTA. There is [are] questions, serious deeply troubling questions. You must distrust it. You have to distrust it. You cannot render a verdict in this case of beyond a reasonable doubt on this kind of evidence, because if you do, no one is safe, no one.**

The key words "There is something wrong" in essence carries

the defense team's entire efforts. To raise a reasonable doubt about the evidence. Scheck's last words can be seen as a special appeal to black people's fear of not being safe at the hands of police officers and other public authorities. This also leads nicely up to Cochran's civil rights appeal.

Scheck goes into minuet details and displays a tenacity and vigor that has often characterized lawyers in court. As this criminal lawyer did, defending his client against murder charges:

> *Doctor, before you performed the autopsy, did you check for a pulse?*
> *No.*
> *Did you check for blood pressure?*
> *No.*
> *Did you check for breathing?*
> *No.*
> *So, then it is possible that the patient was alive when you began the autopsy?*
> *No.*
> *How can you be so sure, Doctor?*
> *Because his brain was sitting on my desk in a jar.*
> *But could the patient have still been alive nevertheless?*
> *It is possible that he could have been alive and practicing law somewhere.*[90]

It was no coincidence that the defense team chose Cochran and Scheck to address the jury in the final argument, as can be seen in this comment from Gerald Ulmen, a lawyer on the defense team:

> I thought that Barry's logical and methodical carving up of the evidence would complement Johnnie's more emotional style, and it was extremely important that we appeal to *both* the hearts and minds of our jurors.[91]
>
> Cochran is most effective when he is extemporizing, and he frequently departed from the structure of the outline. Barry Scheck is almost surgical in his logical precision. He had excellent recall of the precise details of the evidence and could weave

a tapestry that pulled it all together in a very credible way.[92]

If we look at the order Scheck and Cochran chose to present their individual closing statements, it looks like this:

DATE	PERSON	TIME	APPEAL	EFFECT UPON THE AUDIENCE
27. Sept. 1995	Cochran	1:35 PM	Ethos	We would like to listen to you, because we trust you, and we like you.
28. Sept. 1995	Cochran	9:01 AM	Ethos	
28. Sept. 1995	Scheck	10:10 AM	Logos	You speak to our reason, and convince us that this is the way things are.
28. Sept. 1995	Scheck	1:30 PM	Logos	
28. Sept. 1995	Scheck	2:45PM	Logos	
28. Sept. 1995	Cochran	3:50PM	Pathos	You speak to our emotions. We want to do something about it.

This is in line with a traditional buildup of an argumentative speech. First we try to win our audience's trust and good will. Thereafter we appeal to their intellect, and we end up with trying to win their feelings.

Not only was the defense team well aware of the importance of appealing to *logos, ethos*, and *pathos*, and the order in which this is best done, we also see that the rules of effective communication have not changed since the birth of democracy and the creation of law and rhetoric as scholarly disciplines. We as a society have unfortunately moved away from the knowledge and wisdom of what good reasoning contains, a knowledge that was acquired before the birth of Christ.

As Cicero used his knowledge to protect the republic against Catelina's attempts to harm the democracy, we too should cherish this knowledge in order to protect our society. This applies equally to the law as to politics.

14. MARCIA CLARK'S ARGUMENTATION

...it is not the case, as some writers of rhetorical treatises lay down in their "Art," that the worth of the orator in no way contributes to his powers of persuasion; on the contrary, moral character, so to say, constitutes the most effective means of proof.

Aristotle

It would make no sense to only look at the defense's argumentation if one wants to determine why they won the case. To do that would be like showing how someone won in chess by only showing how to move the white pieces. It is therefore necessary to look at the main aspects of the prosecution's argumentation.

Characteristic of the prosecution's argumentation is that they lacked an overall focus in their reasoning. The result was that they spent undue time on details of minor importance and took undue chances on insignificant matters such as letting Simpson try a glove on in front of the jurors. (The glove in question was found near O.J.'s house and was part of the evidence against Simpson. On this glove there was found remnants of blood from Ron Goldman and Nicole Simpson.) If Simpson's hand fit the glove it would not prove it was his. In contrast, if the glove did not fit, it proved it wasn't his glove. The prosecution's lack of focus makes them defenseless against Johnnie Cochran and Barry Scheck's attacks. Almost all the evidence is presented by the prosecution without any particular emphasis. This was an invitation to Cochran and Scheck to help themselves; this meant, that the defense team was able to make sure that the attention was kept on the weakest part of the prosecution's evidence.

So what does it mean to be able to focus one's argumentation? First of all, it is important to realize that *aim and focus are not the same*. In this case, Marcia Clark's *aim* was to *get Simpson convicted.*

What ought to have been the *focus* for her argumentation was *the theme or argument that most effectively enabled her to reach her goal,* with ethics and long-term consequences taken into consideration. You have not found your focus before you can sum it up in one sentence. In the Simpson case, the defense team was very focused, their focus was:

To destroy the police credibility (ethos).

After you have found your focus, all the rest of your arguments have, directly or indirectly, somehow to support your main theme. In this way you can present all your evidence and still be focused. The problem most people have is that they think that their aim is their focus. In this way their focus becomes so wide that it is the same as not having a focus at all. In the Simpson case, the prosecution thought that their focus was to convict Simpson. This is why they didn't have an overall theme for their argumentation. After the rhetorical situation had been changed by the defense team, the prosecution's new focus should have been to protect the police's ethos and destroy the defense team's credibility. This would have been the same strategy as the defense team employed in reverse.

In addition, Marcia Clark made an error choosing to counterargue all of Cochran's arguments. Had she not done so, she would have been able to focus her argumentation and thereby set the agenda.

It's one thing to be prepared for counterargumentation. Another thing is whether to start counterarguing in *the given situation.* In some cases the wisest thing is to "kill" your opponent with silence. The decision on whether to engage in counterargumentation must always be taken based on the question: Is this issue of such great importance to the recipient that support for the principal claim is dependent on it?

The prosecution headed by Marcia Clark knew very well they had a problem and tried to narrow their main arguments down to eight points.[93] This vague attempt at focusing their argumentation, however, no way near solved their problems with focusing. After the trial, critics said that, paradoxically, the prosecution's problem was that they had too much evidence.

It is important to focus your argumentation. You want to make sure that your main points and strongest argumentation are not lost in a stream of reasoning. On top of that, your points or text becomes more interesting and easier to understand if you narrow down what you are talking about.

It is also important to be aware that weaker arguments can lessen the strength of the strongest argumentation by their mere presence. By bringing up a whole list of arguments you somehow imply that you don't believe that any of these arguments has sufficient strength or worth in themselves. It can also easily seem like you have searched for all the good reasons for a point of view that you, for other reasons, have had all along.

The lawyer who knows how to unite his entire reasoning under one overall argument will have a greater chance of winning than the one who levels several arguments co-ordinately. This means that all the different arguments you present have to be united underneath one overall theme. A person that uses such a tactic is perceived as a person that really believes in what he says. One strong argument or theme supports the common belief that the truth is simple, as expressed in the saying, "The obvious truth."

It is hardly a wise rhetorical strategy to use a lot of arguments in support of one's case, as it has been proven that one good argument is more convincing than a lot of arguments in support of the same view. This may be due to the fact that by using a number of arguments it is easier to attack the weakest argument and thereby discredit the other arguments, than it is to reject a strong unambiguous argument.

By this, I do not indicate that the prosecution should not have presented all their evidence, but that they should have had one overriding argument. This would have prevented their main arguments from being lost in details, and thereby their most important arguments from being overlooked. In this case, the prosecution team's main argumentation could have been centered around the key words: "This is about murder, money, and manipulation." All the prosecution's evidence and argumentation should then have been directed towards backing up these key words.

It is the issue of ethos that is the core reason why Marcia Clark's argumentation didn't have any effect on the jury. Unlike in science and math, where the scientist is irrelevant, evidence and argumentation cannot stand alone. Or as Cochran said: "Watch out for the messenger." *The evidence, logos, needs ethos to support it, and pathos to drive it forward*. We can illustrate this by saying that logos is the car. Ethos is the road supporting the car, and pathos is the gas necessary to drive the car forward.

The prosecution started loosing their ethos foundation when the defense started attacking Fuhrman. The prosecution defended Fuhrman vigorously until the Fuhrman tapes. Then they turned their backs on him. Clark thought that it was enough to appeal to logos, thinking that Fuhrman's credibility or ethos was irrelevant. As can be seen from this quote from Clark's book: "I told the jury what Mark Fuhrman had done right. I showed them how impossible it would have been for him to plant evidence-which was, after all, the only thing about Mark Fuhrman that mattered to the case."[94]

Ethos is needed to uphold the credibility of the logical and especially the emotional appeal. This can be seen from this quote from an article published in the *Michigan Journal of Race and Law*:

> Having argued successfully to suppress evidence of all but the smallest hint of Mark Fuhrman's character, Marcia Clark demonstrated nothing less than unmitigated gall when she remarked in closing argument, like Captain Renault in the classic, Casablanca, that she was "shocked, shocked to learn" that her key witness had admitted to casual observers that he could not stand blacks, especially those involved in interracial relationships, that he would fabricate reasons to stop and harass blacks, and, most significantly, that cops needed to lie and plant evidence to meet trial evidentiary standards[95]

This quote illustrates how the emotional appeal can be hard to carry through, if it is not supported by a strong ethos. This is why the same speech can be viewed entirely differently within the black and the white community. Since Marcia Clark had lost her credibility with many people within the black community, what Marcia Clark said could easily have sounded like a hollow display of emotions. If you, on the other hand, saw Marcia Clark as a very credible person, as many within the white community did, her speech probably sounded really good.

The first part of Marcia Clark's closing statement is a good example of the way she lost her ethos foundation, and thereby the support for her entire reasoning. Therefore we are now going to look at excerpts of Marcia Clark's closing statement presented in the chronological order they occurred in her speech.

It is important to realize, that each lawyer's closing statement took several hours. Therefore things that are not repeated or otherwise thoroughly stressed are often lost on a jury that struggles to stay attentive for that many hours in a row.

Marcia Clark's Closing Argumentation:

> **Just like every trial, some evidence has been presented to you that really is not relevant to answer the core question of who murdered Ron Goldman and Nicole Brown. And <u>it is up to you, the jury, to weed out the distractions, weed out the side shows</u> and determine what evidence is it that really helps me answer this question.**

Clark's attempt to sound impartial stems from her presumption that logic and strict reasoning, are the ideal form of reasoning.

Unfortunately, this leads her away from an effective rhetorical approach. In order to be as effective as possible, one does not leave it up to the audience to figure out what to weed out in a debate the simple reason being that what may seem obvious to you, may not be obvious to your audience.

> **The side shows may be very interesting, they present very important issues, very serious issues, <u>but issues that really</u>**

<u>do not relate to who committed these murders</u>. And they should be dealt with outside this courtroom, because here now in this courtroom <u>we are here to decide who murdered Ronald Goldman and Nicole Brown.</u>

Clark is trying to hold onto the original rhetorical situation. Since she does not know how, from a rhetorical perspective, her argumentation was being undermined, she was not able to stop it.

Now, you as jurors sit as judges of the evidence. You are called the trier of fact. And as such your job is to be neutral and to be impartial as you examine the testimony presented.

And in this regard you are guided, just like any judge, by the law. And the jury instructions that were read to you on Friday is the law that you will apply to the evidence to determine the answers to the question that is posed here, who murdered Ronald Goldman and Nicole Brown.

The instructions discuss a wide range of topics. They talk about guidelines for the determination of credibility of witnesses, both expert and lay witnesses, and they talk about what the people are required to prove to establish the defendant's guilt, but they go beyond that and they also tell you the frame of mind that you should adopt when you look at all the evidence.

Clark further tries to hold onto the rhetorical situation by telling the jurors what they are suppose to do. Clark is afraid that the juror's conscious biases will stand in the way of a conviction of Simpson. What Clark was not aware of is that it is the *undermining of her ethos foundation* and the juror's *unconscious biases* (predisposition's acquired by certain life experiences) that prevented the jurors from convicting Simpson.

And one of the first instructions that was read to you by the judge on Friday, if you will recall, concerned your duties as a jury and it stated in part: "You must not be

influenced by pity for a defendant or by prejudice against him, you must not be biased against the defendant because he has been arrested for this offense, charged with a crime or brought to trial." Of course <u>that makes sense. It is logical</u>. And that means that we have to present proof to you. We just don't come in and say it is so. I have to prove it to you with evidence beyond a reasonable doubt, so <u>that makes sense</u>.

Clark goes on telling the jurors that they cannot be biased. This of courses only has an effect on what you could call conscious biases, since you cannot be told to let go of something that you are not aware of that you have. The only way you can get ride of unconscious biases is if:

1. Your biases are shown to you.

2. You build your argumentation on some more basic beliefs than the ones that you are trying to get around.

3. You combat the audience's unconscious biases on their own terms. (When you combat something on its own terms, it means that you build your argumentation upon the same underlying core belief, but you reach other conclusions than your opponent's.)

We can furthermore see Clark's emphasis upon the logical appeal.

All the way through her speech Clark talks about you (the jury) and I/we (the prosecution). In contrast to Scheck and Cochran who mainly talked about we (the jury and defense team). In this way Clark created distance between herself and the jury. This made it more difficult for the jury to identify with the victims that Clark represented. Without some kind of identification, there will be no persuasion This distance was enlarged by Clark's tendency to lecture. This made it seem awkward when Clark later tried to be informal with the jury.

In the course of this trial you have heard some <u>testimony of a very emotional nature</u>. I expect that during the

> **course of argument you are going to be hearing very impassioned (passioned?) Speeches, fiery speeches that may stir up feelings of anger or pity. Although your feelings may be aroused, as may be natural and understandable for all of us, as the instruction tells you as the trier of fact, you, the judges, are to remain neutral and impartial and not be influenced by such passion or sentiment, no matter how sorely tempted you may be to do so. And this applies to both sides, both sides.**

Clark is trying to make the jurors' feelings go away by telling them that they are not appropriate. A neutral mathematical scientific approach seems to be Clark's ideal. It is not possible not to have any feelings, or not to let them influence us, since it is part of being a human being. Feelings are suppose to influence us, that is why we have them. Many times we do not understand something, if we have not felt it ourselves. A person without feelings, especially for other people, is not going to make it in our society, and is dangerous for all of us. It is a misunderstanding to think that it is our feelings that lead us astray. But like anything else, our feelings can be messed up or led astray.

> **Although the brutal and callous way in which Ron and Nicole were murdered may understandably make you feel sorry, pity, even anger, it would be wrong to find the defendant guilty just because you felt sorry for them. On the other hand, although it would be completely understandable if you were to feel angry and disgusted with Mark Fuhrman, as we all are, still it would be wrong to find the defendant guilty — not guilty just because of that anger and disgust.**
>
> **So as you listen to the arguments of counsel, please remember when you weigh the evidence and you consider all of the evidence, remember that appeal to passion and emotion is an invitation to ignore your responsibility as a juror. To be fair we must examine all of the evidence in a calm and a rational and a logical way.**

Clark sees emotions as opposite to responsibility. Clark tries to restore the original rhetorical situation by combating feelings. This does not have any effect, since it is her ethos that needs mending. If the jurors do not believe in the credibility of the evidence she is presenting, it doesn't matter how much this evidence points at Simpson.

> **Let me come back to Mark Fuhrman for a minute. Just so it is clear. Did he lie when he testified here in this courtroom saying that he did not use racial epithets in the last ten years? Yes. Is he a racist? Yes. Is he the worse LAPD has to offer? Yes. Do we wish that this person was never hired by LAPD? Yes. Should LAPD have ever hired him? No. Should such a person be a police officer? No. In fact, do we wish there were no such person on the planet? Yes.**

By attacking Fuhrman's ethos, Clark is making it worse for herself, by further undermining her own ethos foundation. In fact the defense could not have done a better job of cutting her ethos foundation. Clark comes through as a school teacher lecturing a group of children, and thereby further distances herself from the jury. The rhetorical technique Clark is using here is the rhetorical conversation. This is a good example of the fact that it is not just the mere application of a rhetorical technique that benefits argumentation.

> **But the fact that Mark Fuhrman is a racist and lied about it on the witness stand does not mean that we haven't proven the defendant guilty beyond a reasonable doubt. And it would be a tragedy if with such overwhelming evidence, ladies and gentlemen, as we have presented to you, you found the defendant not guilty in spite of all that, because of the racist attitudes of one police officer.**

We here see that Clark is not aware that her evidence no longer has any foundation in the eyes of the audience. Clark is creating distance between the jury and herself by addressing them very formally.

> **It is <u>your duty</u> and it would be <u>your challenge</u> to <u>stay focused</u> on the question you were brought here to answer, and the only question that you were brought here to answer, did the defendant commit these murders?**

The problem Clark is running into here is that the jury already thinks that they are focused upon whether the defendant committed these murders. This is not a case of jury nullification, therefore the jury can only nod their heads to what she is saying. In other words this does not advance nor subtract from her case. Clark is raising her fingers towards the jury, telling them what they *ought* to do, instead of creating within them the desire to *want* to do it or should we say *feel like doing it.*

> **Because the defense has thrown out many, many other questions. They have thrown out questions about whether LAPD has some bad police officers, does the scientific division have some sloppy criminalists, did the coroner's office have some sloppy coroners? And the answer to all these questions is sure, yes, they do. That is not news to you. I'm sure it wasn't a big surprise to you. But those are not — they are important issues. You know, we should look into the quality control, things should be done better, things could always be done better in every case at every time. There is no question about that. We are not here to vote on that today.**

Here Clark saws further into the branch she is sitting on by helping the defense spread the incrimination of the police, from Fuhrman to the rest of the police force. Clark comes forward with such statements because she doesn't think that she needs anything else then "her" evidence and logic.

> **The question is what the evidence that was presented to you that relates to who killed <u>Ron and Nicole</u>, what does that tell you? Does that convince you beyond a reasonable doubt?**

Marcia Clark has just gotten through telling the jurors that they can not trust the police, criminalist, and coroner. And now she is telling the jurors to base their decision on the evidence these people have provided.

Clark thinks that the evidence she is presenting can exist detached from the source or providers. Within the mathematical paradigm the scientist, as a person, is not important. But when we are not discussing math and logic, the person is everything. We also see that Clark suddenly goes from being very formal, to being very personal, which makes it seem awkward. This personal tone towards Ron Goldman and Nicole Brown may be because she identifies with the victims, but not with the jury. This is not a good position to be in, and a formula for a lost cause.

No matter how much more qualified or how much better they could have done their job, still and all, <u>did they present enough evidence to you, did the evidence come to you in sufficient quantity</u> and convincing force to convince you that the defendant committed these murders beyond a reasonable doubt? <u>Ladies and gentlemen</u>, I submit to you that we have more than met our burden in this case.

Clark here thinks that the sheer amount of evidence is going to help her, but if you have already condemned somebody as notorious, it doesn't matter how many new stories he or she tells, you are not going to believe them anyway. Clark again addresses the jury very formally. This may be good in an opening statement, but she has known these people for nine months, and this is her closing statement. This may be one of the best indications that Clark did not connect with her audience at all.

Now, the defense has thrown out a lot of possibilities to you, the merest of possibilities, and a lot of them were just there to scare you.

You heard Dr. Gerdes talk about it could be this, it could have been that. I see the validation studies, you know, kind of like reminds me of a doctor, when you have

> **to go in for an operation, they give you all this list of things that <u>could possibly happen to you, could possibly happen to you.</u> Nevertheless, they have to give you that warning, right? They got to tell you that because otherwise you cannot give an informed consent and say, yes, knowing the risk, I'm going to go and do this.**

This example does not sound reassuring to people who don't want to convict an innocent man. Not to mention a jury that will only convict Simpson if they are totally sure that he is guilty.

Mock trials and opinion polls had shown that black women in general liked Simpson. If you like somebody, you will not convict them, unless you are sure that they did something wrong. The only repetition Clark had, was not exactly to her advantage. In fact, the defense team could not have done a better job of subconsciously undermining what she wanted to say.

> **Now, if you really believed that all these horrible things were going to happen, no one would have an operation. You wouldn't take the risk. But you know, they have got to tell me everything no matter how remote the possibility, and indeed you go and have the operation and you are fine and none of that stuff happens.**
>
> **Well, in this case it is actually they have raised all the possibilities of things that could happen in an effort to scare you away from the evidence, but we have done better than you could ever do in an operation, because we have proven to you that nothing in this case did happen. We have proven to you that it was not contaminated. We have even proven to you that it was not planted, for lack of a better term. And I'm going to go through the evidence and demonstrate how we have proven that to you.**

You have to be careful which metaphors you choose to use in your argumentation, since a carelessly chosen metaphor might work against the message that you are trying to get through to your audience. Even though Clark ends up claiming that they have proven Simpson's guilt beyond doubt, the metaphor she chose, the warning about the possible side effects when you undergo an operation, works against her conclusion of total certainty.

By comparing the conviction of Simpson with the risks we take by undergoing a operation, the jurors' unconscious fears are working against convicting Simpson. This may not be something the jury members are aware of, they may just feel that it is not right to convict Simpson. Clark's last sentence is not exactly the best way to stress the beginning of the presentation of her evidence.

> **So why were these issues raised? Why were these questions raised? Well, they are all questions and issues that were raised as a distraction. They were roads raised, roads created by the defendant to lead you away from the core truth and the issue that we are searching for the answer to, which is who murdered Ron and Nicole?**

It is good that Clark stresses that the defense team is trying to distract them from the facts in the case. The bad thing is that she describes it as a search for who killed the victims, when in fact she is trying to communicate to the jury that there is no doubt who killed the victims. We again see that Clark suddenly tries to be personable.

> **But these roads, ladies and gentlemen, these are false roads. They are false roads because they lead to a dead?end.**

This is again not a good metaphor, since a dead-end in an investigation does not necessarily mean that what you are getting at is wrong, just that you are not able to get any closer to the truth through that avenue.

> **The false roads were paved with inflammatory distractions. But even after all their tireless efforts, the evidence stands strong and powerful to prove to you the defendant's guilt.**

In this sentence Clark redefines her metaphor. It now fits the purpose of showing that the defense's propositions lead away from the truth she is presenting to the jury.

> **Now, I would like to show you a jury instruction that is very important. I think that both the prosecution and the defense will agree. Reasonable doubt. Okay. This is an instruction that we will talk to you about, they are going to talk to you about. This is a real important instruction. It is at the real heart of a case, every case, every criminal case.**
>
> **Because it is the burden of proof that the people have. We don't guess anybody guilty. We prove it beyond a reasonable doubt, which is what we've done in this case.**

Clark is here getting ready to go against the defense team's definition of reasonable doubt. We again see how Clark talks down to the jury treating them as children.

> **Now, to tell you about reasonable doubt, it is kind of a funny definition because it talks to you about reasonable doubt in very negative terms. It says: "that state of the evidence which, after the entire comparison, you cannot say that you have an abiding conviction." It is very weirdly worded and it is going to take you a while to go through this, so I'm going to go through it pieces at a time to try and give you a little hand here.**

This is abstract and difficult to understand. It also tilts towards talking down to the audience.

> **First of all, let me point out the first paragraph talks about the fact that it is our burden of proof. I think that one is fine. That is pretty easy.**
>
> **Now, it talks about how reasonable doubt is defined. This is real important. "it is not a mere possible doubt," okay, "because everything relating to human affairs is open to some possible or imaginary doubt." That is very important. It is a doubt founded in reason. I'm going to amplify more on that with examples when we talk about the actual evidence in this case, but bear that in mind, a**

possible doubt.

Clark is trying to communicate to the jury that beyond reasonable doubt doesn't mean beyond *any* doubt. This is an important point. Unfortunately, it doesn't come through very strongly or clearly.

I have a possible doubt that the sun will come up tomorrow. Do I have a reasonable doubt about it? No. I have no doubt founded in reason that that is going to happen, just for a very basic example, so think about that, too. We are not talking about what possible doubt is. It is reasonable doubt.

It is a very good idea to illustrate what she means by using a concrete example. Unfortunately, this example is so extreme that it carries little effect. One could imagine that the jury would have a lot more doubt about the evidence presented than if the sun comes up tomorrow.

The qualities of a good analogy are that it is interesting and able to create pictures in our imagination that favor our point of view. This could have been something like this:

If you come home unexpectedly, and you see your husband sleeping naked in your bed with another woman, there is a theoretical possibility that they are not having an affair, but is there a reasonable doubt about it?

If they try to prove something to you, their witnesses, their evidence gets evaluated by the same rules ours do. The same jury instruction applies.

You will see a jury instruction in your packet back there that talks about how to evaluate the credibility of witnesses, both expert and lay witnesses. There is no distinction made in that jury instruction for defense witnesses or for people's witnesses. It is all the same. You determine their credibility and the relative convincing force of the proof in — by the same rules, okay? So that is the first thing to remember. When you look at every-

thing, you look at all of the evidence.
What have they shown you? What have we shown you? We have the burden of proof. But you look at what they have shown you when you want to consider what was proven to you. We have pieces of boards and exhibits everywhere in this courtroom.

This is a vague attempt by Clark to address the fact that the defense has turned the case around- that they have become the accusers, though still claiming that they don't have to prove anything, since they officially are called the defense. It was not possible for Clark to state this any clearer, because she had not acknowledged this herself. This is why it came through so confusingly.

The evidence has conclusively proven that when detective Mark Fuhrman said he did not use racial epithets in the last ten years, he lied, but it is also conclusively proven that the defendant is guilty beyond a reasonable doubt.

Here Clark takes another stab at her ethos foundation. It was not very good for her to keep drawing attention on her weakest point. The defense talked about it all the time because it was their strong point. She needed to focus on her own strong points. This is what is called "letting your opponent set the agenda."

We are now going to look at some examples of how Marcia Clark presented the evidence against Simpson, and countered the defense teams allegations.

The cut is on the left hand, but he's right?handed. And the killer lost his left glove at Bundy. Now, we know that the killer cut his left hand because we have the blood drops to the left side of the bloody shoe prints. So now we have the defendant getting his hand cut on the night of his wife's stabbing, cut on his left hand, which just happens to be the hand that the murderer cut that same night. That's an <u>alarming coincidence</u>. And there's more.

Here Clark presents a strong argument about Simpson's guilt on the issue of Simpson's hand injuries. In order to make her argumentation stronger, the word "coincidence" should have been replaced with a word that reflected her total conviction about Simpson's guilt. What she was trying to say is that there is no doubt that Simpson did it. The use of the word coincidence may reflect Clark's desire to come through relatively objective and neutral. However, it made her come through as insecure in her position, but overall this was strong argumentation.

Instead of using the word coincidence, Clark could have said something to this effect: If we just look at the blood trial alone, we can conclude that either Simpson is the most unlucky ex-husband in the world, or he is guilty.

> **<u>You know, I can see getting one cut, maybe two on your hand. But four cuts and seven abrasions?</u> And we're supposed to believe that that's unrelated to a murder in which the killer's left hand was cut and bleeding as he left the crime scene. But there's more. When the defendant got the call in Chicago from detective Phillips, he tells him of Nicole's murder, he realized he had to come up with an explanation for the cut on the middle finger, and that's why we got to hear from the Chicago detective, Berris. He recovered the broken glass in the sink.**

Clark's argument is here built upon common sense, which goes well with her audience. In order to strengthen her argumentation she should not have given so much to the defense in the first couple of sentences. This way of arguing usually reflects a desire to seem reasonable and objective. It often occurs when one thinks that one has a lot of leeway, and can afford to be generous with one's opponent.

> **If you recall, there was a picture shown to you of that hotel room where the defendant checked in on the morning of June the 13th. Now, the story that they wanted to sell you is that the defendant got that big cut on the middle finger when he broke the glass after hearing of Nicole's murder. But there's a couple problems with that**

story. First of all, how do you cut yourself on the back of your finger by slamming a glass down? I mean, I have a real hard time picturing how that could possibly happen.

This piece of strong argumentation is built on commonsense.

<u>Using your life experience</u>, stop and think about the blood at Rockingham just for a moment. Sure people get their fingers cut. May not happen every day, but it happens. It's happened to me. I'm sure it's happened to you. And I don't know whether anybody's ever gotten their finger cut on a cell phone. That might be a little bit more of a rare occurrence, but the thing is, when we do — when we cut ourselves and we drip blood, what do we do? We clean it up. You drip blood around the bathroom, you drip blood in your kitchen, you drip blood in the foyer, you get a napkin, you clean it up. It's just a natural — it's something that you wouldn't even think about doing, but you would do it.

Now, <u>in all the months that you've been sequestered, how many blood trials have you left in your rooms from the bathroom to the hallway? How many times in your life have you left a trial of blood around your house or your apartment and not cleaned it up?</u>

This is a strong common sense argument concerning Simpson bleeding in his house and in his driveway.

And we had evidence from the defendant's maid that he is a very neat and tidy and clean person. And he leaves blood on his bathroom floor and he leaves blood on his foyer? So the cuts in this case, cuts to the defendant's hand and the blood that he leaves around that doesn't get cleaned up, these are very important points.

And I am going to summarize for you. <u>The hand injuries occurred at the time of the murder on the left hand, a left hand glove was lost at Bundy, a left hand.</u>

This is a nice summation of her main points. She should have spent a little more time picking up the threads, making the overall picture easier to grasp.

> **There's what's called the DNA evidence. There's the defendant's blood trial at Bundy to the left side of the bloody shoeprints. Defendant leaves the blood trial at Rockingham, but he does that, he doesn't clean up and the defendant makes the statement to DR. Baden <u>admitting bleeding, bleeding in the murder vehicle shortly after the murders</u>. These are all very significant points that <u>demonstrate conduct by the defendant</u>, actions as well as words that <u>show you consciousness of guilt</u>.**

Clark is wrapping up the issue of Simpson bleeding at the time of the murders. This could have come through stronger, if Clark had not felt the need to use the two abstract legal terms conduct by the defendant and consciousness of guilt. A poignant summation of her main points, showing the common sense of what she was saying, highlighting the defense teams claims as ridiculous, would have come through much more powerfully.

> **Now, detective Phillips testified that he told the defendant Nicole had been killed. And what did the defendant do? Did he ask how? No. Did he ask who? No. Did he ask where? No. Did he ask when? No. Did he ask whether it was a car accident? No. Now, think about the reasonable response. Someone is informed that the mother of their children has been killed and a detective calls and says, "I'm sorry to tell you this, but the mother of your children has been killed." What do you do? Wouldn't you think that the first reaction — I can understand shock. Wouldn't you think that the first reaction would be one of disbelief? No. First response, deny it, no, that can't be because you don't believe — you know, you don't believe someone close to you can be met with violence. Even if it's a car accident, you have a sense of disbelief about can't be, you know, someone I know doesn't die that way. Can't**

be. And so in your effort to make it where it might be real or to test the truth of the statement, you ask questions. How did it happen? When? Who do you think did it? Where did it happen? What was the cause of death? How could this be?

Clark addresses the fact that Simpson *never* asked any questions concerning the fact that his ex-wife had died. In other words, he was distressed without really knowing why he was distressed. This is a strong point that Clark could have gotten more out of. She could have asked the jurors if they had ever been in a situation,where somebody close to them suddenly died, and they had not asked how they died.

They hint that the blood was planted. They have tried to create the impression that multiple other bloodstains were contaminated and that somehow all the contamination only occurred where it would consistently prove the defendant was guilty.

Clark is trying to show how the defense team has constructed their defense.

Obviously <u>it is common sense, if contamination is going on you are going to see it going on all over the place</u>. As a matter of fact, if what they are saying is true with this aerosol effect, flying DNA all over the place, then Mr. Simpson's blood type ought to be showing up in other cases somewhere. You know, somewhere out or down in another department in a rape case Mr. Simpson's type should be showing up because it is everywhere.

Here Clark is addressing the defense team's weakest point, the issue of selective contamination. Since the defense can always make the argument that the reason that there was contamination with Simpson's blood in only this case was because it was here the police had been tracking it around and so on, it weakens the argument when Clark talks about why Simpson's DNA doesn't show up in other cases. This is a good example of what can happen when one is not able to see the issue from the opponent's point of view.

In order for Clark to focus the arguments on the defenses' weakest point, she should concentrate only on the fact that selective contamination occurred only in the test results, and not in the control tests. And, according to the defense theory, contamination only occurred in the places where the blood was not planted or degenerated. On top of that, all the places where contamination is suppose to have taken place, all the DNA from the real killer is suppose to have totally vanished, but Simpson's DNA is still intact. The DNA issue came through in the Simpson case as relatively complicated, but this should be relatively easy to understand.

> **Or even let's confine to it this case. Talk about that. That how come if the argument is that his blood is flying all over the place, DNA is flying all over the place, why didn't we find his blood type showing up where obviously it shouldn't be? What I mean is this: They took samples from the pool of blood by Nicole's body. They took samples of blood that was near Ron Goldman's body. Obviously the blood came from them because they were lying there.**
>
> **And then of course you know you have the blood drops leading away from the crime scene that had to be left by the killer. There is no question about that. That was left by the killer because they are next to the bloody shoeprints. So you know, why is it that the samples of blood they took from her pool of blood didn't come up with the defendant's blood type if the defendant's blood type DNA is flying all over the place? If it is flying all over the place, then it ought to be all over the place. Why isn't it in the pool of blood sample that was taken from Nicole Brown? Why isn't it in the pool of the blood sample that was taken from near Ron Goldman's body?**

Clark now confines her arguments about contamination to the Simpson case. The idea is good, but it is hard to understand, because it comes through in a rambling and confusing way. It doesn't matter how good your argument is, if your audience doesn't understand it.

And what you have here is they are trying to get you to believe that only the killer's blood was contaminated and it was consistently contaminated with only the defendant's blood typing. Does this make any sense to you? What you ought to have, if you have contamination, if you've got a problem here, is that some of the blood drops come back to the defendant and some don't; they come back to the real killer. That is what you ought to get, because it can't be this consistent.

Here Clark addresses her strong point in a more clear and straightforward way.

And you know, that is the other part of their — of their scenario that makes no sense, no sense. You have all these police officers that were there on June the 13th, officer Riske saying his partner, young rookie names officer Terrazas, shined his light on the rear gate to show him the blood on the rear gate. You have officer Riske seeing the blood on the rear gate. You have officer Rossi seeing the blood on the rear gate. You have detective Phillips seeing the blood on the rear gate, all of it early on.

Dennis Fung, whom you can see is not the model of efficiency, forgot to collect it, and from this we get a theory that they seem to imply that the blood was planted. Why do they say that?

Clark is addressing the defense team's claims that the blood on the gate was planted.

Here again it would have been better to say that Fung overlooked the bloodstains, instead of putting him further down, as irritated as she may be with him.

Now, first of all, I want to hear Mr. Cochran actually stand up in front of you and tell you he believes the blood was planted. I want to hear that. Because that is incredible. That is absolutely incredible. When you think about

> **that, think what evidence have you been given to show you how that blood was planted, to show you when that blood was planted, to show you who planted that blood?**
>
> **Now, the reason that they have to come up with this story about contamination and planting, and I want to hear if they really, really do that, say that to you, is because they can't get around the result.**

Clark addresses the overall reason for the defense team's theory. We see Clark trying to vaccinate the jury against the framing theory. This would be a good place for Clark to state, i.e., if the defense team wants to become the accusers, they have to bear the same burden of proof as the prosecution.

> **From the fact that you have higher molecular weight DNA on blood collected later, July 3rd, they want you to infer that somehow it was planted. But they are inconsistent, because if you remember, now if you plant the blood, aren't you going to plant it close to the time you collect? What are you going to do, plant it and hope somebody finds it later? You plant it when you expect someone to find it, right?**

Clark is addressing the defense team's claims that the blood found on the gate leading up to Nicole Brown's house was planted. The controversy was around the fact that the blood on the gate was collected three weeks later than the rest of the blood evidence and that it seemed to be in a better condition than the other blood samples collected. The defense team says that the blood drops should have been in a worse condition than the rest of the blood collected from the crime scene, the prosecution says that it has to do with the surface that it landed upon.

> **If you are going to say that the blood was planted, then you are going to say that was planted at or near the time of collection, in which case the EDTA would not break down, in which case the EDTA should be intact, in which case you should see the kind of high smooth arc that the**

graphs showed you from the reference tubes, instead of the jagged noise that you actually saw.

And they brought in Dr. Rieders to try and tell you that that jagged noise looks just like that high arc which is ridiculous, which is insulting to your intelligence.

This again is hard to understand, and is easily overlooked in a several hours long argumentation. One has to understand the medium. In an oral argumentation lots of specific details are hard to grasp. This is easier to understand if presented in a written text. Scheck can better get away with going into minute details, because it is in his best interest to confuse the issue.

But the reason that they have to say this, <u>defying logic, defying common sense</u>, is because, ladies and gentlemen, his blood on the rear gate with that match that makes him one in 57 billion people that could have left that blood, I mean there is what, five million people on the planet, that means you would have to go through 57 billion people to find the DNA profile that matches Mr. Simpson's. There is only five billion people on the planet. Ladies and gentlemen, that is an identification, okay, that proves it is his blood. Nobody else's on the planet; no one. Now, they know that.

Clark is here getting into why the defense team claims that the blood evidence has been planted and contaminated.

Now, the blood on the socks, Nicole's blood on the socks. Again RFLP match, very powerful. Showed from Cellmark that was a five?probe match and I believe found to be one in 6.8 billion people. Again, more than — there are people on the planet. Identification. And 11?probe match by DOJ showed that it was one in 7.7 billion people. Again, her blood and only hers on this planet could be on that sock. Now, how do you get around that? It wasn't wrong and they couldn't find an expert who would say it was contaminated because there is too

much DNA. That is the blood. That type is the type. It is her blood. How do you get around that? And if you know that that is true, if you know it is her blood on his socks that they find on the morning of June the 13th, that alone with the rear gate stain convicts him. You can't believe otherwise. You have so much proof now how do they get around that? They have to find a theory to get around that. And what do they do? This is what they come up with. So <u>if it is low volume DNA, it is contaminated. If it is high volume DNA, it is planted</u>, and it is also very convenient and ridiculous.

Here Clark gives a strong argumentation against the defense team's contamination and planting theory.

No, did, did get contaminated, and they could have come here and told you and pointed out the evidence that showed why only the blood drops left by the murderer got contaminated and shown you why they consistently only got contaminated in a way that showed the defendant's DNA type, not that they possibly could have. Yes, possibly we are all sitting on Mars right now, you know, and I'm from Venus and I'm talking. Anything is possible. Let's talk about what did happen. Let's talk about what we've got.

Another example of a good point that gets lost in a clumsy presentation.

They could have shown you proof that the Bundy blood drops were contaminated, not the mere possibility. No, I'm talking about evidence that gives you a reason to conclude that that happened, and that they never could do. And they could have done it if it were true, but they didn't.

Here Clark makes another good point, trying to hold the defense team responsible for their accusations.

So they took you through all this tortured and twisted road one moment saying that the police are all a bunch of bumbling idiots. The next moment they are clever conspirators.

And now ask yourself did they ever prove who planted, when, how? And it is a fact that the defense doesn't have to prove anything, that is a fact, but once they do decide to put on a case, once they decide and proof something, their witnesses are subject to the same scrutiny as the people's witnesses are. Your jury instruction, as I've told you, makes no distinction.

Here Clark actually defends the police, and clearly refutes the defense team's efforts both to be the accusers and claim that they don't have any burden of proof. This represents what Clark's argumentation is desperately in need of, an ethos foundation.

They have got to make you believe that blood was planted. It is the cornerstone of their defense, it really is, because as I've pointed out, if you know that is his blood left on the rear gate, if you know that is her blood on those socks, what are you left to conclude?

Here Clark puts forward a strong argument against the contamination theory.

Now, what do they do to show you, to prove to you the cornerstone of their defense? What do they do? They take our tests, our tests, and they have some other expert, who neither did the test himself nor could come in and try and interpret those graphs for you. Not only that, but he does it inconsistently. He writes a report. If you recall, he wrote a report in which he said he found one parent ion and one daughter ion, not the full daughter spectrum that would permit identification of EDTA, but the same finding of one parent ion, one daughter ion that Mr. Martz said he found in his own blood, in his own unpreserved blood, which tends to prove — no, which does

prove — that the blood on the rear gate, the blood on the socks are just like again Martz' unpreserved blood, natural blood, not from a preservative tube.

Here Clark addresses the defense team's claim that the blood collected at the murder scene comes from the blood sample taken from Simpson; that the blood drops come from preserved blood.

I don't ask you to take my word for anything. That is why we present evidence. That is why we call witnesses. If it isn't in the record or it doesn't make sense to you as a logical inference from what you've heard, reject it. I don't care who says it. Reject it. But <u>do the same for the defense. Hold me to that standard. Hold them to that standard</u>. When you hear them try to tell you that all this evidence was either contaminated or planted, ask yourself does this really makes sense? Was — what evidence was I given to prove that? Is there any evidence that really shows that? <u>Or is it smoke and mirrors? Is it all just smoke to cloud everything, cloud all the issues, distract you? Take a little piece here, take a little piece there.</u>

Clark again tried to hold the defense team accountable for their accusations. Furthermore, she tried to communicate to the jury that the defense team was trying to confuse the issue, in order for it to seem more complicated, and therefore more uncertain if Simpson was the killer. Clark needed to explain further what she meant by "take a little piece here, take a little piece there." Another option was to cut it away. Clark needed to tighten up her argumentation by cutting away unnecessary stuff. Her argumentation needed to be trimmed up by cutting away the fat.

But <u>what they have done systematically is fragmented the case</u>. This is not new, you know. They did a very good job of it. They are fine lawyers and <u>they challenged the people's case as they should and that is good</u>. You put the state to their proof. That is what we have to do. We have

to deliver. That is our job.

And we have been aware of what is happening, hearing their fragmenting. They take little pieces out of context and focus on only that little piece and take a little piece of a picture focus on only this little piece of a picture. And forget about all the rest that puts it all in context. Give Henry Lee second generation photographs that he can't see anything on instead of the good stuff, the original photographs that would show him what is going on on Bundy walk there.

Clark explains what she means by little pieces. The sentence: "They challenged the people's case as they should and that is good" was again what I would call fat. It was superfluous and needed to be cut away. Too much fat in one's argumentation makes it sloppy. The active ingredients drown in irrelevant stuff.

Now, back to DNA. I'm sorry, I digressed. Even when it is analyzed using the PCR method, it is not quite so easily contaminated as the defense would have you believe. As you have heard, it is used every day to save lives and you always use it, you have learned, in very non?sterile conditions. What does that mean? War dead, soldiers who die in jungles and in deserts, those are not sterile environments, ladies and gentlemen. Those are very dirty environments, but they use the PCR test to go identify those soldiers.

And why do they do that? So they can notify next of kin. That is a very serious responsibility. You better be right. You better be right. Now, if it is good enough to go and notify next of kin that their son, their daughter, their husband, their father, has been murdered or killed, excuse me, on a battlefield, then it better be good and reliable stuff. So if it is good enough for that, on body parts being recovered from jungles and deserts, it is pretty hearty, pretty durable.

Here Clark tries to counter the defense's claim that the DNA has deteriorated due to rough treatment that it should have deteriorated further on the gate at the murder scene, because it was collected three weeks later.

And by the way, when DNA degrades, as you've been told, it doesn't turn into someone else's type; you get no result.

Here we see, that one of Clark's *most important* points gets lost in the abundance of issues addressed in Clark's closing statement. This is a good example of what can happen when one does not adequately focus one's argumentation, and thereby determine what are the most important issues. Clark really needed to get into this point. We should have seen paragraphs upon paragraphs where Clark addressed this issue.

She says really they have got to be touching. The swatches would have to come in contact. A swatch of somebody else's type would have to come into physical contact with a swatch where the DNA had completely degraded. She could not envision flying DNA, as they have tried to sell you in the defense, because DNA just doesn't jump or fly.

It is here worth noting that the defense team overcomes this argument by implying, that the DNA got on the samples when the test tube with Simpson's blood was upended, and some of the blood squirted out.

<u>If you have contamination, the controls should come up showing DNA. And the controls on the Bundy walk did not.</u> And there you go.

Oh, I wanted to go over an instruction with you. This is a long instruction that has particular relevance to this case. (brief pause.) Ms. Clark: It is called — this is the instruction about circumstantial and direct evidence.

Here we again see how the important issue drowned in words. In this instance it simply gets pushed aside by another issue.

So what do we find on the Rockingham glove, the one he

drops? We find everything. Everything. We find fibers consistent with Ron Goldman's shirt. We find the hair of Ron. We find the hair of Nicole. We find the blood of Ron Goldman. We find the blood of Nicole Brown. And we find the blood of the defendant. And we find Bronco fiber from the defendant's Bronco. We find blue black cotton fibers just like those found on the shirt of Ron Goldman and on the socks of the defendant in his bedroom. And on this glove he is tied to every aspect of the murder; to Ron Goldman, to Nicole Brown, to the car, and of course that is why the defense has to say that the glove is planted, because if they don't, everything about this glove convicts the defendant, where it is found, what is found on it, what is found in it, even a black limp hair found inside the glove. Everything about it convicts him.

This is a good and strong argument put forth by Clark concerning the planted glove theory.

Whatever you think of Mark Fuhrman, nobody thinks much of him, <u>he couldn't have done this. Why couldn't we have done this?</u> It is not just the fact that all the other officers who were there before him saw only one glove. Think about what he knew at the time he went out to the south pathway? He didn't know whether or not there were eyewitnesses to the crime that would say somebody else did it. He didn't know if there was going to be someone who said I heard voices. They weren't his. They weren't Mr. Simpson's. He didn't know if the defendant had an airtight alibi and had maybe left on the nine o'clock flight to Chicago. He didn't know any of that.

He could have — what he could have done, by planting evidence, is been wrong and completely fouled up the solution of the case, because he is doing something like that without knowing anything about the case, subjecting him — himself. Think about his own self?preservation, so incredible and in — an incredible felony. He is in big trouble, in big trouble. And all that has

to happen is that an alibi is disproven or an eyewitness comes forward, neither one of which he knows anything about. They can be out there for all he knows. Probably thinks they are. So think about that when you consider this theory of the defense.

You know, I mean, <u>it is like dismissing logic and reality and reason all at once</u>, throw them out the window, because nothing makes sense about that theory, <u>nothing from even Mark Fuhrman's point of view.</u>

Clark states that Fuhrman could not have planted the glove. It is interesting to see how she goes from *he* to *we* when she refutes the defense team's framing theory. It shows that the defense had already spread the allegations far beyond Fuhrman, an aspect that the prosecution was aware of, but did not address or accept. By acknowledging this the prosecution would have had a better chance of coming up with an approach to counter this development in the case.

But the bottom line is, and I think that you will reach the same conclusion, no one planted that glove. You know why? Because they are his gloves. They are his gloves.

Think about all the evidence you heard now. Remember that he is a size extra large. The gloves are a size extra large. The glove at Rockingham is a mate to the glove at Bundy. They are a pair. A pair that are the same exact type purchased by Nicole on December 18th, 1990, one of only 200 pair sold that year. Gloves that are cashmere lined, gloves that cost $55.00, rich man's gloves, gloves that were exclusive to Bloomindales, gloves that were not sold west of Chicago, gloves that the defendant was wearing at football games from January of 1991, just a few weeks after she bought them, until the last football season before the murders.

We here see Clark providing more evidence to counter that the glove found on Simpson's property was not planted.

So with all of this blood evidence, what we have done, and

> **fiber and hair, look at all we have traced, look at all we have proven, we have linked the defendant to the crime scene, we have linked the defendant to the victims, we have linked the defendant and the victims to his car and that link has reached from Bundy into his bedroom at Rockingham.**

Clark delivers a nice summation of their concrete evidence against Simpson, evidence that if it would have had a solid ethos foundation would have been hard to beat.

Marcia Clark's argumentation is not outright bad. It is rather a reflection of a number of common misconceptions of what good argumentation is, as for example that logical argumentation is always the best form of argumentation, or that the more arguments you have for your point of view, the better. These misconceptions include a lack of understanding and knowledge of what is convincing and what forms the basis of consensus. We are dealing with a prosecution confronted with a group of handpicked defense lawyers composed of some of the country's best legal minds. We are seeing a lack of symmetry in the balance of strength, which opens up the possibility for manipulation. A possibility would have been for Marcia Clark to play on her own weaknesses. But, on the other hand, this would have called for a certain understanding of the rhetorical situation.

A way to play on her own weaknesses could have been the theme:

> I am just an ordinary lawyer, working in this courtroom on an everyday basis. And I am up against a bunch of hand-picked wildly successful lawyers from all over the country. Poor me, I am just an average lawyer, but at least I tell the truth.

An interesting thing here is to see that Johnnie Cochran actually uses this topic to his own advantage. He did this by emphasizing that they, the defense, were up against the entire state of California, represented by Marcia Clark and Christopher Darden.

A topos which would have been obvious for the prosecution to bring forward was:

> There's another law for the rich than there is for the rest of us.

I believe that the rhetorical situation called for the use of this topos. This topos was not used, however, since the prosecution was not able to respond to the new rhetorical situation. Instead the prosecution carried on with their logical, quantitative reasoning while at the same time they came staggering behind Cochran's race arguments with clearly defensive argumentation.

It is important to focus your argumentation and only have one key argument. Making use of a whole group of arguments creates the impression that you lack sufficient confidence in any one of them. The way to have one main argument, without loosing out on the rest of your argumentation, is to subordinate the rest of the arguments so they directly support the main argument.

The deployment of arguments is often even more dangerous in refutation, as it suggests that what may have been a casual remark by one's opponent had ample justification since no stone is left unturned in combating it. There is a further consideration. Since a speaker is supposed to be aware of the dangers of weak arguments capable of harming his prestige, making use of them raises the serious presumption that he has no better arguments available, or even that there are no others. Without realizing it, a speaker who advances weak arguments may destroy other stronger arguments, which might have spontaneously entered the hearer's mind. Silence can have the same effect as a weak argument and make people think there are no good arguments. An unfortunately chosen argument and silence can thus both have the same disastrous effect.[96]

The prosecution did indeed succeed in refuting most of the allegations put forward by the defense. Unfortunately, they did not gather the threads and show an overall picture or theme to the jurors. It is important to have an overall theme that runs through your whole argumentation. By always connecting your arguments to your overall argumentation, you make sure that the significance of all the facts and information you present fall into a overall picture that you are presenting to your audience.

Unfortunately it is a very common mistake not to put the refutation of one single point into the wider context. As sender of the message one tends to believe that the recipient is able to follow one's thoughts, and see the overall meaning, the red thread that runs throughout the points refuted. One must not as a matter of course rely on this. Instead it is wise to draw the conclusions of the individual refutation continuously.

This is probably one of the most common reasons why an otherwise good and well-founded reasoning does not attain the effect or sympathy it warrants.

Another important issue was that the prosecution didn't focus on rehabilitating their police witnesses since they did not think that their own credibility was closely connected to the credibility of the police. By not rehabilitating their one witness, they also missed out on getting the last word on specific issues, as the trial progressed.

What happened to Marcia Clark and Christopher Darden could have happened to many lawyers in their situation. The law schools have let lawyers down by not providing adequate education in rhetoric. These lawyers did everything they were taught, and it was not enough. The most tragic thing about this is not the effect it has on the lawyers, but the consequences it has for the people they represent and the community in general.

Aggressive behavior is one of Marcia Clark's characteristic traits. In evaluating her effectiveness towards the jury, we have to look at how this effected her abilities as a prosecutor.

Generally it is not in one's advantage to appear aggressive. I am referring to actual aggression, not to be confused with being committed, forward, and energetic. A committed and energetic personality has a clear advantage when one seeks to convince an audience.

Aggressiveness is a clear disadvantage when you want to convince an audience of your point of view. You can win with an aggressive behavior, but you are actually winning in spite of the aggressive behavior. A good example of this is Barry Scheck, who has so many other abilities, that he wins in spite of this negative trait.

Often the reason for the aggressive behavior can be found in the metaphors a person applies to a subject. The way we perceive a situation is reflected in our use of metaphors. The metaphor we choose to use in a certain situation reflects our way of viewing the situation, and it further influences the way we understand the event.

If we choose to use war metaphors we will more-or-less consistently use the standard of war in adjusting and acting upon the situation.

In American society the use of violent metaphors is very common. Many people "kick, shoot and hit" their way through life. A web site does not receive clicks or hugs, but hits! The use of metaphors might seem a trivial and unimportant issue that at best is getting into unnecessary details. To illustrate the importance of which metaphor one applies, we are going to look at three areas influencing the Simpson case, where the appliance of the war metaphor had devastating effect.

1. Marcia Clark's aggressive attitude.
2. Cochran's ethical standards.
3. The reputation and behavior of the police.

Marcia Clark interprets her role as prosecutor through the war metaphor, as can be seen in the following quotes from her book *Without a Doubt*: "...verbal dexterity and strong opinions are welcomed at the bar. There are clearly delineated rules of combat, rules that favor reason."[97]

As Clark mentions in the following quote, she is not alone in interpreting her role through the war metaphor: "The cheap metal partitions had been rearranged to convert it to what Bill Hodgman liked to call the War Room. (Prosecutors love military talk. I, like many of my fellow deputies in Special Trials, had a big old metal cart that I'd load with briefs and haul down to court. Everyone called it the War Wagon.)"[98]

The negative effects of using the war metaphor is that it leads to aggressive behavior that stifles the prosecution's ability to convince a jury.

What makes the negative effects of employing this metaphor more extreme when it comes to Marcia Clark and many other female prosecutors is their feeling of having to be better then their male colleagues. As Clark states: "I've never been one to cry sexism. But I know the score. I know I have to be tougher and better than the guys I work with. My attitude has always been, So what? Having to be tougher and better makes me just that, tougher and better."[99]

This feeling of having to be better often leads to extreme behavior. Since men have set the standards, being better than the men is often perceived as being more male than the men. This is a real shame, since the female nonaggressive consensus-seeking traits is actually more effective when one wants to convince a skeptical or neutral audience. Female lawyers should be aware of that, just as any minority or suppressed group must stop imitating white men and seek strength in their own abilities. The main reason for that is that white men will always be best at being white men.

By trying to live up to the perceived male ideal, female prosecutors who actually start out with an advantage in their abilities to communicate with a jury end up being the least effective in convincing a jury. This aspect has been well commented upon by Jeffrey Tobin:

> The office's losing streak in big cases was well known. What was less known or at least less commented upon in the media was that most of those cases had been lost by women prosecutors with pugnacious demeanors, among them Lael Rubin in McMartin Preschool; Lea D'Agostino in *Twilight Zone*; and Pamela Bozanich in Menendez. All of these prosecutors came across as aggressive and outspoken, just as Marcia Clark did...[100]

Johnny Cochran also uses the war metaphor. Both in his closing statement and in the book he writes after the trial is over, Cochran talks about being at war against the LAPD, in order to rut out racism within the police. This did not effect Cochran's effective communication skills, but it did affect his ethics. When one is at war, the goals often justify the means. The greater good is often used as justification for the means. This can, to some degree, explain the length Cochran is willing to go in order to achieve his goal. In general this attitude determined the defense team's sole emphasis upon effect. Winning by any possible means.

The war metaphor has been very popular in describing the police strategy against crime. "war on crime" warrants a military type of policing that begs police misconduct and brutality, since there are no rules in war. This alienates minority groups, since they are often the ones that live in the area where the rough police methods are employed, and are often looked upon as potential suspects or enemies. Using this metaphor for police work has had two major disadvantages. First, one cannot solve nor eliminate crime without the support of the local community. Secondly, the potential jurors taken from this jury pool will not convict the defendant, if they have no trust in the police. In other words, the criminals may be caught, but they will not be convicted.

We have in this case seen how the war metaphor influenced the prosecution's ability to achieve support for their case, how the war metaphor influenced the extent of the conduct the defense was willing to engage in, and how the war metaphor influenced the ethos foundation for the entire case against Simpson.

15. CHRISTOPHER DARDEN'S ARGUMENTATION

...the rich think they are worthy to rule, because they believe they possess that which makes them so. In a word, the character of the rich man is that of a fool favoured by fortune. At the same time there is a difference between the character of the newly rich and of those whose wealth is of long standing, because the former have the vices of wealth in a greater degree and more; for, so to say, they have not been educated to the use of wealth. Their unjust acts are not due to malice, but partly to insolence, partly to incontinence, which tends to make them commit assault and battery and adultery.

Aristotle

"He killed her out of jealousy," Christopher Darden tells the jury during the prosecution's opening statements. "He killed her because he couldn't have her."

Christopher Darden, a black public prosecutor who was second to Marcia Clark, played the decisive part in the argumentation towards the jurors. Darden and Clark divided the argumentation among them. Darden speaks to the issues of motive, and Clark mainly argues the material evidence.

In his speeches to the jurors, Darden was the most emotional of the prosecution's attorneys. His use of pathos was intense and seemed honest. The biggest problem with Darden's speech was that he did not firmly connect the issue of spousal abuse to the probability that Simpson committed the murders. You cannot presume that the jury shares your knowledge.

Darden had a really good account of the domestic violence, and the events that led up to the murders. Unfortunately, one tends to become irritated at him because he is so long drawn-out and repetitive. This has to be seen in connection with the jury wondering what relevance the domestic violence had to the actual murder case, since they were not convinced that spousal abuse had any relevance in a murder case. This combination undermines the effect that Darden's speech could have had on the jury's verdict.

In order to determine the effectiveness of Darden's argumentation, it is necessary to have a look at his closing argument to the jury. We are therefore going to look at excerpts from Darden's closing speech presented in the right chronological order. In the beginning of his speech Darden said:

> **All you have to do is use the tools God gave you, the tools he gave you to use or utilize whenever you're confronted with a problem or an issue. All you have to do is use your common sense. And the defense would have you believe that this is a complex series of facts and evidence and law and science and all of that. Not really. Not really.**
>
> **You have to question or wonder how it is a lawyer can summarize a case in eight hours when presenting the case took eight months. It's a simple case, but there's been a lot of smoke, a lot of smoke screens, a lot of diversions, a lot of detractions, a lot of distractions, and in some respect, there's been an attempt to get you to lose focus of what the real issues are in this case. And that takes time.**

Darden looses a strong grouping of three here; diversions, detractions and distractions because he repeated unimportant words, which only made him seem wordy and lessened the strength of his argumentation. Besides Cochran, Darden was the only one to make references to God, probably because Darden and Cochran were the only ones that fully knew how much this issue meant to the predominately black female jury.

Darden supported the straightforward interpretation of the evidence by accusing the opposite side of manipulation. Darden was trying to expose the opposite side's techniques. In order for this attempt to be effective, he needed to be more *concrete* and *precise* in his claims, at least initially. In this way he would *show* the jury what was going on, instead of *telling* them.

To convince somebody by telling them about it demands a good ethos from the onset, especially if there are competing opinions. If you can show the audience what you are claiming, it can actually reinforce your ethos.

We believe that this evidence of domestic violence is very important. It's important that you understand the nature of this man's relationship with one of the victims in this case. It's important because when you consider it, it may help explain to you or it may suggest to you his motive for killing Nicole Brown and perhaps his motive for killing Ron Goldman as well, and the law allows you to use this evidence as you attempt to determine whether or not there was a motive to kill.

You can use this evidence to help in the sense of your deciding whether or not the killing was premeditated. And if you find that it helps in terms of identification, the identification of this defendant as the person who killed these two people, you can use it.

This was about as close as Darden got to tying the relevance of the domestic violence into the murder case. Unfortunately, Darden never came forward and refuted the defense team's claim that there was no significant link between domestic violence and murder. The defense team said that there was no connection between spousal abuse and murder, because under one percent of the men that beat their wives actually end up killing them. Therefore it was irrelevant to the murder case that Simpson physically abused Nicole Brown.

Darden needed to make it clear to the jury that the relevant way to apply this statistic was to look at the women who have actually been murdered. If they have been battered by their husband, boyfriend, ex-husband, or ex-boyfriend, the statistics show that there is a 35 to 50 percent chance that this man is the murderer. By not doing this, Darden allowed the defense team to cut the logos foundation for the domestic violence argumentation. This could have been excellent to use in his attempt to show that the defense team used manipulative techniques

The kind of manipulative techniques that the defense team used here were a big gamble.

Either one benefits greatly from them, or one looses big time if exposed. From a purely effective standpoint there are two issues to take into consideration before one employs such techniques:

1. How symmetrical is the balance of strength between the opponents.
2. What kind of odds does the case face.

In order for this kind of manipulation to be successful, the balance of strength between the opponents has to be more-or-less unsymmetrical. And in order for it to be worth the chance to employ this kind of technique, the odds have to be pretty bad from the onset. We have seen that both these criteria were fulfilled from the onset in the Simpson case. So from the defense team's point of view, this was a good choice, since they were only concerned about effect.

> **And when I spoke to you back in January, I told you — I promised you I think that I would expose to you the other side of this man, of this defendant. I promised you that I would expose to you the private side of him, that part of him, the side of him that was capable of extreme rage, jealously and violence, and I said to you back then, I said to you and I asked that you consider the nature of their relationship, with Nicole, because <u>to understand what happened at Bundy, you need to know what happened between them during the 17?year period that they were together off and on, because when you look at that, you see a motive for killing.</u>**

Darden was trying to support the relevance of the domestic violence evidence. Since Darden was not specific enough in his reasoning this argumentation was more vote-gathering than vote-moving. In other words, the ones that already agreed with him would get more riled up while not effecting the ones that are skeptical.

I'm sure the defense is going to get up here at some point and say, uh, that domestic violence evidence, it's irrelevant, and they may say to you that just because this defendant had some marital discord or violence in his marriage to Nicole Brown, that it doesn't mean anything.

Well, this isn't a "just because" issue. This is a "because" issue. It is because he hit her in the past and because he slapped her and threw her out of the house and kicked her and punched her and grabbed her around the neck, <u>it's because he did these things to her in the past that you ought to know about it and consider it</u>, and it's because he used a baseball bat to break the windshield of her Mercedes back in 1985 and it's because he kicked her door down in 1993.

You remember the Gretna Green incident. Remember the 911 call. It's because of a letter he wrote her — he wrote to Nicole rather around June the 6th talking about the IRS. It's because he stalked her, because he looked through her windows one night in April of 1992. They may say the defendant is just looking through a window late at night. We say that's stalking.

This was generally a good argumentation, except for Darden saying to the jury that the domestic violence was relevant because of the nature of the domestic violence evidence itself. This is what is called a ring argument. "It is important because it is important." This is not an argument but a statement. This can be seen by putting it into the argumentation model. We will then realize that the claim and the reasoning are the same:

Reasoning--	**Claim**
Because he did these things to her in the past, you ought to know about it and consider it.	The domestic violence is important

Pure statements do not have the ability of moving votes, since they do not provide any reasoning for changing one's mind. Since Darden was not able to firmly connect the relevance of the domestic violence to the murder case, Cochran was able to say:

> **He is a human being and he is not perfect. He is not proud of some of the things he did, but they don't add up to murder.**

Darden further stated:

> **It's because of all those things and because all of these things alongside the physical evidence at the scene, the bloody shoeprints in his size, the blood drops at Bundy, the blood on his sock, the blood trial at Rockingham, it's because when you look at all of that, it all points to him.**
>
> **I'm not afraid to point to him. Nobody pointed him out and said he did it. I'll point to him. Why not? The evidence all points to him.**

Here Darden was arguing coincidences. How likely is it that the physical evidence in this case would point to a man who had a history of domestic violence? This argumentation may win the case for Darden in a civil case, but it is not adequate in a criminal case, where the burden of proof is higher.

The last part where Darden points Simpson out as the killer strengthens his argumentation, in the sense that it shows conviction.

> **And it's also because when you look at the bloody ruthlessness...of these murders and when you see, as Miss Clark pointed out, that <u>these killings were rage killings</u>, rage — I mean, you have to say to yourself, well, who in the past has ever raised a hand to this woman? Who during the days and the hours leading to her death was upset with her?**

Here Darden provided a reason for his claim that the domestic violence was relevant because of the way the murders were conducted. This was a lot better than the ring argumentation, but it still didn't specifically tie Simpson to the killings.

And as Miss Clark alluded to earlier, the killing was personal, the way it was done. The way it was done, this is personal. Somebody had a score to settle. Who had a score to settle with Nicole? When you look at all of that, you look at the domestic violence, the manner of the killing, the physical evidence, the history of abuse and their relationship, the intimidation, the stalking, you look at it, it all points to him. It all points to him.

Now, they may not think this evidence is important. But it was important to Nicole Brown.

There was no doubt that being beaten was an important issue to Nicole, but this still didn't address the issue of its importance in the determination of who actually killed her.

You heard detective Mark Fuhrman testify about the 1985 incident. Let me say Fuhrman, Fuhrman, Fuhrman, Fuhrman. All right. I've said Fuhrman about 50 times. Let me let you know this. We're not hiding Fuhrman. He's too big, especially now, to hide. So hey, Fuhrman testified.

Fuhrman described for you a 1985 domestic violence, domestic abuse incident or incident of violence or incident of abuse or disturbing — what do you call it — disturbing the peace incident, whatever you want to call it. But in 1985, detective Fuhrman was not a detective. I just called him detective, geez. Fuhrman was a patrol officer. He went to 360 North Rockingham in response to a call.

We here see how Darden was choking on Fuhrman. Darden may think that it was because of Fuhrman's racists views, which undoubtedly appalled him, but the deeper reason was that Fuhrman was the way Cochran had chosen to discredit Darden, and thereby level the playing field for his racists conspiracy theory. Darden had to become an "Uncle Tom" in order for the racist conspiracy theory to seem credible. This was necessary because Cochran needed to expand the racist framing theory from Fuhrman and out to other people involved in the case, in order for it to seem theoretically possible. Darden was caught in a bad place, between a black icon (O.J. Simpson), and a tremendously popular black lawyer. In order to survive he had to defend a man that he despised. Without the rhetorical insight it is no wonder that Darden didn't choose this approach.

> **Remember that time at the Red Onion when he grabbed her by the crotch in front of a bar full of strangers and said, "this is where my babies come from. This is mine." Remember that testimony? <u>This relationship between this man and Nicole, you know, it is like the time bomb ticking away. Just a matter of time, just a matter of time before something really bad happened.</u>**
>
> **You know, you meet people in life and there are people with short fuses. You know, they just go off. And there are others with longer fuses, you know, takes them a little while longer to go off. And relationships are the same way sometimes, you know, especially a violent abusive relationship like this one. <u>This thing was like a fuse, a bomb with a long fuse. And there were incidents along the way, and along the way as each incident occurred, that fuse got shorter.</u>**

Here Darden introduced the bomb metaphor that he was going to build his presentation of the domestic violence evidence around. It was a well-chosen metaphor in the sense that it lent credibility to why the domestic violence evidence was important, and it provided an explanation about why Simpson chose to kill his ex-wife now, and not on one of these earlier occasions. Here the bomb metaphor gave Darden the possibility to tie the domestic violence evidence onto the evidence leading up to the murders themselves.

The biggest problem Darden had in his presentation of the domestic violence evidence was that he was too drawn-out and repetitive. In Darden's use of a bomb metaphor, he kept stating that the fuse was getting shorter and that the bomb was close to going off. But the bomb never goes off. Darden didn't bring his speech to the point of an explosion, the murders. This made it difficult not to get irritated with him, or fall asleep during his presentation.

Because Darden didn't make it totally clear for the jury why the domestic violence evidence was relevant, it enhanced the irritation over Darden's long presentation. From the comments given by the jury shortly after the trial was over we can see that this was exactly what happened. Not only did the jury not find the domestic violence relevant to the murder case, but their aggressive responses to this question reflected their irritation at having to listen to many hours of repetitive and "irrelevant" argumentation. We are going to look at one example of the domestic violence that Darden presents. We can see that Darden had some really strong evidence of the domestic violence that took place. This argumentation was weakened by the fact that approximately 40-50 percent of the words Darden used could be taken away, and he would still be saying the same thing. The superfluous words are between the bolded words. If we take just the words that are bolded, we don't have to add another word for Darden to be saying the exact same thing in a coherent way:

> **Let me say this to you. We submit to you that the hand that left that imprint five years ago is the same hand that cut that same throat, that same neck on June 12th, 1994.** It was the defendant. **It was the defendant then, it's the defendant now.**
>
> **And at that point, Nicole Brown made a — she said a series of things to officer Edwards**. Remember, keep in mind that she was hysterical, she was upset and she was panicked, and I'm sure that she was in fear because she must have been in fear because she was running through the night covered with mud in a bra and in her pajamas.
>
> And she said to officer Edwards — **she said something very important** to officer Edwards. She said, "**you never do anything about him**. You come out here, **you've been out here eight times and you never do anything about him**." That's what she told officer Edwards that day. She said, "you've been out here eight times."
>
> **They want to tell you that the police conspired against O.J. Simpson**. Nicole says they had been out there eight times before and never did anything to him. I don't know.

Well, let me ask you this. How many times does it take? **If they'd been out there eight times before that night, then that night was the ninth time**. No one had ever done anything to him before. I don't know why that is. But **what do you think?** Do you think it's time to think that perhaps this time, we ought to do something? Eight is enough. If eight isn't enough, nine — nine is certainly enough.

Nicole said it with her own mouth back then, "he is going to kill me, he is going to kill me." **And sure enough, he has**, long after she makes these spontaneous statements to officer Edwards, after she complains they have been out there eight times before and they've never done anything to him, **this man, the defendant, see.**

And we're seeing the defendant at home at this point, you know. **We're seeing the private side of him**, the private side I told you I'd show you. **He comes out of his house** and he's **wearing a bathrobe** 4:00 o'clock in the morning. Nothing wrong with that. **And he speaks to officer Edwards**. Now, when he speaks to officer Edwards, **does he ask him, "how's my wife"? No. Does he say, "I hope I didn't hurt her too badly"? No**. What does he say? What does he do? **He humiliates her**. Remember what he said. **He said, "I don't want that woman in my bed anymore. I got two other women**. I don't want that woman in my bed anymore." That was his response. And **this was** Nicole, **his wife. She had been his wife four years.**

..."responsibility" is an important word, one of the words we teach our — I know I teach my **kids** about responsibility. You know, you have to tell them — you have to let your kids know, hey, **you do an act, you've got to accept responsibility**, okay. **You've got to accept the consequences. Well, he didn't accept the consequences** that day. **He didn't accept responsibility**. He jumped in that Bentley, he drove away, **he snuck off**. He avoided responsibility. He got away from the police. They tried to catch him. They couldn't. Well, we caught him this time. **Well, after the defendant got away, Edwards asked Nicole to go down to Parker Center**, to come from Rockingham all the way downtown to Parker Center **so he could have some professional photographs taken of her injuries, but she refused**. Remember what she said? **She said, "no. I just** want my children. I **want to stay here with my children. I don't want to leave my children." And she was beaten** and she was **bruised and** she was hurt. **She still wanted to stay with her kids**. She wanted to be with her kids. **And Edwards said, "well, will you do this for us? Will you just go down to West L.A. station and let us photograph your injuries? It only takes a few minutes."** It seems as if she was more concerned about her kids than she was doing anything to the defendant. She didn't — she didn't care about documenting her own injuries at that time. She just wanted to be with her kids. But **Edwards took her to West L.A. station and he took some Polaroid photographs of her**. Remember those photographs? Back in February I think it was, I think I marked those people's 4 and 5.

Now, what set this whole thing off? **What happened in 1989 that caused him to** get to the point that he **beat this woman up?** Well, Ron Shipp testified about his conversation with Nicole. Now, **if you reflect back for a moment on the defendant's statement to Edwards, that he had two women**, right, what does **Shipp tell you** about his conversation with Nicole? **She found out about the other two women. She didn't want to have sex with him**. She didn't want to be with him. **That's what led to this whole thing in 1989,** his passion, his emotion. And when that passion and that emotion gets out of control — and he was out of control in 1989 — and when that fuse starts burning, ladies and gentlemen, and it starts getting shorter and shorter, sets him off.

Even though African American preaching and speaking style often uses repetition to reinforce the meaning of the words, it is confined to key words or sentences, not the entire text. Repetition of key words and sentences in an oral speech can be very powerful, but used randomly it becomes exhausting.

The fuse is burning and getting shorter, but Darden never gets to the explosion. If you are very repetitive it is even more devastating not to get to the point, since this can make people even more frustrated over the time they spent listening to you. Darden further stated:

> **It shows that he is not just a murderer, but he is a double murderer, and that is unfortunate. It is unfortunate that I have to stand here and tell you this because I <u>would rather be somewhere else. I'm sure would you rather be somewhere else.</u>**

When you want to convince somebody of something, it is not beneficial to say that you would rather be somewhere else. You have to show that you are emotionally committed to what you are saying.

This stood in sharp contrast to how Cochran let the jury know that he didn't want to be anywhere else:

> **...That is why we love what we do, an opportunity to come before people from the community, the consciences of the community. You are the consciences of the community. You set the standards. You tell us what is right and wrong. You set the standards. You use your common sense to do that.**

Darden continues:

> **Who wants to really have to confront and deal with these issues? But we have to because we have a duty. Marcia and I have a duty and you have a duty as well. Your duty is to look at all the evidence, to be fair, be conscientious, be objective. And your duty is to look at all the evidence, the totality of the circumstances, everything. We don't want you to just look at one piece. Don't just look at the prosecution's case. Look at the entire case. Look at everything. Because when you do, when you do, what can you say except he did it and we have proven it and we have proven it beyond a reasonable doubt.**

Here Darden was trying to refute the defense claim that if they, as jury members, have a doubt about one single piece of evidence, they have to throw the entire case out and acquit Simpson.

It was good that Darden addressed this issue, he just needed to be more concrete and directly address the logic of the defense team's reasoning. He could here have given an absurd example that could have highlighted what he was saying. It could sound like this:

To deny the massive amounts of evidence that shows that Simpson mutilated and killed these two people, because one is in doubt about one piece of evidence, is the same as denying that the Nazis in Germany killed 6 million Jews, because one is in doubt about one piece of evidence.

Ladies and Gentlemen. This is not the way the law works. Judge Ito will be able to tell you that it actually works the opposite way. That if there is one piece of evidence that shows you that he did it, he is guilty!

> **<u>Now, I'm just a messenger. I hate to be the one to stand here and tell you about these things</u>, but this is a murder case. This is what he did. All these things we talked about, these are the things that he did. This is how he lived. This is his life, okay?**

Here Darden sounds as if he were bailing out. In a sense he didn't fully want to invest his credibility (ethos) into the case. This behavior is probably due to Darden feeling squished between the black icon and the black civil rights lawyer. But unlike a science study, the evidence can't stand alone. It needs somebody's credibility to back it up. In this paragraph the evidence has neither the ethos of the ones that provided it, nor the ethos of the one that presented it. Cochran made sure to fully utilized Darden's statement:

> **... Mr. Darden said something very interesting today. He said, "I'm just the messenger." Now, how many times have you heard that; "I'm the messenger. Don't blame**

me, I'm just doing my job?"

There's no way out. He's a fine lawyer, but he can't hide behind just being a messenger. Well, whose message is he sending? Who is he representing in this message? He's a man of integrity. That statement is not going to fly; "I'm just the messenger." He's not any messenger. He's the prosecutor with all the power of the state of California in this case.

We are not going to let them get their way. We're not going to turn the constitution on its head in this case. We are not going to allow it. ...if you can't trust the messengers, watch out for their messages.

Darden further states:

He is a murderer. <u>He was also one hell of a great football player, but he is still a murderer.</u>

This comment about Simpson's football abilities did not work in Darden's favor, since it highlights Simpson as a celebrity, not a man who committed murder. This was again an attempt on Darden's behalf to sound impartial.

And so we have come full circle. There was Ron and there was Nicole and — <u>Ron, he was just at the wrong place at the wrong time. Nicole, she was in the wrong place for a long time, and there is this common factor, this common element between the two of them, one thing they had in common with this man, this defendant</u>. And so we began with them, two very much alive, vibrant human beings.

Here Darden ties the two victims together by pointing out what they have in common. This lent credibility to the claim that Simpson killed not only Nicole Brown, but also Ron Goldman. It was a piece of strong argumentation also when it came to the way it was presented. It is worth noticing the use of the words: *Wrong time - Long time*. They make Darden's statement elegant and catchy. It also makes the sentences rhyme.

> **And I told you when this began that I <u>had the hardest job. Nobody wants to do anything to this man. We don't. There is nothing personal about this</u>. But the law is the law and it applies to us, it applies to you, it has to apply to him.**

Darden wanted to communicate that nobody wants to frame Simpson, of all people. That if somebody was going to be framed, it was definitely not going to be Simpson. But because he was not concrete and precise enough, it sounded as if not even the prosecution wanted to convict Simpson. When Darden said that he has the hardest job, he was hinting at his position in between the icon and the civil rights lawyer. An appeal to pity was not going to save his reputation among the black population, nor grant him a conviction.

> **Let me say that what you do in this case is entirely up to you. You are the jury. When I sit down, I sit down. I'm done. I have completed my duty. I have done what the law requires me to do. I have lived up to the oath, my oath as a member of the district attorney's office.**
>
> **And I presented, we hope we presented the best evidence we could. And if we didn't present the best evidence we could, don't hold that against us.**

Here Darden once again did not want to fully invest his ethos. It sounds like Darden was saying to the jury, Hey folks, I am just doing my job. This approach does not convince anybody.

In a sense Darden was fighting as much for his own reputation as trying to get Simpson convicted. Since a good ethos is the foundation for believability, this was not a good situation to be in.

So what could Darden have done in this situation? Well, first of all, Darden needed <u>not</u> to focus on himself. You never win a case if you focus upon yourself. It is your belief in the case that will carry your message, not your concern for yourself.

After Darden securely connected the relevance of domestic violence to the issue of murder, there is an interesting way he could have elaborated the issue of domestic violence:

Love may also pervert so you declare that you love a person madly and beyond all bounds but forget the respect. In the wedding ritual it says that one must "love honor and respect", and respect may be the most important word. Respect is to view the other as an adult different from yourself and that is important to keep in mind as love is indeed dangerous and you can get seriously burned. If there is no respect, and you exceed the other person's bounds, the great love may then prove to be a display of power where you want to possess and in the end destroy the other. And this is unfortunately what happened in this case. This is why we see the patterns of domestic violence before we end up with murder. Now, thank God, it usually doesn't go that far, but in this case it unfortunately did.

> **I would just like you to use your common sense when you do. When you do that, when you use your common sense, when you try to be objective, <u>when you remove all of the emotion out of this case</u>, when you remove all of the sympathy and passion and when you just look at the facts, the evidence as best you can, you will come up with the right decision.**
>
> **<u>The world is watching and everybody wants to know what you are going to do</u>. Marcia Clark and I know you are going to do the right thing under the law. <u>And whatever you do, the decision is yours, and I'm glad that it is not mine.</u>**

We see that Darden was combating feelings in general. Since all decisions are based on feelings, this attempt was bound to fail. Instead of being afraid of feelings, one has to help the audience understand one's point of view through their feelings. This may not have been so bad for Darden, if his opponent had made the same mistake. Argumentation is like playing chess:

How dearly you have to pay for your mistakes all depends upon your opponent's ability to take advantage of the situation.

We see how Cochran attempted to help the jury members understand his point of view through their feelings:

> **And so you know when you talk about this whole concept of reasonable doubt...it is how you feel inside about this evidence. It is how you feel inside about these messengers and their message. It is when you have that queasy feeling, you can't trust this evidence.**

To mention that the world is watching only contributed to politicizing the case, something that did not benefit Darden. The following shows how Cochran seized the opportunity to further utilize this statement made by Darden, at the same time as he assured the jury that he didn't want to be anywhere else. He was, in other words, totally committed:

> **Your verdict goes far beyond these doors of this courtroom. As Mr. Darden said, the whole world is watching and waiting for your decision in this case. That is not to put any pressure on you, just to tell you what is really happening out there.**
>
> **So we talked about all of those things, hopefully in a logical way. Hopefully something I said made some sense to you. Hopefully as a advocate, you know my zeal, you know the passion I feel for this. We've all got time invested in this case. But it is not just about winning, it is about what is right. It is about a man's life that is at stake here.**

By Darden saying to the jury that he was glad that the decision was not up to him, Darden was communicating to the jury that the case wasn't really as simple as he wanted them to believe it was. But even worse, it showed lack of conviction on his part. Maybe not as much concerning the legal issues, if Simpson killed the two victims, but concerning the political issues, what are the wider consequences of the verdict going to be. Not to mention the personal consequences for the jury members. In the end of Darden's closing statement he got into a lot of issues that he should have addressed in the beginning of his speech, before his main argumentation concerning the domestic violence. In the end of his argumentation he needed to spend time pulling the strengths together, not asking more questions. Generally one never introduces something totally new in one's conclusion; it only contributes to confuse the audience. This is why it was not good for Darden to come up with all these new issues at the end of his speech. Darden either needed to address them earlier on, or not address them at all. In the end of your speech you should only stress the points that you have already raised earlier in your presentation.

It is important to remember, that in an oral presentation you start out with:

> Saying *what* you are going to say.
> Then you *say it*.
> You then end up with saying *what* you have said.

Johnnie Cochran also came up with a whole string of questions near the end of his closing statement. Since his aim was to create confusion and raise doubts about the prosecution's case, it worked out better for him.

Here are some of the otherwise good arguments that Darden introduced in the end of his speech:

> **I hope you keep in mind that, you know, people made a lot of money testifying in this case and you should consider that on the issue or question of whether or not those witnesses are biased.**
>
> **They can[t] explain to you what happened to O.J. Simpson's Aris Light 70263 gloves, the gloves found at the murder scene, the same style of gloves purchased by Nicole, the same style of gloves you see him wearing in that January 6, 1992, game photo. Where are his gloves?**
>
> **Insist that the defense explain to you just who does — who kills two people wearing $200.00 leisure shoes if it ain't this man, if it ain't this defendant?**

Ask them to explain to you why the bloody shoeprints leading away from the body are size 12, his size.

They put on a defense and you would expect that if the man that Allan Park saw entering the defendant's house that night was not the defendant, would you have expected them to call that man to tell you that, hey, it was me. It wasn't the defendant, right?

A major, major question in all of this is what happened to that little black bag, the bag on the driveway, the one that Kato offered to go get that night just before the defendant left for the airport? The defendant said "I will get it, I will get it." What happened to that bag? Has it been seen since?

And ask them to explain to you, hey, if this is a rush to judgment, why then did the police go out to that house eight times prior to 1989? Why didn't they ever arrest him? And if this is a rush to judgment, why did the police stand out in front of the house, in front of 875 South Bundy that night for a couple of hours doing nothing, as the defense has asserted, doing nothing but waiting for Vannatter and Lange? That is a rush to judgment? This is no rush to judgment. Unfortunately this is just how things go.

Those cops got out there to conduct a murder investigation and that investigation led them to Rockingham. They followed the blood trial. Using your common sense and when you evaluate all the evidence, you should do the same thing, take a look at the crime scene and follow that blood trial, because when you do, you are going to follow it right into his house, into his yard, into his bathroom, into his bedroom, right into his lap. And that blood trial went nowhere else. It didn't go anywhere else and it didn't go to any other person.

Darden ended up with addressing the defense team's claim, that this was a rush to judgement. This was really good, in the sense that he finally defended the police, and thereby his ethos foundation. This issue needed to be expanded and addressed in the beginning of his speech.

Darden ended his closing statement with a metaphor that reflects upon the division of strength in the case, and the defense team's efforts to confuse the issue. This was a good metaphor. Unfortunately, some of its effect was reduced by Darden's long-windedness and repetition.

> **The people put on their case, the defense put on their case, and I assert that the defense case is a bunch of smoke and mirrors, all about distracting you from the real evidence in this case.**
>
> **So imagine the smoke and imagine a burning house. Imagine that you are standing in front of a burning house, and from inside that burning house you can hear the wail of a baby, a baby's cry, a baby in fear, a baby about to lose its life. And you can hear that baby screaming. You can hear that wail. Now, that baby, that baby is justice. This is baby justice. Usually justice is a strong woman, but in this case justice is just a baby. And you hear that baby and you hear that wail and you see the smoke, you see the defense. There is all this smoke in front of you and you feel a sense — you have a sense of justice and you have a sense of what the law requires and you have a strong commitment to justice and to the law and you want to do the right thing while justice is about to perish, justice is about to be lost, baby justice is about to be lost.**
>
> **And so you start to wade through that smoke trying to get to that baby. You have got to save that baby, you have to save baby justice, and you happen to run into smoke, find your way through the smoke, and if you happen to run into a couple of defense attorneys along the way, just ask them to politely step aside and let you find**

> **your way through the smoke, because the smoke isn't over, okay? The smoke is going to get heavier because they are about to talk to you. Let's use your common sense. Wade through the evidence. Get down to the bottom line. And please do the right thing.**
>
> **It has been a honor to appear before you and we will wait for your verdict.**

The following shows how much stronger Darden's argumentation becomes if we wipe out the repetitive words, and generally tighten up his argumentation:

> I assert that the defense case is a bunch of smoke and mirrors, all about distracting you from the real evidence in this case.
>
> So imagine the smoke and imagine a burning house. Imagine that you are standing in front of a burning house, and from inside that house you can hear the wail of a baby, a baby in fear, a baby about to lose its life. Now, that is baby justice. Justice is crying, and unless you react, Justice is dying. There is all this smoke in front of you and you have a sense of justice you have a sense of what the law requires and you want to do the right thing.
>
> And so you start to wade through the smoke. You have to find your way through the smoke to save the baby, and if you happen to run into a couple of defense attorneys along the way, just ask them to politely step aside. Wade through the evidence. Get down to the bottom line. And please do the right thing.

That Darden's argumentation was more vote-gathering than vote-sliding was seen in this quotation from Darden's rebuttal, where he tries to copy Cochran's use of the Bible: "These … things doth the Lord hate:… A proud look, a lying tongue, and hands that shed innocent blood." And he says about Cochran, "A false witness that speaketh lies, and he that soweth discord among brethren." These statements are so general that they just as well could be turned against Darden himself, depending upon what opinion the audience had from the onset.

If Darden in his reasoning had chosen to focus on the topos rich against poor, he could have chosen this passage from the Gospel of

Matthew, verse 19:

> Jesus said unto him, If thou wilt be perfect, go and sell that thou hast, and give to the poor, and thou shalt have treasure in heaven: and come and follow me. But when the young man heard that saying, he went away sorrowful: for he had great possessions. Then said Jesus unto his disciples, Verily I say unto you, That a rich man shall hardly enter into the kingdom of heaven. And again I say unto you, It is easier for a camel to go through the eye of a needle, than for a rich man to enter into the kingdom of God.

Then Darden could have said to the presumably deeply religious, mainly black women on the jury:

> You, Orenthal James Simpson, will be held accountable for your crime, for your violation of the Commandments thou shalt not kill, and thou shalt honor thy neighbor. Not only here will you be held accountable, but also before God! Jesus in his almighty wisdom is right that someone like you will find it difficult to enter the Kingdom of Heaven.
>
> And God has put you jurors in his place, for you to judge his will on earth. Do not listen to the rich and greedy people's siren song. Do not forget your true task and do not betray the trust God has placed in you.

Cochran did in fact in his closing argument say to the jurors that God was watching them. In other words, it was an ill-concealed threat that they also would be held responsible for their decision in the Simpson case.

Where Clark's concrete evidence lacked an ethos foundation, Darden's domestic violence argumentation lacked a logos foundation.

As can be seen from Darden's argumentation, it is not only a question of *what* is said, but also a question of *how* it's said. The impact of examples and points is dependent on the speaker's aptitude for profiling. Time and again a potentially good example or point is lost and fades into a gray mass because the debaters forget to stress the meaning of them or gather the thread from the isolated example to the key issue. In this way you can say everything, while your audience understands nothing.

16. CHRISTOFER DARDEN & MARCIA CLARK'S REBUTTAL

Men also pity those who resemble them in age, character, habits, position, or family; for all such relations make a man more likely to think that their misfortune may befall him as well. For, in general, here also we may conclude that all that men fear in regard to themselves excites their pity when others are the victims.

Aristotle

When closing statements are presented to a jury, the prosecution, or in civil cases the plaintiff, starts out arguing its case. Thereafter the defense argues its case. In the end the prosecuting party is offered an opportunity to address the issues raised by the defense. This is called a rebuttal.

In Darden's rebuttal he actually started saying some of the things that his reasoning desperately needed. Darden started to support the police, even Fuhrman got some support. He also started getting into the theme, rich against poor. On top of that he was more willing to invest his own credibility into the issue. With this higher level of personal commitment also followed a less repetitive speaking style. It was as if both Darden and Clark, after listening to Cochran and Scheck's closing statements, had finally understood the new rhetorical situation, and were now addressing the case on those terms. Unfortunately, it is difficult to save a case, that has lasted almost a year in its last few hours.

As mentioned earlier, we usually adapt a paradigm as a way of interpreting certain events. Events and facts can then be fitted into this way of interpreting the world. When certain facts and events start disproving our paradigm, we initially reject them or try somehow to fit them into our paradigm. We display this behavior because we have to feel some continuity in our actions. A paradigm shift is usually something that happens suddenly, after our belief system has been disproven for awhile. It can therefore be difficult to change somebody's opinion about a case on the last day of the trial, especially when the case has lasted for almost a year.

We here see how Darden addresses the topos rich against poor:

> **I have been a prosecutor for almost fifteen years, and if there is one rule that I have lived by, if there is one rule that means a lot to me, it is this one: No one is above the law; not the police, not the rich, no one. And I hope you agree with that. I hope you agree with that rule. I hope you consider that — that motto. O.J. Simpson isn't above the law.**

Besides appealing to the topos "rich against poor," Darden was also strengthening his own image and morals by emphasizing his idealism and qualifications. It was a shame he did not elaborate more on this. He could have said that they should send a message to the rich and famous that their money and fame had not raised them above the law.

This quotation shows that he not only chose not to use efforts in defending the ethos of the police, but actually attacked them by putting the police in line with others that were to be "put in their places." We can here see that he accepted that the system stands accused and indirectly he agrees with the defense in the legitimacy of this.

It would have been desirable for the prosecution not solely to defend their own image and morals when it was attacked, but also displayed some solidarity with the police, the forensic lab, and the other public authorities. A prerequisite would have been to realize that they were mutually dependent when it came to the credibility of their message. It could have barred Cochran from of ever expanding his theories on conspiracies and incompetence to comprise and include still more and more people.

One clearly sees the difference in attitude between the police and the public prosecutors from the quotes stated below:

> The following day, Lange and Vannatter learn from another detective in the office that Darden, apparently on a whim, had decided to call Geraldo Rivera on his CNBC program, *Rivera Live*. Darden wanted to complain that Lange was not being "aggressive" enough on the stand.
>
> "I would like the officers to be a bit more aggressive," Darden said to Rivera. "They are answering the questions being put to them by the defense; and some of the questions, I think, are a bit ridiculous. And I just wish they would point that out to the jury sometimes."
>
> Both Lange and Vannatter have always admired Darden. After hearing this news, they are more baffled than angry. They wonder why Darden, in view of his important role in this trial, would go out of his way to criticize a colleague and one of his key witnesses on a nationally televised program.[101]

This is to be seen in context with the following quote from Clark's book:

> Until then, I'd intended to do the rebuttal by myself. But Johnnie had changed that. "If you can't trust the messengers, watch out for their message," he'd said. He insinuated that Chris and I were both, at best, overzealous; at worst, dishonest. We were both part of a nefarious conspiracy that now seemed to involve all county employees right down to the steno pool. Chris and I *both* had to put in an appearance to defend our honor.[102]

The police saw themselves as a team with the prosecutors, but the lawyers focused mostly on their own credibility. This lack of solidarity is counterproductive in complicated cases. By complicated cases is meant situations where the opponent is capable of utilizing the rhetorical situation. It is worth noticing that this behavior was contrary to the defense's team spirit. The problem in this case was that the prosecution didn't consider the police part of the team. So when the police department was attacked, they thought that they could just disassociate themselves from them.

> **You heard from Scheck yesterday. You heard him talk about our science. They have to attack our science because all the science points to O.J. Simpson, to this defendant. It all points to him as the killer. They have to attack that science. Not only does common sense dictate that he is guilty, but we have proven him guilty to a scientific certainty. We have proven him guilty beyond a reasonable doubt.**

Darden tries to expose the opponent's technique.

> **If you were to acquit him, what explanation would you give the day after that acquittal if someone said why did you acquit him? Would you say racism? Would you say it is because there is racism in the LAPD? That is what they want you to say. That is what they want you to think.**

Darden was challenging the new rhetorical situation.

> **You just need to calm down, take that common sense God gave you, go back in the jury room. Don't let these people get you all riled up and all fired up because Fuhrman is a racist. Racism blinds you. Those epithets, they blind you. You never heard me use that epithet in this courtroom, did you? I'm not going to put on that kind of show for you know who, for people to watch. That is not where we are coming from. We want you to focus on the evidence.**
>
> **...the Constitution says that a man has no right to kill and then get away with it just because one of the investigating officers is a racist.**

Darden was here trying to turn the rhetorical situation back to being a murder case.

> **... It is easy to get lost in the evidence and it is easy for lawyers to get lost in the evidence, and as judge Ito told**

you before, and I think I told you the other day, nothing we say in this argument is evidence. Nothing I say to you today is evidence. Certainly nothing they said to you is evidence in this case. The evidence is what you heard from the witness stand. The evidence is the exhibits.

I listened to one of the lawyers testify in this case. I heard lawyers add things, add facts into the record, or attempt to. The facts are what you heard in testimony by people who took an oath and who sat down in that chair. If you find what they said to be true, then you find the facts. Nothing a lawyer says is a fact. They said yesterday that I'm an advocate. Well, I am an advocate, and they are advocates, too. You've taken notes throughout this trial. We watched you all take notes. Rely on those notes, rely on the court reporter's transcript. Rely on your own recollection. Don't be misled, don't be misled. Because I listened to lawyers argue yesterday, and you know what we do when we start to argue and get caught up, you get in that role soon and pretty soon you just start saying stuff. It may not necessarily be true, it may not necessarily be what is in the record, so rely on the record. Rely on the record.

Darden was attacking Cochran and Scheck's ethos by questioning their credibility. Unfortunately, he puts his own credibility down at the same time. Darden thinks he can do that because he believes that the evidence can stand by itself. This was again due to his use of the mathematical paradigm as a model for his argumentation.

If you rely on the record and use your common sense, you will find your way through the smoke. And I told you there was going to be some smoke. I told you there had been some smoke. Yesterday we heard thee smoke. It was fiery rhetoric, but that is what we do. We are lawyers.

Darden was reminding the jury that he vaccinated them against the opponent's argumentation. But this vaccination was too vague and broad to have any effect. An effective vaccination is precise and concrete. Darden uses the word rhetoric about lawyer's statements. In the way the word rhetoric is commonly used, it means dressing up your statements with empty words, trying to deceive people with something that isn't really there. In other words, Darden was again putting himself down in order to attack the defense attorneys' ethos.

> **I think it is safe to say at this point, after all that I've heard over the last few days, I think it is safe to say that I'm the messenger and I volunteered for that job and I don't mind being the messenger. I told you what the message was. In 1989 the message was that he is going to kill me, he is going to kill me. And Edward said, "who is going to kill you?" "O.J." "O.J. the football player?" "yeah, he is going to kill me." That was the message in 1989. The new message today, there is another message. The message in '89 was that he is going to kill me. The message in '95 is he killed me. That is what this has been all about. That is the message we have been trying to send you the past eight months. The message is he killed her.**

Darden was starting to invest more of his own credibility into the case, though it still doesn't sound totally wholehearted. Darden sounds more as if he had been pressed to invest his credibility into the case by Cochran attacking his lack of emotional commitment to the issue. Cochran attacked Darden for describing himself as a messenger. If Darden wanted to come out of the argument as a winner he needed to get on the offensive position and turn the argument around against Cochran. That could have sounded something like this:

> The defense wants to talk about the messengers - Okay, let's do just that. We as lawyers are messengers. There is nothing wrong with being a messenger; Moses and Jesus were messengers too. You may ask: "So who's messenger are you?" Well we are not the messenger from the police, as Cochran wants you to believe. And Cochran is not the messenger from justice, as he wants you to believe. We are the messengers from the victims, we are their only voice, since they no longer have a voice of their own.

Cochran and the rest of the defense team are O.J. Simpson's messengers and they are obviously his voice. Now, who is more believable? The victims or O.J. Simpson? Who has most to hide? Who has most to lose?

They know that they have a killer on their hands, but a killer with cash and they will do anything to get him off. Why do you think they go through all this trouble of finding other things to talk about? Because they know they have a killer on there hands.

Mr. Cochran is a handsome man, he is a intelligent man, but most of all he is a well-paid man. For his part this case is not about murder and morals, it's about money and manipulation; therefore he will do anything, anything, to get O.J. off although he knows he has a killer on his hands. Just like Judas took the silver coins and betrayed Jesus, Cochran is willing to take the money and betray justice. That's the messenger you should be aware of, ladies and gentlemen, that's the messenger you should doubt. No matter what happens in the end of this trial, O.J. will be judged when his time comes, judged by God. At that time he will have no shield to protect him, no messenger, no Johnny Cochran.

Darden goes on to say:

They want you to believe that if you acquit him that that will be the courageous thing to do. I think the courageous thing to do in this case would be to look at all the evidence. I think that takes courage. I think it takes courage not to jump to a snap conclusion. I think it takes courage to recognize within ourselves that what we heard yesterday was appeal to a certain part of us and it was appeal to some of us perhaps and not all of us, but it was an appeal to a certain part of us that only some of us know about. That is what happened yesterday.

Darden was trying to tell the jurors that the defense team, headed by Cochran, used his background knowledge about them to try and manipulate them.

> **I think it takes courage to recognize that. If you mistrust the police — I spent seven years prosecuting bad policemen. I understand why you mistrust the police. If you have that basic mistrust - Mr. Cochran: Objection, your honor, improper. Mr. Scheck: Objection. The court: Overruled. Mr. Darden: I understand that, and perhaps you ought to, but I think that we have to do is we have to take every case on a case by case basis and every cop on a cop by cop basis. Yesterday they took Fuhrman, this racist, and then they put Vannatter with him and pretty soon they were interchanging Vannatter and Fuhrman. Vannatter has been a detective 27, 28 years. You didn't hear anybody come in here and say he ever used that word. And it is easy to put up a big poster and say "Vannatter's big lies." That is easy to do.**

We see Darden defending the police by trying to limit the ever-expanding incrimination of the police, through Mark Fuhrman. By doing this, Darden was starting to mend his ethos foundation. Cochran and Scheck objected when Darden said that he had been prosecuting bad police officers, since they realized that Darden's credibility was closely linked to the ability of applying the racist conspiracy theme. If Darden was not an Uncle Tom, but an advocate for civil rights, the cover -up and conspiracy theory lost credibility.

> **They talk all this stuff about race and everything. We got one racist cop...and trust me, I am not an apologist for this man — but the last time, according to the evidence, that anybody heard him use this slur was in 1988. They say since he used it in 1988 he must be a racist. Well, the last time that we know of from the stand that the defendant beat up was in 1989. If you say it in '88 and you are a racist in '94, well, what are you if you beat her in '89? What are you in '94? But they want you to apply double**

> **standards.**

Here Darden even vaguely defends Fuhrman. But Darden takes it back in the next statement, where he wants to use the example to show that the domestic violence evidence against Simpson is still relevant.

> **Read along with me what Martin Luther King said about justice: "Justice is the same for all issues. It cannot be categorized. It is not possible to be in favor of justice for some people and not be in favor of justice for all people. Justice cannot be divided. Justice is indivisible." Okay. we can't have a system of law, a system of justice or a concept of justice or a concept of law or a legal standard of burden of proof. We can't have reasonable doubt over here for everybody else and then have another reasonable doubt standard for a particular individual. That ain't justice, okay? That is not justice. That is what he is talking about. That is what he is talking about. He is talking about a double standard of justice. We can't have that.**

Darden starts quoting civil rights activists and the Constitution to go against Cochran's use of maxims and the Bible. Darden is trying to give his argument as broad a perspective as Cochran's claim, and still stay within the legal appeal. Darden stated that everybody has to be treated equally under the law. This argumentation did not affect the juror's point of view, since they did not see themselves as granting Simpson any special favors. From their view they were actually making sure that the law was applied equally, in the sense that they were protecting Simpson from being convicted just because he was black. Mark Fuhrman was supposedly providing false evidence in order to convict black people.

> **As they say, what is done in the dark will come to light. I just heard that yesterday. Remember this photograph? Here is another red herring we all went chasing after. Remember that? The police had contaminated the scene,**

they had traipsed through that scene, crime scene. You remember that. Then what do we do? We went and we got a video. We went and we got a video. Do you have the video? Please. Back it up. (a videotape was played.)

***Mr. Darden*: what did we find out when we went and got that video? We found out that when those officers walked up that walkway that the tape had already been taken down, that the crime scene had already been disbanded. Remember that? They tell you not to believe the messenger.**

Darden was attacking the defense team's ethos by exposing some of their manipulative tactics. This boosted Darden's and the prosecution team's ethos, and it took him from a defensive to an offensive position. Unfortunately, Darden still insisted on using the messenger metaphor, and thereby refused to back the evidence with his own credibility.

Awfully convenient. How many times can one person get cut in how many different states in one night in one morning? They called him. He knew he had to come back. They said, oh, he just came back. Where was he going to go? I find him. And they tell you not to trust the messenger.

This was another good example of Darden being on the offensive, focusing upon his strong points. A place he ought to have been all through the trial.

We see Darden use the sentence-And they tell you not to trust the messenger-as key words. It is usually not a good idea to use one's opponents' words or phrases as keywords, since they still carry the agenda of one's opponent. Darden could instead have said-And they tell you that he is innocent.

You can't send a message to Fuhrman, you can't send a message to the LAPD, you can't eradicate racism within the LAPD or the LA community or within the nation as a whole by delivering a verdict of not guilty in a case like

this. The evidence is there. You just have to find your way through the smoke. You just have to find your way through the smoke. In this case they have interjected this racism and now they want you to become impassioned, to be upset, and they want you to make quantum leaps in logic and in judgment. It is true that Fuhrman is a racist and it is also true that [Simpson] killed these two people, and that we proved that he killed these two people.

Not only did Darden use time and effort admitting that racism exists within the LAPD and in society in general, on top of this he didn't come up with anything that takes the sting out of these statements. The way Darden could have taken the sting out of these comments about racism could have been by using them to build up the opponent's reasoning, only to tear this reasoning down again:

Does Johnny Cochran want to eliminate racism? - *maybe*
Does Johnny Cochran want to save the world? - *hopefully*
Or does Johnny Cochran want to make money? - *certainly*

This is a very effective form of argumentation, since it seemingly takes one's opponent's reasoning into consideration, only to reject it due to an overruling factor.

Darden's statements do not promise them anything, either, if they "buy" his version of the case. This might have been that they could send a message that all are equal before the law with equal rights, and that the rich and famous must not believe that their riches and fame entitle them to treat the rest of us at their discretion. It could also have been something about men should not think that women are their personal property to be treated as they please, etc.

All of this would have added a wider perspective to the verdict and made the jurors feel they carried out a meaningful and noble act. It can of course be claimed that the prosecution's appeal to the jurors to ensure that justice be done partly satisfies these criteria but still it hardly matches Cochran's promises of a better future.

It was disadvantageous to his case that he chose to focus on Fuhrman, the weakest link within the police, and not on the most credible police officers and witnesses. Cochran focuses upon Fuhrman because this was to his advantage, and therefore Darden should have chosen to focus upon something else.

As a rule, in a discussion, the reasons that lead one side to adopt a certain order should normally tend to make the other side adopt a different order.

Darden could have focused on all those people within the police and public authorities that Cochran accused of being parties to this conspiracy, or that necessarily must have been parties to it. Especially it could have been good to focus on the ones that were not white. In that case Darden could have asked what advantages they would derive from participating in this racist conspiracy. A witness that might have been ideal for Darden to focus on was Ron Shipp, a friend of Simpson's, a retired black police officer employed with the LAPD. He testified that Simpson had told him that he beat Nicole and had dreams and visions of killing her. Darden could in this regard have asked the jurors what this man gained from participating in a wide-spread racist plot against Simpson.

Here is what Darden said about Ron Shipp:

But they went after Ron Shipp and they had to go after Ron Shipp. They talk about Ron Shipp, his eyes being red and all of this stuff, you know. When you think about — when you think on the issue of whether Ron Shipp was drunk or something that night, I hope that you go back and you read Arnelle Simpson's testimony. And I will just leave it at that. And I hope that you will reflect on her testimony about Ron Shipp.

It is not very effective not to mention your point. You cannot presume that your audience necessarily understands what you are hinting at. It may not be so obvious for them.

But Ron Shipp, well, they tore into him early on in the trial, right, and that was the first real indication of just

what this whole thing was going to be. And they tore into Ron Shipp. And let me offer to you a reasonable explanation for Ron Shipp's eyes being red the night of June 13th. Could it be because he knew that his friend Nicole was dead and that he knew his other friend had killed her?

This was again a really good argumentation that should have been brought out nine months before, when Ron Shipp was being questioned. This could have been done by asking Shipp questions about his emotional state at the time, and so on. This is another example of the prosecution not adequately protecting their ethos foundation. Because Ron Shipp is a black man, the defense team has to destroy him, in the same way as it was necessary to character assassinate Darden. On the other hand this means that it would have been very worthwhile for the prosecution to protect his credibility, as it eroded the foundation for the defense team's case.

They want to talk about the timer in the video. What did Willie Ford tell you about the time? He didn't even care about the time in the video. He never even check the time in the video. He never adjusted the timer in the video because it had nothing to do with his purpose in being there. And his purpose ?- Mr. Cochran: Misstates the evidence, your honor. The Court: Overruled. Mr. Darden: And his purpose was in videotaping that particular room. It was for civil liability purposes. He didn't want to contaminate the evidence, contaminate the room, so he had to wait until after Fung had collected the evidence from the room. That is Willie Ford's testimony. <u>You heard that brother testify. He looked like a co?conspirator to you?</u> And they say don't trust the messenger.

This is the closest Darden gets to ask why blacks and other minority groups would contribute in a racist conspiracy. Darden should have elaborated extravagantly upon this issue.

We heard so much about the scriptures. I'm not even

going to read it. Just read proverbs 6 one day when this is all over. Now, if I'm the messenger, you know I have delivered the message as best as I could, and the message is that he killed these two people and that is what the evidence dictates.

If Darden did not want to get into the Proverbs, he was cluttering up his speech by mentioning them. Darden continued to describe himself as a messenger, but as Cochran said, who is he the messenger for? The police, the public authorities, God? Evidence has to be collected, interpreted, and presented; it doesn't just stand by themselves.

All I could ever ask from you and all that I ask from you today is that you try and be as objective as you possibly can be, that you not allow any passion or emotion or any bias, any of that human feeling — these human feelings we all have to interfere with the decision you have to make.

We here see Darden's view of feelings as being irrelevant interference in the decision process. This view may be relevant in math, but not in law. The reason we have certain laws is that this is the way we *feel* things should be. When you spend too much time combating the juror's feelings, you just cut yourself out of the decision process. The reason why feelings are combated is because they are viewed as irrational and unpredictable. Feelings are neither irrational nor unpredictable; they always have a reason. The reasoning for feelings are just broader based than a single paradigm.

I just want you to do the right thing. That means the right thing under the law. We believe we have proven this case beyond a reasonable doubt. And it is unfortunate, it is unfortunate what jealousy does to you. It is unfortunate that obsession. It is unfortunate that obsession can do these things to you. It is unfortunate that two innocent people are dead because this got in this man's way. That is the message we wanted to deliver and I'm the

> **messenger and I'm proud to have delivered it.**

In one of the last sentences of his rebuttal, Darden finally fully invested his own credibility into the case.

Darden started to say a lot of the right things in his rebuttal, but it was not only too vague, it is also too late. At this point the patient was too sick to be saved.

Marcia Clark's rebuttal was also a lot better then her closing statement, in the sense that she supported the police by backing up their actions, and she used the police officers whose integrity had not been questioned to support the evidence and the statements made by the police in general.

Clark also pointed out how many people had to have been involved in the conspiracy for it to have been physically possible. First and foremost, Clark started addressing the accusations of a conspiracy directly. Clark said:

> **You have been here. Lawyers spin stories and spin yarns, too, with no evidence to it. Not only no evidence, but no logic, and in that specifically I'm talking about this story about Mark Fuhrman swiping the bloody glove inside the Bronco. That is a story. That is an interesting story, but it has no substance. Not only does it have no proof to it, but it also has no logic to it, and I will show you why and that is what I want to talk to you about now; logic, what makes sense. In this case we have seen what the defendant has done and it has been a very contorted, inconsistent thing. I'm going to point out the inconsistencies to you, but basically they have jumped from we are stupid bumblers and we are brilliant conspirators, and he includes us in this. And I find that particularly painful, ladies and gentlemen, particularly painful, because I have been doing this a lot of years. I didn't start here, I started on that side of counsel table. I was a defense attorney and I know what the ethical obligations are of a prosecutor. I took a cut in pay to join this office because I believe in this**

job. I believe in doing it fairly and doing it right and I like the luxury of being a prosecutor because I have the luxury on any case of going to the judge and saying guess what, your honor, dismiss it, it is not here. ...ladies and gentlemen, I can come to you and I can say don't convict, it is not here. ...if there is evidence of a conspiracy, it would be my obligation to dismiss, pure and simple, and I can go on to the next case.

We here see how Clark started drawing on her own credibility in order to carry her case through. In a way Clark was administrating CPR to a case that had lacked ethos for far too long. All through the case, we saw Cochran supporting his case with his own credibility, and the credibility of highly esteemed persons, at the same time as he was working on cutting the ethos foundation for the prosecution's case.

The argument has been made that when they went to Rockingham, what they really wanted to do was make an arrest, right? Rush to judgment. They had it in mind that they were going to go there and arrest him and he was a suspect. ...let's look back at the evidence that is not contested, the evidence that is — that stands unrefuted.

They were out at Bundy. Commander Bushey told the initial detectives get on out there, go and make notification at Rockingham. You know that would be a problem for somebody who is famous, because if the media find out, it is all over the place, that is a very painful thing, and commander Bushey sure doesn't want it to happen on his watch ... did they? No. They weren't sure if they were going to keep the case. ...detective Phillips did say we weren't sure if we were going to keep the case, if we had the resources. That was a real big problem with this case, because they only had four or six detectives in homicide over in west L.A. So they thought that it might be taken over by robbery/homicide division downtown that has many, many detectives and more resources...

Your first contact with next of kin is to go and make the notification, make that contact, establish that

rapport. And there might be some information that you can get from the next of kin or the person, you know, that would be very helpful to solving the case. The person could be a witness. Okay.

Now, especially in this case where they have children in common, he might know who she is dating or not, because you know, they are divorced, but they still have to have contact. He might know something. It is an important first contact for them to make, so whoever is the handling detective is the one that is supposed to go. This is the testimony you've already heard. I'm not telling you anything knew.

So they waited. They waited until they found out if robbery/homicide was going to take the case, and sure enough, they did. That is what happened. ...when it was finally assigned to robbery/homicide, commander Bushey spoke to them again and said go to Rockingham. You know, how many times do I have to say this? Go and do it. ... even then they didn't go immediately. It wasn't — I think about five o'clock when they finally went to Rockingham, finally went there.

Now, think about this. There were a lot of questions asked about why couldn't you have sent a rookie to go and make notification. Okay.

Now, you know that doesn't make sense. If notification is an important thing, first of all, it has to be handled delicately, sensitively by people who have done this before, many times before, homicide detectives. It is one of the saddest parts of their job to have to make these notifications everyday, but they know how and they know how to deal with it. Bless you.

So they are going to go and do it themselves. It is an important contact. That is their job. That is their duty, okay? So they can't send a rookie out to do it, but what should they do? Think about this now. If it is their intent to go out to Rockingham, make an arrest, because he is a suspect, there are certain things they should have done. No. 1 thing is you take back?up. You don't go by yourself.

You take back? up. You take a couple of squad cars, you make notification downtown, hey, we are going to arrest and this is an important suspect, and you know, this could be a media event. You make plans. You make arrangements. They did nothing.

***Mr. Cochran*: objection, your honor. Ms. Clark: Zip. Mr. Cochran: Misleading.**

***Ms. Clark*: They went out there and they took just the four detectives in their two cars they went over to Rockingham. That is all they did. What else should they have done ask yourself?**

***Mr. Cochran*: Misleading, your honor. The court: Excuse me, counsel. Overruled. They may argue reasonable inference from the evidence that is in the record. Mr. Cochran: If it is misleading? The court: Counsel, have a seat. Mr. Cochran: I will, your honor, but it is misleading.**

***Ms. Clark*: Your common sense will tell you I'm not misleading you. This makes sense. I'm talking logic. I'm talking logic based on what the witnesses have told you. You know it when you hear it. Now, what else should they have done if they are going to go make an arrest that is going to take sometime? Really wrapped up. Do questioning. They could take downtown the things that you know happened when someone gets arrested.**

So if they know they are going to take a long time, they have a crime scene that has to be processed, they have two dead people lying out there and all that evidence around, what would they do? They would go to somebody who is going to stay at the crime scene and they would say call the coroner, we are going to be gone a while. Call the criminalist, we are going to be gone a while. We need you to get this evidence collected and we won't be here because we are going to make an arrest. Did they do any of that? No.

Now, what the evidence has shown is — and what they have testified to and what their actions tell you is true, they expected to come right back. Two of them would stay with Mr. Simpson, taking care of him, taking

him to the station to get his children, making the arrangements, and two would go back to Bundy and handle the crime scene, and their actions totally support that.

If they expected to be gone a long time, they wouldn't all four go or they would tell someone else take care of business for us, we are going to be gone. They didn't do that. What their actions tell you is we are coming right back. It doesn't really matter if somebody isn't taking care of business and calling the coroner and calling the criminalist. Logic. Logic. Look at their actions. Look at their actions. You don't trust the word. Look at what they do. That is what they did.

Clark started defending the police. She was doing this because the accusations now have spread to the whole police force. Unfortunately it is far more difficult to treat an epidemic than it is to vaccinate against the disease, or practice preventive medicine.

Clark was starting to mend her ethos foundation, which was why Cochran felt it necessary to object. An important aspect of Clark's presentation of her rebuttal was that she was interrupted by objections from Scheck and Cochran every couple of minutes. This was done in order to cut the flow of Clark's speech. By doing so, the defense team tried to create confusion at a time when the prosecution was starting to address some of the issues that could have turned the case back into a murder case. The defense needed to create confusion at a time when the prosecution was starting to mend their ethos foundation, and questioning the defense team's ethics and morals.

Thano Peratis. Remember, that was the nurse. He drew the blood. That was their witness. Now, he was their witness because he was the cornerstone of their case. Very important to make you believe that there is missing blood.

But then — now I think defense counsel made some reference to that, the notion that we — Hank Goldberg secretly went out and interviewed him. What secret? You know, if you have a question about this, ask the judge. No attorney for either side is required to give notification to

another side, oh, I'm going to go interview my witness. That makes sense, doesn't it? They don't notify us and we don't notify them. We talk to them, we give them evidence of it. We give them a statement, here, we talked to this guy. Here is the statement. That is what we do. Hank Goldberg went and talked to him. Mr. Peratis said, no, I didn't measure, no, I didn't look, and I realize I was wrong. I was trying to be very precise. Okay.

Now, here is the syringe. You are going to have this back here. You can look at it. And what he said was I turn it over, I had it turned over and I couldn't see the number. And you will see when you look at the numbers and all these little lines as are sitting there like this, you are this going to be able to measure precisely how much you have got in there, but if you have it turned over, you are really not going to know. Okay.

But beyond all of that, it kind of makes sense, if no one tells you must take this much blood, you are not going to look to take that much blood. You are going to take enough. You take enough for sampling, for testing, and that is what they did.

Clark was trying further to mend her ethos foundation by rejecting the claim that there was any missing blood from Simpson's blood sample. If Clark could convince the jurors, that there was no missing blood, she would cut the defense's logos foundation. This was therefore one of the more important parts of her rebuttal.

...You have to view very, very carefully the experts, see if they make sense, see if you can rely on them, see if they are believable, see if they are logical, and consider the fact that they are for hire. Sure, that makes a difference.

Dr. Baden, DR. Baden who came and told that you gravity doesn't work, paid over $100,000 in this case. He is very charming, he is very affable, I enjoyed seeing him in court, but hearing him was something else. Over $100,000 he got paid in this case.

Clark attacks the credibility of the defense experts. This was something that she needed to have done earlier, at the latest in her closing statement. When different experts go up against each other, it is more their ethos than the evidence itself that determines who the jury is going to believe.

If you are standing behind somebody cutting their throat, they are bleeding out and they are not bleeding on you, so you will get some on your hands, maybe you will get a little bit of the spatter, but you are not going to be covered in blood and you are certainly not going to be covered in the kind of blood in the Bronco because it is not on your back.

When you think about this, think about it logically, but don't let the record mislead you. If you want it read back, they will do it for you. They will do it for you. Don't hesitate to ask, ladies and gentlemen.

Defense has raised the issue about there being — why wasn't there dirt, why wasn't there mud at Rockingham tracked in the — tracked in the house on that light carpet. There wouldn't be — there was ?- you saw the bloody shoeprints, and they faded out halfway down the Bundy walk to the point where there were no visible bloody shoeprints on that walk at the end of the walkway. Then you saw the imprint in the Bronco, so that whatever blood was left on the shoe was picked up by the soft tufts of the carpet.

By the time he gets back to Rockingham, there isn't much left there. Whatever blood, whatever mud, whatever dirt he's got on his shoes, he's tracked off. This is common experience, you know. Either blood or mud, whatever you get on your shoes doesn't stay there forever. You walk, it comes off, and as you walk, more comes off. By the time he gets home, there's not a lot of excess there. Maybe there's some trace amount, but you're not going to notice that on a carpet. And so that in itself says nothing, and the testimony of their expert, Mr. MacDonell, I think even DR. Lee does not dispute that.

> ***Mr. Cochran*: objection. Misstatement, your honor.**
> **The court: Overruled.**
> ***Ms. Clark*: Of greater importance and I think actually—Yes. Dr. Lee even testified—he was asked specifically if somebody walked through dirt, walked through berries, would you necessarily see it, and his answer was you might see it and you might not. The absence of evidence is not evidence of absence, and that's what their witnesses have said.**

Clark goes against the defense claim that there wasn't enough evidence. In this situation Clark could have said something like this:

> The defense asks why Simpson didn't track dirt and blood into the house? We don't know everything that this man did. Maybe he took his shoes off before he walked onto that white carpet, maybe the dirt and blood had already rubbed off his rubber soles before he entered his house. Who knows? We just know that he dripped blood inside his house, and that he forgot his socks on the floor.

This way of arguing takes Clark from the defensive to the offensive. At the same time Clark doesn't have to commit to a specific set of facts that she in reality doesn't know anything about. By not committing to unnecessary details, you cover your back when it comes to counter-argumentation. You can not so easily be proven wrong. In this instance Clark would be able to cover herself against counter-argumentation in the jury room.

The prosecution had to pay a high price for their desire to be precise when it came to the time line issue (when exactly Simpson committed the murders). Because they wanted to be able to say exactly when the murders happened (10:15 pm) they lost several witnesses whose testimony suggested that the murders happened later. These witnesses were instead turned into witnesses for the defense. This is another example that the scientific approach as an ideal is not always appropriate.

Here are the reasons why you can have faith and you can rely on the validity of the results of the testing of the Bundy blood trial. No. 1, you've heard us talk about it too many times, substrate controls were clean. They should have showed contamination and they didn't, and they were tested and they came up clean. And what that gives you is quality assurance. You know you can rely on the result because you have this. The bindles were closed. That's very important. Remember if you will the testimony concerning opening of the blood vial, the defendant's reference vial. And they were saying that when the blood vial was opened, that that somehow contaminated the bindles and the swatches that were taken from the Bundy walk, that there was some aerosol effect, that his blood was spraying all over the place.

Well, the problem with that is that Collin's testimony was, when he opened the blood vial of the defendant's reference blood, he was 10 to 15 feet away from the swatches and these swatches were in closed bindles. And not only that, but the bindles were inside envelopes that were closed.

Now, what testimony have you heard in this trial that DNA can fly from a test tube into a closed envelope through a closed bindle onto the swatches? None. In fact, there's testimony to the contrary.

And that brings us to next, there was no vacuum in this test tube. This was not a vacutainer. This was a syringe, and it's already been shown to you and the testimony was ?- *Mr. Scheck*: Objection. The court: Sustained. Excuse me, counsel. Not a syringe.

***Ms. Clark*: Thano Peratis.**

***Mr. Scheck*: No. It's a vacutainer tube. The Court: No.**

***Ms. Clark*: He said it was a syringe. The Court: I stand corrected. Syringe.**

***Mr. Scheck*: No vacuum in the tube. The Court: Proceed.**

***Ms. Clark*: You have the tape there. It was not a vacutainer that was used. It was a syringe. And there was testi-**

mony concerning this from Collin Yamauchi as well.

And by the way, while we're at it, let me point out something else. Mr. Scheck argued yesterday that Collin Yamauchi, when he opened up the defendant's reference vial, he spilled blood on his gloves and spilled it on the chem?wipe. And it sounds to me like if it was spilled, I guess then it is true that there is no missing blood because it got spilled. But the truth of the matter is and the testimony was that, as Collin Yamauchi told you, when he opened it, he thought he might have gotten a little bit when — a little bit on his gloves and that he immediately changed his gloves and threw them away before he went to handle anything. So you don't have any problems with flying DNA and you don't have the kind of — you don't have the contact that you need to have in order to show contamination.

And by the way, I should indicate to you that Gary Sims, whom the defense endorses to be a very good scientist, indicated he too has had the experience of opening a reference vial and getting a little bit of it out and then you wipe it off, you clean up, it's fine.

This argumentation sounds really good if you trust the forensic scientist. If you distrust him, it doesn't sound so convincing. This is why ethos is everything.

All of the swatches that were tested on the Bundy walk were consistent. They all came back to the defendant. That's important for the following reason. If you have contamination, what you should expect to find are results that are out of succinct, willy?nilly if you will. What should have happened is, you should have seen the defendant's blood type coming up, for example, in the sample that was taken from the pool of blood under Nicole where it shouldn't be, you know. Remember, I told you about 41 and 42.

***Mr. Scheck*: Your honor, objection.**

***Ms. Clark*: 41 came from—The Court: Overruled,**

counsel.

***Mr. Scheck*: Objection.**

***Ms. Clark*: — From the area near Ron Goldman.**

***The Court*: Overruled.**

***Ms. Clark*: There was a tree stump that he was curled around and there was blood on that tree stump, and they recovered it as a representative sample from the crime scene of what his blood type would be. If this was in fact contamination and the defendant's type was flying all over the place, why don't we find it in Ron Goldman's crime scene sample? Why don't we find it in the sample taken from the pool of blood underneath Nicole? We don't.**

***Mr. Scheck*: Objection. The Court: Overruled.**

***Ms. Clark*: If you had contamination, it should be in other places, places where it doesn't belong. But you don't have that. You only have the defendant's blood type coming up in the places where the killer dripped blood. This is the other point that was made by the defense. And in order for you to believe that the results of the Bundy blood trial were the result of contamination, you must first believe that all of the DNA on all of the swatches completely and totally degraded.**

Now, when you think about the fact, as was brought out in testimony, that you can recover DNA through PCR analysis from Egyptian mummies, then how can you possibly buy this story about stains that were recovered a few hours ago completely and totally degrading every single one of them, all of these swatches for all of the drops

***Mr. Scheck*: Objection. The Court: Overruled, counsel.**

***Ms. Clark*: — Completely degrading to the point where they're able to pick up contamination? It makes no sense. It's completely illogical. It stands science on its head.**

This was part of Clark's strong argumentation, which she needed to elaborate more upon so it wouldn't drown in the argumentation. It would also have been good to have brought it up regularly in her argumentation, at the latest in the closing argumentation, where it could have been used as a vaccination against claims on behalf of the defense team. Since this was what the defense team's case had to rest upon it should not have been so hard to anticipate. Instead, it was again brought up too late.

> **Now, there's -- something else that you should know about this is the following. We did conventional serology, if you recall, on one of the blood drops on the Bundy walk, item no. 49. We did conventional serology. That means no DNA stuff. That's just regular what we call PGM markers. You've heard them talk about that. We did a PGM test on item 49. That came back to the defendant. It put him within .5 percent of the population that could have deposited that blood. So even if you do not take into account the DNA, even Dr. Gerdes, their expert, conceded that conventional serology is very hardy stuff and he said no problem with contamination for PGM typing. That testimony is in 40198 to 40199 if you want to review that.**

This was again one of the prosecution's strongest points that needed more exposure and attention. This is what is meant by being able to focus. By focusing, one is able to set the agenda, in other words, what issues are being taken into consideration.

> **But then I think it was really the most telling of all, officer Riske, the first officer on the scene — it's been a long time since you've seen his face. He was very early on in this case, but he was very honest. He was very candid. Even defense counsel agrees. And this is what he had to say about that, page 14068.**
>
> **"Question: now, when you went out towards the — out through the rear gate, were you able to see any other blood drops? "Answer: I met with my partner at the rear gate and — yes, I did. "Question: How much and how did you happen to see those? "Answer: My partner directed my attention to them. "Question: And how did he do**

that? "Answer: He just told me he saw blood on the gate and on the driveway and he showed me where they were with his flashlight. "Question: Shone his light on them? "Answer: That's correct. "Question: Was he staying away from them? "Answer: Yes." Officer Riske is describing the actions of his partner, officer Terrazas, who saw blood on the rear gate. They were the first officers there in the early morning hours — excuse me — just shortly after midnight, June 13th, 1994.

We here see how Clark started defending the police by backing the evidence with testimony from police officers that had not directly had their ethos questioned. This again should have been elaborated upon far more extensively and introduced earlier in the case.

Now, what they're trying to tell you is that the defendant dripped blood on that side somehow with his cut left hand, dripped over on the console and that later, Mark Fuhrman came in and just happened to take the bloody Rockingham Bundy glove that did not have the blood of the defendant on it, but swipe exactly where the defendant had dripped on the console, and somehow, that's how his blood got mixed up with Ron Goldman's blood on the console. If you wanted to sell this story in Hollywood, they wouldn't buy it because it's so incredible. It's not even funny. It's ludicrous, okay. This is ludicrous.

But above and beyond that, they're also saying this. They are saying that Dennis Fung collected all of the blood on the console and it was all gone. Then someone came back later and planted blood exactly in the same place as it had been before to look exactly the same way it had looked before. This is ridiculous. Talk about makes no sense? Talk about — just unbelievable.

You'll have the pictures. You need to look at the pictures. Look at the pictures yourself. You will have them back in the jury room. Compare — look at all the pictures you can get your hands on. Compare the blood patterns on this console from the photos that were taken.

This one's later, September 1st, down here and this one up here was on June 14th (indicating). Compare them. You ask yourself, you ask yourself how could this possibly happen, how could it happen that they can duplicate exactly the way the blood looks on June 14th on September 1st? It can't happen. But you need to go back and look at it. You need to get your hands on this stuff yourselves and talk about this because this is so far beyond the pale that only your seeing yourself and holding this in your hands is believing that they're actually, actually saying this to you.

This is an example of how Clark goes against the conspiracy theory. This is one of Clark's strong points, which she needs to get into more. Show them the pictures and ask the jury how this could happen. When it is one of your strong points, you don't just rely upon the jury to understand the evidence. As said before, the evidence cannot just stand by itself. The reason why Clark doesn't feel like she has the time to get further into this issue is probably because she feels the need to address all the aspects that the defense team raised. In this respect it is important to, that it is the defense team's aim to create confusion, and the prosecution's job to create clarity.

He's got Ron Goldman's blood in his car. What's it doing there? That's it. That's it. He's guilty. So they have to find an excuse. That's why you have these — this flailing about. You have contamination, you have planting, you have contamination and planting and/or planting, you got everything, everything to explain it all away, everything. But the theories get wilder and wilder because the proof is so devastating. There's so much of it and there's so much to explain.

This is a strong effort by Clark to expose the defense team's tactics. Well presented, this often works in one's favor, since it is an attack upon one's opponent's ethos.

And by the way, the blood that was collected that's shown

here in the bottom photograph that has the number 26 on it on this exhibit, that blood was collected and sent directly to the department of justice. It didn't go through that cesspool they want to call the LAPD. It went straight up to DOJ, and it was tested and it came back with the RFLP result of Ron Goldman and the defendant.

This is a strong point that needed far more attention. The prosecution can build upon a strong ethos foundation for their argumentation.

We have the Bruno Magli going down the Bundy walk in blood and then we have a bloody imprint right there (indicating) where you'd put your foot if you were the driver. And what does that look like? That's very highly incriminating.

Now, they want us to explain this one away by saying that Mark Fuhrman stepped in the blood of Nicole Brown because — actually this is all woven in, a bunch of stuff together. That photograph where you see him pointing to the evidence at Bundy, that really wasn't taken at 7:00 or 6:30 or something as was testified to. No, no, no, no, no. That was taken before he left to go to Rockingham. And the blood on his shoe dried. He was standing there — he was marching around in her pool of blood.

That's what you have to believe. Then he went out on Rockingham, he stepped on the wet grass, he got it wet again, and when he got into this Bronco, which I guess he must have had a slim Jim with him to break into it because it was locked, he got in and he put his foot on that carpet right where you would put it if you were driving it. But he didn't have the keys. So why would he be sitting that way? I don't know, but that's the story. That's what you're supposed to believe.

Now, there's a bunch of problems with that story that make it impossible. <u>It doesn't fit. It doesn't make sense and it didn't happen</u>, and here's why. No. 1, there was testimony from Mr. Bodziak concerning the characteris-

tics of this stain. And that means 33 where the imprint is. And what he said was that there were the "s" squiggles that were very distinctive of this Silga design of the Bruno Maglis. He said there was not distinguishable characteristics for him to make an absolute positive identification.

But you can see. I'm going to show you. I'm going to show you that logic and common sense in your own powers of observation tell you that's the Bruno Magli shoe. And Mr. Bodziak told you that he excluded the shoes of all of the officers including those of Mark Fuhrman from the bloody shoeprints at Bundy.

***Mr. Scheck*: Objection. The court: Overruled.**

Clark presents a strong argument against the contamination/planting theory. It is interesting that Clark was starting to use Cochran's effective speech pattern, with the use of three and figures of speech like the anaphor. Rhetoric is an equally practical and theoretical science.

What you see, ladies and gentlemen, is a very elaborate effort to make you disbelieve a great wealth of evidence, and what you've heard is basically a conspiracy that extends from officer Riske to commander Bushey. Do you realize how many people would have had to have gotten involved in a conspiracy within an hour? Can you imagine how this could happen?

Detective Vannatter and detective Lange never even knew Mark Fuhrman until they met him that night at Bundy, and yet the allegation by the defense is that they got together that night, meeting the first time, for the very first time, and everybody's covering up and conspiring all of a sudden. Impossible. Not only that, but there are other people involved as well, people we don't even know who they are, according to the defense, who are willing to get involved in this. You realize how many people have to be involved? I mean it boggles the mind. We don't even know who they're talking about.

But that's the contortion you have to go through to believe in this conspiracy theory. That's the contortion

you have to go through to step away from the very obvious truth you can see when you look straight on and clear? eyed at this evidence. If you look at it straight on, you can see the truth. It's very clear and it's very obvious. Mr. Simpson committed these murders, ladies and gentlemen. We don't like it and it's hard, but it's true.

We see Clark get into how many people would have to have been involved in the conspiracy. Clark was here trying to mend her ethos foundation. Even though it was a strong argument, she was still on the defensive. This could have been avoided if she had vaccinated against it in her closing statement. Then Clark could have spent more time attacking the defense for presenting such an accusation. This would have kept her on the offensive. It would have been good if Clark had mentioned all the people that would have to have been involved in the framing/cover-up. She could have mentioned them by name, and pointed out some of the good deeds these people had done.

Since we are here trying to save a dying patient that has been neglected far too long, we would have to do something drastic in order to turn the case around. In this situation we could do as Cicero did in his defense for Murena and Sulla. We could turn the opponent's argumentation into a comedy. We need to employ the persuasive effects of humor if we, on such a short notice, are going to change the way our audience views the issue. Only humor can change the soul and move the mind in such a limited time.

The way we are going to convince and entertain at the same time is by taking our opponent's arguments to the absurd. Employing this technique, Clark could have said something like this:

They have put on an act for you. The act is called: "If you got the dough - they run the show." It all has to do with a conspiracy. First a police officer decides that he wants to blame Simpson for the murder, "*Of course, why not*!" Then he walks around the crime scene collecting evidence to place at O.J.'s house. He thinks "Now I can't do this alone," and so he convinces all the other officers on the scene to join him in his scheme, "*Off course*," they say, "*Why not*?" Then he and the others plant the evidence in and outside O.J.'s home, but they think, "We have to be sure he is convicted" and so they persuade the people at the lab that they should tamper with the evidence "*Yes, sure*" they say, "*Why not*?" Now we have a real good conspiracy going for us, about fifty people that don't know each other are agreeing to put their jobs, integrity, and freedom at risk by lying and cheating, by planting evidence and withholding information. "*Sure, why not*?" They decided that because he has so much money and is so famous, it is time to frame him. "*Sure, why not*?" They all decided to frame him, because they have treated him as a star for so many years, "*Sure, why not*?"

- "I think not," but it is a fine story…

Marcia Clark further states in her rebuttal:

The shoeprints at Bundy were from a size 12 Bruno Magli shoe. There is no contradiction for that testimony. The defendant wears a size 12 shoe. That testimony is uncontradicted. The bloody shoe impression on the Bronco carpet is consistent with the Bruno Magli shoe. That testimony is uncontradicted. That's the one we just showed you.

The left glove at Bundy and the right glove at Rockingham are Aris Light gloves, size extra large, uncontradicted. Nicole Brown bought two pair of Aris light gloves at Bloomingdales in New York on December 18, 1990.

***Mr. Cochran*: Objection again.**

***Ms. Clark*: Testimony that is uncontradicted.**

***The Court*: Overruled, counsel.**

***Ms. Clark*: The defendant wore black and brown Aris Light gloves between December 18th, 1990 and June the 12th, 1994. Let me make one further point about that. If the gloves you saw him in in these photographs that we showed to you, ladies and gentlemen, were not the ones purchased for him by Nicole Brown, why is it we have no photographs dating before the day she purchased those two pair of gloves?**

Mr. Cochran: Your honor, I object to the form of that. The Court: Overruled. It's a fair inference from the evidence, counsel.

Ms. Clark: Which only shows, ladies and gentlemen, and highlights one further point for you. Where are they? If they are not the gloves you have here in court, where are they? They are here.

Mr. Cochran: Your honor, again, objection. We have no obligation ?- The Court: Overruled. No. That's not correct, counsel.

Ms. Clark: The killer dropped blood to the left of the shoeprints at Bundy. That's testimony that's uncontradicted.

The defendant had a fresh cut on his left hand during the week of June the 13th, 1994, uncontradicted. A blood drop on the Bundy trial was typed the same as the defendant's. And this is the conventional serology I was telling you. This is the PGM typing that they did, not the DNA. This is uncontradicted. No one — no one contradicts the accuracy or the integrity of that. No one claims that's the product of contamination.

Mr. Scheck: Objection. The Court: Overruled, counsel.

Ms. Clark: Blood transfers were visible in the defendant's Bronco. Don Thompson, officer Don Thompson, who was at Rockingham that morning said he saw blood in the Bronco. Blood drops are on the street, in the driveway, 360 Rockingham, uncontradicted. Blood drops were found in the foyer and in the master bathroom at Rockingham, testimony that's uncontradicted. It's also uncontradicted that it's his blood. ... fibers consistent with the carpet from the Bronco found on the Rockingham glove, uncontradicted. Blue black cotton fiber found on Ron Goldman's shirt, the defendant's socks and the Rockingham glove, uncontradicted. Fiber consistent with the carpet from the Bronco found on the dark knit cap at Bundy, uncontradicted. Hairs consistent with the defendant found on the dark knit cap at Bundy,

uncontradicted. Hairs consistent with the defendant found on Ron Goldman's shirt, uncontradicted.

Mr. Cochran: Misstates the evidence.

Ms. Clark: On this, I refer to head hair as well as limb hairs.

The Court: Overruled.

Ms. Clark: Motive, you know. Full circle. Spousal abuse, domestic violence against Nicole Brown. Unrefuted. You can see, ladies and gentlemen, this is just what hasn't been contested.

Now, you add to that the fact of all of the evidence that they've tried to claim was contaminated or planted. I've shown you how it wasn't. Add all of that to this. It is truly overwhelming.

Clark here states the facts that still stand unrefuted. This was a strong argument presented by Clark. Unfortunately, it takes awhile to get people to change the way they interpret certain events. It was therefore too late to get the jurors to totally change their minds about what the case was about, especially when it is an opinion that they have acquired over nine months.

And if you'll think back to this time of jury selection when all of you were first together, you will remember that we talked about the United States Supreme Court building in Washington, D.C. it's been so long, I wonder if you remember that, the highest court in the land. And we asked if you knew what was inscribed on the facade of the Supreme Court building up above the steps, up above the pillars. If you think back, we told you what was written above those marble pillars, "Equal justice under the law." We talked about what that meant, "Equal justice under the law." You may recall, that means the law is to be applied equally to all persons in this country regardless of whether one is rich or poor or race or creed or color, famous or otherwise. Not even the President of the United States is above the law. You all agreed with that.

> **We asked you if you had courage to be just to a person. Each of you, each of you said yes, some individually, some responded as a group. And we asked you, you may recall, what equal justice under the law meant to you, and you replied that is the way it should definitely be. And that's right. That is the way it should definitely be. But you see, equal justice under the law is an ideal. It's an abstract principle and it takes you to make this principle a reality. Only you can make this ideal real.**

Clark finally starts appealing to the topos rich against poor. Unfortunately she does not get into this topos before the last few minutes of a nine-month long trial.

Like Darden, Clark says a lot of the right things in her rebuttal, but it is hard to mend nine months worth of damage in one day.

17. WHAT THE NEW RHETORICAL SITUATION CALLED FOR

Hence the answer of Simoneedes to the wife of Hiero concerning the wise and the rich, when she asked which was preferable, to be wise or to be rich. "Rich,: he answered, "for we see the wise spending their time at the doors of the rich."

Aristotle

In order to find out how to best argue your case, you need to get an overview of your own and your opponent's argumentation. This is best done by applying the argumentation model to your own and your opponent's argumentation. You start with writting out both. Regarding your opponent's argumentation, you will generally have a feel for what he or she is going to say from depositions, letters, conversations, or common sense.

After you have written out both argumentations, you use this flow chart:

Find the overall claims in the written material
Find the reasoning and warrant that belongs to these claims
Pinpoint the main argument in the text
Find the weaknesses or strengths in the reasoning and warrant that supports the overall claims

If you are going to improve your own statements

1. Throw out possible weak arguments

2. Improve your focus by making sure that all argumentation directly supports the main claim

3. Vaccinate against counter-arguments in the weak areas of your argumentation

If you are going to address another person's statements

1. Address yourself either positively or negatively to the strong or weak points in the statement

2. Build your counter-argumentation up either as a critic of the reasoning and/or warrant that has been presented, or as a further addition/support of the presented reasoning and warrant

You basically go through this process both with your own and with your opponent's argumentation. Then you go through your own argumentation a second time taking your findings concerning your opponent's argumentation into account.

Using this argumentation model we are now going to work our way through the defense team's arguments. Using this technique we will eventually discover the defense team's weak points. From those weak points we can begin to construct the most effective rhetorical response. I have underlined the weak points.

On an overall level the evidence against Simpson can be divided into two categories, the physical evidence against Simpson and the psychological motivation-seeking evidence consisting of evidence of spousal abuse.

The defense team's reasoning concerning the physical evidence:

Reasoning	**Claim**
The evidence is: 1. planted. 2. contaminated. 3. deteriorated.	Simpson is innocent.

Warrant
You cannot be convicted upon false and useless evidence.

The defense team's reasoning concerning spousal abuse:

Reasoning---**Claim**
Spousal abuse is irrelevant in a murder case. Everybody has occasional problems in their marriage. — Simpson is innocent.

Warrant
You cannot be convicted upon insignificant and vague evidence.

In order to find the weak point in an argument, we usually have to dig a little deeper underneath the surface of what is said, the reason being that if the weak point was obvious from the beginning it wouldn't be such a good argument. The way we do that is by further examining the reasoning or the warrant in the argumentation model. When we want to examine the reasoning or the warrant we make them the claim in the argumentation model, and then find out what is the new reasoning and warrant in the argumentation model. If we still have not found the weak point, we repeat the process one more time, and make the new reasoning or warrant the claim in another argumentation model. This can be repeated as many times as necessary, until we reach the weak point. Usually, we don't need to dig more than two or three layers down before we find the weak spot in the argument. By digging down through the different layers in an argument, we are able to find the foundation that the argument rests upon. These core beliefs are often more easy to reject. We are now going to dig our way down through the different layers in the defense team's reasoning concerning the physical evidence against Simpson:

Reasoning---**Claim**

1. Mark Fuhrman has racists views.
2. There is not enough blood evidence.
3. Blood is missing from the test tube.

The evidence is planted.

Warrant

When the evidence doesn't add up, and people have wicked opinions, the evidence has been manipulated, and there may be a conspiracy going on.

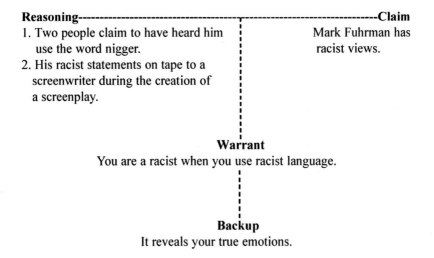

Reasoning---**Claim**

1. Two people claim to have heard him use the word nigger.
2. His racist statements on tape to a screenwriter during the creation of a screenplay.

Mark Fuhrman has racist views.

Warrant

You are a racist when you use racist language.

Backup

It reveals your true emotions.

Because Fuhrman is not defended by the prosecution, it allowed the defense to take their allegations one step further.

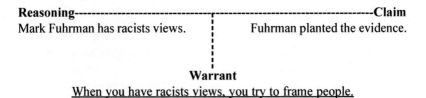

Reasoning---**Claim**

Mark Fuhrman has racists views.

Fuhrman planted the evidence.

Warrant

<u>When you have racists views, you try to frame people.</u>

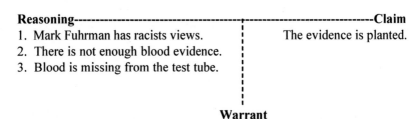

Here we see that there is a possibility of defending Fuhrman on the different levels, working our way down to the final claim that Fuhrman planted evidence against Simpson. The prosecution only addressed the leap in assumption between the reasoning and the claim in the last argumentation model. This is also the biggest leap in assumption. But by working on the different levels of assumption, we can better mend Fuhrman's ethos and block the defense team's argumentation.

Reasoning	**Claim**
1. Only smaller blood drops were found. 2. There was not enough blood evidence found in Simpson's car. 3. There were no blood drops going up the steps to Simpson's bedroom.	There is not enough blood evidence.

Warrant

<u>If only a small amount of blood drops are found, (blood not found in "sufficient" amounts), and if the blood trail stops in certain areas, there is not enough blood evidence.</u>

Reasoning	**Claim**
1. The nurse that drew Simpson's blood said that he drew 8 ccs, when in fact only 6.1 ccs can be accounted for.	Blood is missing from the test tube.

Warrant

When there is a difference between what the nurse said that he drew, and what can be accounted for, there is missing blood.

This time we are going to go further by analyzing the warrant, not the reasoning, since the presumption in the warrant this time is the most interesting.

Reasoning--**Claim**

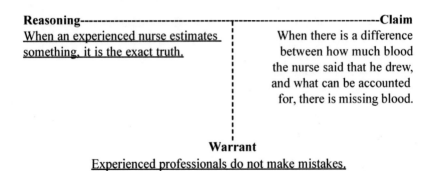

<u>When an experienced nurse estimates something, it is the exact truth.</u>

When there is a difference between how much blood the nurse said that he drew, and what can be accounted for, there is missing blood.

Warrant

<u>Experienced professionals do not make mistakes.</u>

We here see that it sometimes is just a question of going down deep enough into the foundation of an argument, for us to find the weak point.

We have now found the weak points concerning the argument that the evidence against Simpson was planted. We can therefore go on and examine the defense team's second overall claim that the evidence against Simpson was contaminated. We are again going to work our way down through the different layers in the argument:

Reasoning--**Claim**

1. The blood samples were collected incorrectly.
2. Police officers were cross-contaminating the murder scene, Simpson's car, and Simpson's house.
3. The blood samples were analyzed and handled at the same time as Simpson's blood was handled.
4. The evidence has gone through the LAPD's laboratory, which is a "cesspool of contamination."

The evidence is contaminated.

Warrant

<u>When this many things are wrong, the evidence has to have been contaminated.</u>

Reasoning--**Claim**

The two people who collected blood evidence collected it without wearing gloves. You

The blood samples were collected incorrectly.

contaminate the evidence
if you don't wear gloves.

Warrant

When the evidence has been contaminant, it cannot be used.

The reason why the warrant is a weak point, is that the DNA profile of the "real" killer doesn't disappear in the blood samples just because it has been contaminated with another DNA type.

Reasoning--Claim

1. Video of police officers tramping through the crime scene (Later shown to be after the collection of evidence had ended, and the evidence scene was being washed down.)
2. The same detectives that showed up at the crime scene went directly to Simpson's house to notify Simpson, investigate Simpson.

Police officers were cross-contaminating the murder scene, Simpson's car, and Simpson's house.

Warrant

When the police go directly from a crime scene to a suspect's house and car, they contaminate the evidence.

Backup

They tracked blood from the murder scene to Simpson's car.

The reason why the warrant and the backup are weak points is that it would not have been possible for the police to track this much blood into Simpson's car since they had to travel all the way to his estate in order to get in contact with Simpson's car and there could not possibly have been so much blood left underneath their shoes that they could have left a huge bloody footprint inside Simpson's car.

Reasoning--Claim

1. A lab technician said that he took Simpson's blood sample out to analyze it. Then he put it away and took out some of the blood drops

The blood samples were analyzed and handled the same time as collected at the murder scene in order to analyze them. Some blood was supposed to have spurted out of the test tube when the technician opened the tube.

Simpson's blood sample.

2. We do not believe the lab technician when he claims that he wiped the table off, nor that he changed gloves when he went to handle the blood drops. We also do not believe that he put Simpson's test tube away before he started to handle the blood drops. Because they do not care about following the correct procedures at the LAPD.

Warrant

When somebody has not done things according to the procedure, they are liars.

Backup

We do not believe what this man says, because he has done several things wrong in the way he went about examining this evidence. He has not followed the correct procedure.

Reasoning---**Claim**

1. They made mistakes in this case.
2. They made mistakes in other cases.
3. They do not have a written manual that they go by.

The evidence has gone through the LAPD's laboratory, which is a cesspool of contamination.

Warrant

When you have made mistakes, and you do not have a set of correct guidelines (manual), you are a cesspool of contamination.

The reason why it is often the warrant that is the weak point in the argument is that you often don't have to mention the warrant in your argumentation. Therefore it can be easier to get away with a flaw in the warrant.

Now that we have found the weak points concerning the contamination argument, we can go back to examining the defense team's last overall reasoning supporting their claim that Simpson is innocent:

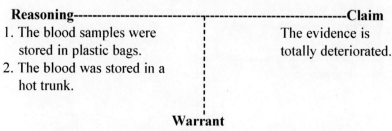

Reasoning---**Claim**

1. The blood samples were stored in plastic bags.
2. The blood was stored in a hot trunk.

The evidence is totally deteriorated.

Warrant

When the evidence is stored wrong, it totally deteriorates.

DNA is very hardy material, therefore it would be very unlikely that all the DNA deteriorated because it was not stored correctly.

This is the first time that we only have to dig one layer down to find the weak point for the entire reasoning. This indicates that this is the weakest of the defense team's arguments. Therefore, this is one of the prosecution's strongest points.

We only have to look at the defense team's arguments concerning spousal abuse in order for us to have mapped out the defense team's entire argumentation. The defense team's arguments concerning spousal abuse look like this:

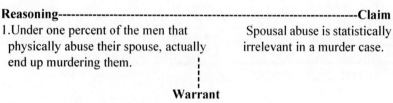

Reasoning---**Claim**

1. Under one percent of the men that physically abuse their spouse, actually end up murdering them.

Spousal abuse is statistically irrelevant in a murder case.

Warrant

If it is not statistically significant, it is irrelevant.

The reasoning in this argumentation model is weak because the starting point is not who has been physically abused, but who has been murdered. In this way we get a 35 to 50 percent chance that the one who physically abused the murder victim committed the murder.

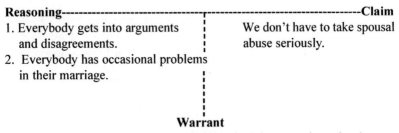

Reasoning--**Claim**

1. Everybody gets into arguments and disagreements.
2. Everybody has occasional problems in their marriage.

We don't have to take spousal abuse seriously.

Warrant

Problems that everybody encounters we don't have to take seriously.

Backup

Since everybody gets into problems in their relationships, we don't have to take domestic problems seriously.

Cochran mentioned the reasoning but not the claim, which was left unsaid because it was too outrageous to say aloud.

We have now mapped out the defense teams arguments and are ready to build up the prosecution's new argumentation, based upon the new rhetorical situation that has been created by the defense team. The first step is to line up the defense team's weak points:

Warrant

When you have racists views, you try to frame people.

Warrant

If only a small amount of blood drops are found, (blood not found in "sufficient" amounts) and if the blood trail stops in certain areas, there is not enough blood evidence.

Warrant

Experienced professionals don't make mistakes.

Reasoning

When an experienced nurse estimates something, it is the exact truth.

Warrant

When these many things are wrong, the evidence has to have been contaminated.

Reasoning

The two people who collected blood evidence collected it without wearing gloves. You contaminate the evidence if you don't wear gloves.

Warrant

When the evidence has been contaminated, it cannot be used.

Warrant

When the police go directly from a crime scene to a suspect's house and car, they contaminated the evidence.

Backup

They tracked blood from the murder scene to Simpson's car.

Warrant

When somebody has not done things according to the procedure, they are liars.

Warrant

When you have made mistakes, and you do not have a set of right guidelines (manual), you are a cesspool of contamination.

Warrant

When the evidence is stored wrong, it totally deteriorates.

Reasoning

Under one percent of the men that physically abuse their spouse actually end up murdering them.

Backup
Since everybody gets into problems in their relationships, we don't have to take domestic problems seriously.

Claim
We don't have to take the spousal abuse seriously.

If your opponent, as in this case, has a lot of weak points, you pick out the weakest points. This is where you begin the selection of your strongest points. In this case this would be:

Warrant
If only a small amount of blood drops are found, (blood not found in "sufficient" amounts) and if the blood trail stops in certain areas, there is not enough blood evidence.

Reasoning
When an experienced nurse estimates something, it is the exact truth.

Warrant
When the evidence has been contaminated, it cannot be used.

Backup
They tracked blood from the murder scene to Simpson's car.

Warrant
When somebody has not done things according to the procedure, they are liars.

Warrant
When you have made mistakes, and you do not have a set of correct guidelines (manual), you are a cesspool of contamination.

Claim
When the evidence is stored wrong, it totally deteriorates.

Reasoning

Under one percent of the men that physically abuse their spouse, actually end up murdering them.

Claim

We don't have to take the spousal abuse seriously.

We now have the facts that we are going to build our new argumentation around. I call this technique a spider web, where we weave our argumentation around our opponent's weak points. The question then is, how do we counter these weak arguments in the most effective way?

There are nine basic ways of counter-arguing. If we know about these nine ways we can attack our opponent's weak argumentation and determine what technique would be the most effective in order to make our point. We are here going to see how the Simpson defense team's weak arguments can be countered by using the different forms of counter-arguments:

(1) Refuting Point by Point

One refutes the opponent's argumentation by taking the arguments and statements up individually and rejecting them one by one. One can, for example say, that my opponent's main positions is: …, and her reasons are: 1 …., 2 …. and 3 …. Thereafter you tear the arguments apart, in order for the main claim to collapse. The aim of attack can switch from argument to argument since you switch between the different methods that are stated below. The point by point method is viewed as one of the most effective methods, especially when it is followed up by a positive argumentation of your own opinion. A prerequisite is that the specific points are of importance to the audience.

(2) Pure Denial

You are on the defensive and denying the opponent's claim without presenting any counter-arguments. The method is only effective if the burden of proof rests upon the opponent, and if the audience is in agreement with your position.

Pure denial will only generate support among the ones that already are of the same opinion. The exception is if the one delivering the statement has an authority or ethos that in itself persuades the audience.

(3) To Dispute It

One refutes something that the opponent says, and claims the opposite. This method demands that one argues for one's own counterpoint, and provides one's counterpoint with specific documentation. If, for example, one's opponent has quoted an expert, one can dispute her claim by stating that the quote is wrong or misunderstood. This usually only works when one has precise information to refer to. Otherwise it starts resembling the Pure Denial. This will be a strong counter-argument, if one can present the expert's own denial of what one's opponent has quoted.

The To Dispute It method can be used on all types of argument, contrary to the Reject The Authority that can be used only on authority arguments.

(4) Reject the Authority

One can refute an authority argument by challenging the mentioned authority. When one uses this method, one can also include counter-authorities in support of one's own viewpoint.

In order for this method to be effective, one has to be thorough with one's documentation, otherwise it sounds more like an assertion.

(5) Present A Dilemma

One points towards two possibilities that are equally destructive for the opponent. If one, for example, wants to refute the point of view that women in leading positions are as well off as men, one can present the dilemma: They lose if they behave as men, and they lose if they don't behave as men!

The dilemma builds upon the "damned if you do, damned if you don't" effect. It demands wide and linguistic creativity, and hits the spot if it is presented with the right intonation. In such cases it is hard to counter.

(6) The Exclusion Method

One presents a list of options, preferably three points, where the first two are designed to benefit the opponent. One then starts to refute them one by one, until one reaches the last one that speaks in one's favor. This one then has to be right, since the other possibilities have been excluded. It is only the last point that is seriously meant, and the strategy is that one doesn't have to present arguments for one's point of view, since all the other options seemingly have been excluded.

This method is quite entertaining, because it has a built-in climax effect. At the same time it has a false aura of objectivity, because it seems as if one proceeds logically. Usually it is an distorting refutation method, since there rarely are only a limited number of options as claimed, and the method can then be attacked by the opponent, if he is quick enough.

(7) Leading It into the Absurd

This method that traditionally is called "reductio ad absurdum," consists of accepting one's opponent's point of view, and then further developing it until one ends up with a outrageous consequence.

Often the ones that use this method attribute to the opponent a more extensive point of view then the spokesperson's. But this method can also be used seriously. It is appropriately used in the cases where the opponent either has not thought out the wider consequences, or is trying to hide them.

(8) To Reveal Contradictions

One takes two of the opponent's claims and compares them with each other, and thereby shows that they are contradictory.

This method is especially effective when one wants to reduce the opponent's credibility, and support for his point of view. If one, on top of that, is able to force the opponent to take back his statements time and again, this method alone can destroy him.

(9) To Attack the Argumentation Form

One criticizes the opponent's way of arguing. This can either be specific arguments, or the entire argumentation.

This method is only effective if the audience feels committed to the set of rules for argumentation that one is promoting. One has to be especially careful about attacking the argumentation form on the basis of purely logical rules of reasoning.

So if we apply the nine different ways of counter-arguing to the defense team's weakest points, it could look something like this:

<u>If only a small amount of blood drops are found, (blood not found in "sufficient" amounts) and if the blood trail stops in certain areas, there is not enough blood evidence.</u>

Counter-argumentation techniques used:

(8) To reveal contradictions.

(3) To dispute it.

They say that we have not found enough blood from Simpson in the blood trail that was left behind, from the murder scene, into his car, and all the way into his house. At the same time they say that the wound on Simpson's hand isn't big enough. What in their opinion is a sufficient amount of blood, and how big does a wound have to be?

The fact of the matter is, that if we had found more blood, it would not have fit with the size of wound Simpson had on his hand, and if the wound had been bigger, it would not have fit with the amount of blood that he left behind. In fact, the amount of blood that Simpson lost, and the size of the wound that he had, fit perfectly together.

Just think about it. It would have been useless to plant a blood trail using Simpson's blood, if Simpson had not had a bleeding wound at the time of the murders.

<u>When an experienced nurse estimates something, it is the exact truth.</u>

Counter argumentation techniques used:

(8) To reveal contradictions.

(3) To dispute it.

Scheck claims, that when an experienced nurse estimates something, in this case how much blood he drew from Simpson, it is the exact truth. At the same time Scheck claims that this nurse is wrong when he later claims that he overestimated the amount of blood that he drew from Simpson.

Scheck claims that when an experienced nurse claims something, then it is the exact truth. But in this case we even have the nurse himself denying this claim.

Now they complain that we didn't drag the nurse into court a second time to state this, but instead videotaped his statement from his sick bed. We all know that the nurse got suddenly ill with a serious heart condition. Though we would like to set this matter straight, we do not want to kill this man in the process.

When the evidence has been contaminated, it cannot be used.

Counter-argumentation techniques used:

(1) Refuting point by point.

First of all, if the blood had been contaminated, we would have seen not only Simpson's DNA in the blood samples, but also the mysterious "real" killer's DNA. Therefore we could still have used the blood samples to narrow down the possible killer.

Second of all, if this blood had been contaminated, we would have seen all kinds of DNA profiles in the blood drops, and not just Simpson's DNA; therefore it is not likely that the blood got contaminated in the first place.

They tracked blood from the murder scene to Simpson's car.

Counter-argumentation techniques used:

(6) The Exclusion Method.

We know that the victim's blood was in Simpson's car. To this the defense team mentions the possibility of the police tracking blood from the murder scene to Simpson's car. They say that it could have gotten on, say, Fuhrman's sleeves, or on the sole of his shoes, leaving the bloody sole imprint on the driver side of Simpson's car. This means that there are three ways the blood from the victims could have gotten into Simpson's car:

One from blood stuck to the cloths of the police.
Two from blood stuck underneath the shoes of the police.
Three from blood stuck to the cloths and shoes of Simpson.

By the time the police got from the murder scene to Simpson's house and car, let alone supposedly broke into it, any blood on their clothes would have coagulated, and it would not have been possible to wipe it off on the inside of the Bronco. And there certainly would not have been enough blood left underneath their shoes to leave such a distinct and clear bloody shoe imprint on the driver's side of the Bronco, not to mention that the bloody sole print does not fit any of the shoes the police were wearing. It does, however, fit a size 12 Bruno Magli shoe.

This leaves only one possibility, Simpson tracked the victim's blood directly from the murder scene into his car, stepping in Nicole Simpson's blood as he leaves the crime, leaving bloody footprints as he walks towards his car and steps into his car. Ladies and gentlemen, this is not only the straightforward explanation of what happened, it is also the only thing that could have happened.

When somebody has not done things according to the procedure, they are liars.

Counter-argumentation techniques used:
(5) Present a Dilemma.
(9) To Attack the Argumentation Form.

Scheck says that we can't believe anything the forensic scientist says. He claims this because the scientist testified that he did not follow the correct procedure in one area when he analyzed the blood. He says that by not following procedure in one area we can't believe he did so in other areas. If you follow Scheck's reasoning we can't even be sure if he did not follow correct procedure when he said he did not. Not to follow the exact procedures is not the same as being a liar. In fact, since he did admit to not following procedures it shows him to be an honest man, just the opposite of what Scheck wants you to believe.

It seems to me that Scheck needs to brand this man a liar for his claims to be even theoretically possible. To deliberately character assassinate somebody like this is not only extremely immoral, but also shows a complete disrespect for the truth. Scheck gets up here and gets offended about this and that, but he apparently doesn't think that sticking to the truth applies to him. Where do you buy these kind of morals, at a two for one kind of discount store?

When you have made mistakes, and you do not have a set of correct guidelines (manual), you are a cesspool of contamination.

Counter-argumentation techniques used:
(4) Reject the Authority.

He says that you are a cesspool of contamination when you have made mistakes and not followed a written guideline, Scheck, the man with the two for one kind of morals. Scheck wants to use DNA evidence to free wrongly convicted prisoners, but when the evidence points at his client, he rejects the value of the DNA evidence, claiming that it was not collected correctly, and that it wasn't stored correctly. Funny that he would never pose any of these questions when he wanted to free his clients. Scheck claims that it is easier to exclude somebody then it is to determine whose DNA profile it is. I don't know about you, but this sounds a little thin to me, when we have a positive DNA match. Not even their own experts are able to claim that the kind of minor mistakes that occurred in this case would have been able to change the outcome of the entire load of evidence.

When the evidence is stored incorrectly, it totally deteriorates.

Counter-argumentation techniques used:
(6) The Exclusion Method.

The defense claims that because the blood from the left hand of the killer that was dropped as he left the crime scene was stored incorrectly and was totally deteriorated. Otherwise there would have to have been traces of the so-called real killer's DNA in the blood drops that they claim were later contaminated with O.J.'s blood. Now this has never happened before, neither for Mr. Fung, nor for anybody else collecting blood evidence. Which means that either Simpson is the world's most unlucky ex-husband, or he is the one who killed these two people!

Under one percent of the men that physically abuse their spouse, actually end up murdering them.

Counter-argumentation techniques used:
9) To Attack the Argumentation Form.

This is a totally irrelevant piece of statistics that the defense team comes up with here. We don't start looking at who has physically abused their spouse, but who has been murdered. After all that is what we are dealing with. If the murder victim has been physically abused by a spouse or former spouse, there is a 50 percent chance, that the spouse is the killer. If there is any additional evidence, that statistic only goes up.

We have heard that the defense team has been called the dream team. We find it more appropriate if they were referred to as the con team. Cochran says that this has been a journey towards the truth. What Mr. Cochran didn't tell you was what side he is on. Unfortunately, the only kind of journey that they have taken us on is a detour.

We don't have to take the spousal abuse seriously.

Counter-argumentation techniques used:
7) Leading It to the Absurd.

So Scheck says that spousal abuse is massively irrelevant in a murder case. If we were to follow this line of argumentation, it would mean that in a murder of passion, the fact that there was a love triangle going on would be massively irrelevant.

When it comes to the arguments concerning Fuhrman, we have to address these issues, even though none of those arguments belongs to our opponent's truly weak points. We have to address these issues since they are a threat to our entire ethos foundation. Since this is our weak point, we don't want to be locked into discussing specific incidences and statements on Fuhrman's behalf that are hard to defend and can give the opponent an excuse for stirring up the sore feelings of our audience. Instead we are going to go straight to the point, and start building up Fuhrman's ethos by the use of credible people's ethos. Preferably, we have to have blacks and other minorities to vow for his credibility. In Fuhrman's case, this did not seem to be a problem, since there seemed to be lots of police officers, former victims, and even defendants from minority groups that were willing to defend Fuhrman.

Now the defense team's arguments have been broken down to their weakest points and our own strong points have been established. The process of creating the entire speech is the next task. We can choose to tailor our speech after a presentation model, which is an overall standardized disposition for our speech. You don't need to follow a standardized disposition, but it can help you give your speech some structure, and maximize the effectiveness of your arguments.

There are many kinds of presentation models. Which one you want to use depends upon what kind of speech or presentation you are giving. In our situation, where we are creating a legal argumentative speech aimed at winning support for our point of view, a classical Greek disposition model can be used. Our audience, the jurors, and the original Greek jurors are very similar. The classical Greek legal disposition goes like this:

Opening

Here one needs to interest the receiver in the subject and get them to feel goodwill towards you, if these things have not already been accomplished. This one can do by starting with something concrete, an event that is an example of the subject, or the like. If this event shows something like an unjust situation, it calls for audience sympathies, and thereby it indirectly shows that one has one's heart "in the right place."

In this situation, where the jurors know the lawyers and the case well, the story that is aimed at creating goodwill, should be about Fuhrman. This would address what the new rhetorical situation is about. In this case, I would choose the story about Fuhrman saving a black man that is accused of murdering a white man. It could sound like this:

> One day in downtown L.A., a white man was murdered, shot to death.
>
> Shortly after this, a black man was accused of committing the murder. This black man was in deep trouble, because his fingerprints were on the murder weapon. Everybody thought that this man had killed the victim. But then a detective came forward and got the charges dropped against the defendant because he had gotten reliable information that somebody else had committed the murder with the defendant's gun.
>
> This detective's name is Mark Fuhrman!
>
> Now if Fuhrman is hell-bent on framing black people, as the defense wants you to believe, why would he go out of his way to save a black man that everybody else thought was guilty?

The Story

This part builds on the beginning and tells about the subject one wants to do something about in a more broad and general way.

In this case it would be a further elaboration of Fuhrman's good deeds and relationships with people from minority groups. Furthermore, it would entail a general attempt at turning the case back to being a murder case, not a civil rights case, since this would be the general aim when we address the new rhetorical situation.

Dividing

Here you deliver a more analytical explanation for what you have talked about in the story part. One divides, distinguishes, shows cause and effect and so on.

In our example we would go back to talking about the evidence against Simpson, since this is the rhetorical situation we want to get back to addressing.

Confirming

You offer your solution, proposal, and the like, to what needs to be done. You back it up with thorough reasoning that shows that this will solve the problem, or improve the situation explained previously.

Refutation

You take the opponent's counter-arguments into consideration, and list the most important ones-the ones that have already been put forth, and/ or the ones that presumably will be put forth. You should not attack the motives behind them, but instead show that they do not work, will have the wrong effect, are too expensive, have big side effects, or the like. Here we would be putting in our counter-arguments concerning our opponent's weak argumentation. We would only attack our opponent's motives indirectly, where we have chosen to use the counter-argumentation form labeled "attacking the argumentation form." By primarily attacking the argumentation form, this in itself legitimizes the indirect accusations against the opponent's motives.

Conclusion

Here you conclude, that the solution you have come to is the best, when everything has been taken into consideration. You can end up with going back to the beginning that will be changed if the solution you have put forth is implemented.

In our case, it would emphasize that justice will be served, no matter if you are rich or poor. Everybody is equal under the law. In order to know what to stress in the end, it is necessary to go back and look at your main theme. In this case it is rich against poor.

There is no doubt that it would have been difficult to win a case against Johnnie Cochran and the other meticulously picked defense lawyers as they undeniably were able to squeeze the most out of this case and get as much as they could out of the rhetorical situation.

A subject such as race may be difficult to handle as it is such a delicate issue in America, especially at a time when political correctness rages throughout the country. However, I still believe that it would have been possible if top priority had been given to defending the image and morals of the police, and if the large-scale conspiracy theory had been attacked as illogical and improbable. A meek attempt was made to this effect when it was stated that logically it was not possible to falsify all the evidence, and, secondly, if there were a slight substance to the allegations it would have taken a giant conspiracy, including scores of people, to effect. These statements were drowned in the abundance of arguments.

Moreover, the defense lawyers' image and morals should have been attacked. That would have been an efficient way for the prosecution to get out of their defensive stand and at the same time it would have been possible to raise their own image and morals by tarnishing the opponent's ethos. For instance:

> Here's this hand-picked group of defense lawyers who are making tons of money by searching their minds to come up with alternative theories to get a rich murderer acquitted. If this man isn't made to pay for his crimes, it's due to one thing only. He's rich.

There were also excellent possibilities for laboring the theme "There's another law for the rich than for the rest of us." It would have provided an opportunity for cutting the strings of identification and solidarity that Cochran tries to tie between the black jurors and O.J. Simpson. This would have exposed some of Cochran's rhetorical strategies:

> Here's Johnnie Cochran bringing out both God and the devil. Here he is trying to talk like Martin Luther King and comparing himself to Malcolm X. This man is not Martin Luther King. This man is not Malcolm X. This man is not even a lawyer. He's an actor making loads of money manipulating you. I'm no match for him as I'm simply a lawyer and only capable of stating facts.

In this respect the opportunities for the prosecutors to make a virtue of how inferior they are were excellent. The theme "I'm not too clever but I am honest"- I'm not a speaker ...

Included in this argument is an attack on Cochran's image and morals by insinuating hubris-that he compares himself to Martin Luther King-and thereby abuses a highly esteemed person's good reputation. On this basis this could be taken a step further to attack the theme racism:

> This is not a case about racism, it's not an instance of white supremacy over blacks. It's an instance of a man's supremacy over a woman. This is not a case about blacks vs. whites. It's a case about rich vs. poor. Look around, do you believe that there'd have been all this fuss had it been a poor man? Look at the defense team-the dream team. Do you believe any of them would've been here had it been a poor man? I tell you who'd have been here had it been a poor man. *I'd have been* here and *Darden* would've been here. It's our job to make sure that murderers get their punishment whether they're rich or poor -a murderer is a murderer.

As public prosecutor Marcia Clark may emphasize her idealism to improve her image and morals. The sentence "rich or poor-a murderer is a murderer" could have been used as a sort of key word. The contrast and the repetition could have carried the theme: "There's another law for the rich than for the rest of us" at the same time it could have carried the ideal: we are all equal before the law. Another good slogan could have been: "This is about murder, money, and manipulation." This alliteration could have been repeated throughout the prosecution's closing statement like Cochran's "If it doesn't fit, you must acquit." The accusation against the police could in this respect have been turned 180 degrees:

> The only thing the police may be blamed for in this case is turning a blind eye to O.J.'s violent and psychopathic behavior towards this young woman simply because the man was rich and famous. No, we're all color-blind when it comes to wealth. Then we're not talking about race, we are talking about power. This man could beat his wife in public places and no one interfered. Was it because he was black? Hardly. No, ladies and gentlemen, it was because he was rich. They say the police did nothing to find other suspects. But, ladies and gentlemen, it's not only the police that were unable to come up with an alternative suspect, this million-dollar defense team as well has not been able to come up with another suspect. Why is that? Because there isn't any! Why do their explanations sound far-fetched? Because they are far-fetched!

I believe that the prosecution should have consistently and efficiently refuted the accusations of racism and bias on the part of the police. It would have been a wise tactic to take the offensive instead of being on the defense. I also do not think that the actions of the police in this case have been racist in any way. The police officer, Vannatter, neither said nor did anything racist. Still, he and Mark Fuhrman are called the twin devils of deception. This is because Vannatter was the one to collect and keep Simpson's blood sample until it was handed over to the forensic expert. Therefore, it is inevitable that he is linked up with Fuhrman if the conspiracy theory is to hold water. No one verifiably said or did anything racist in this case. Concerning Mark Fuhrman, it is true that he had made racist and derogatory remarks about blacks, but there is nothing to indicate that he acted in accordance with these statements in this or previous cases.

The tactic of being straightforward and blunt may be employed when, as in this case, we have a favorable case. In addition to contradicting the concrete statements made by Cochran, Marcia Clark could have turned them 180 degrees and thereby enabling herself to respond to some of Cochran's postulates and still be on the offensive:

> Johnnie Cochran claims it's odd that we haven't found more of Nicole Brown's and Ron Goldman's blood in Simpson's house and car. He says that since we're not swimming in blood, it's planted. Of course we're not stamping around in blood, even though Cochran seemingly wants us to do that. The man wants to hide his crime. It would've seemed odd had he left obvious traces. Simpson wanted to erase all traces of the crime he had committed, but that's not easy.

Cochran's words about Hitler, Mark Fuhrman, and the like, could have been turned around by pointing out the audacity of comparing the police and the prosecution with Hitler seeing that one of O.J. Simpson's victims actually was a Jew. And so his Jewish family has to sit here and listen to the case against O.J. Simpson being compared to the murder of five million Jews, something, which evidently did offend Fred Goldman, the murdered Ron Goldman's father.[103]

These were some examples of what could have been done to remedy some of the shortcomings of Marcia Clark's closing speech. It must, however, be held in mind that it is always easy to be wise in retrospect. At the same time we cannot know whether this change of response actually would have changed the course of events. It is, however, interesting to see how Daniel Petrocelli, the leading counsel for the Goldman family in the subsequent civil case, actually used a lot of the themes and rhetorical strategies that are suggested here: "Their defense to all of this should start with the 'D' words... It's desperation. It's deception. It's dishonesty."[104] Petrocelli asked the jurors what a guilty man does when confronted with massive evidence:

> What does he do? What does this guy do? He hires an army of lawyers, experts, investigators, consultants... They sit down and they figure out what to say about all this evidence... What you have heard in this courtroom, ladies and gentlemen, for the last four months, is what a guilty man has to say in response to all this

> evidence: It's all planted. It's all contaminated. All the photos are fake... Every witness is lying or mistaken. There is a conspiracy the likes of which never before has been witnessed-all to get me... That's what a guilty man does.[105]

The prosecution in the criminal case against Simpson only superficially touched upon the ludicrousness and physical impossibility of a mega-conspiracy against Simpson personally. They mainly indirectly tried to refute these conspiracy theories and prove Simpson's guilt by using logic and logistic as when it came to the time aspect, whether Simpson had time to commit the murders or not. As opposed to the criminal case, we here see that Petrocelli takes the offensive both regarding the accusations he makes against Simpson of having committed the double murder and regarding the accusations made against the police and the public authorities. Not only is this position better to be in, it is in addition a far more appropriate role for a public prosecutor or in this case a lawyer for the plaintiff to be in. He must change the state of affairs and convince the jurors that Simpson is liable for the murders in essence convict him in a civil sense. As that is a change of the status quo, his arguments must overcome the principle of inertia, which is our natural resistance against change, and show weightier arguments in support of his point of view than those the defendant's lawyer will have to come up with to maintain the status quo.

The reason why we have to come up with better arguments when we want to change something is that we know things as they are, but we cannot totally predict what a change will bring. It is also often easier to maintain things as they are. Status quo also often represents lots of work and adjustments that have occurred over time. We protect the work and efforts we have put into shaping things into the way they are. This could be everything from wanting to change the law, to arguing about how to go about doing the housework. In certain circumstances our tendency to want to maintain the status quo springs from our reluctance to admit that we have done something wrong, or that we, in the past, could have done things in a better way. Sometimes, asking someone to accept new methods or new ideas is to ask them to admit past failings.

So we can say that the argumentation in the criminal case was divided in two, an accusation against Simpson and an accusation against the police and the public authorities. Marcia Clark and Christopher Darden only acted as prosecutors when it came to Simpson's guilt but were made to act as defense lawyers for the police and public authorities, a battle they lost because they did not take it seriously, while at the same time being unable to sweep this aspect off. In that respect, the roles of prosecutor and defense lawyer were reversed. When the prosecution lost the battle over the morals and ethics of the police and public authorities, the arguments against Simpson were sapped like a tree with its roots cut.

In his closing statement Petrocelli made it clear that it was not only a prerequisite of the conspiracy theory that dozens of people had collaborated in committing a miscarriage of justice against Simpson, it was indeed the very same people who had treated him like a hero and looked the other way for years while Simpson beat up his wife. He was, as Petrocelli pointed out, the last man they wanted to convict. Petrocelli made this clear by focusing upon it in both his closing statement and his rebuttal. Petrocelli said it directly instead of stressing the evidence. But it must though be kept in mind that Petrocelli had the benefit of hindsight.

To sum up, we can say that Marcia Clark's response to the new rhetorical situation should have been more focused and included a defense of the image, morals, and ethics of the police and public authorities. At the same time, it would have been to her advantage had she, to a greater extent, taken the offensive by questioning the morals and ethics of the defense. Moreover, her case would have benefited had she focused more on the impossibility and ludicrousness of a gigantic conspiracy against Simpson personally. That all these people's efforts and all this work was only to get a single person.

It is in this respect important to be aware of the defense team's sliding argumentation reaching all the way from, "they are deliberately trying to frame this man," to "they are just trying to cover-up for each other."

Ways of explaining away the evidence

Willful intent	The Big Conspiracy-O.J. was being framed by all the police The Code of Silence- not all police officers were involved in framing O.J. but those that were not were either *covering up* for those that were and/or *turning their heads*. Evidence Manipulation-The police were either *boosting their case* by planting additional evidence or *covering up for incompetence*.
No intent	The police were *incompetent*.

Since the prosecution didn't close all the entrances to this argumentation, the defense team was able to slide right by the prosecution's counter-reasoning. In the prosecution's rebuttal, they worked hard at trying to close the door to the argument that it was a deliberate conspiracy. But they didn't acknowledge the argument, that the police were just trying to cover up for each other's incompetence. After the trial, several jury members stated that they didn't believe that it was a deliberate attempt to frame Simpson, but that the investigation had just started out badly, and that the police had been trying to cover up for that ever since. Because the racist framing theory was so inflammatory, it was easy for the prosecution to overlook this lesser allegation. An attempt on Clark's part to close this door could have sounded something like this:

> All these people, who in most cases didn't even know each other, do not suddenly start covering up for each other. Why should they? They are civil servants! When have you ever known them to take such a course? There is probably more imagination in Johnnie Cochran's head than there has ever been in our work. Now these are good people, but they do not have the ability to perform nor preach in front of a nationwide audience.

In the last statement, there's a small amount of humor. Clark can say these things about civil servants, since she herself is a civil servant. This statement would fall under the topos: "*He is not to bright, but he is a good person.*" This is the topos that Darden and Clark also could have used concerning themselves, as compared with the defense team. By using the same topos throughout their argumentation, the prosecution presents a coherent view to the jury members. In this way the prosecution can present themselves as *dumb but good*, contrary to the defense being *smart but evil.* If one wants to seek acceptance for one's point of view, it is better to be perceived as dumb but good, than smart but evil, since kind and dumb people are not so threatening as smart, but evil persons.

Because of the nature of the case, too much humor would seem distasteful. Certain kinds of humor can be used to move people from one opinion to another since humor often puts two things together that haven't been paired before. This opens up the possibility of seeing things from a new perspective, and thereby the possibility of changing one's mind.[106]

Clark needed to defend the two key players on her team who were being character assassinated, Darden and Fuhrman. Here is an example of how she could have defended Darden, and still be on the offensive:

> Now Cochran wants to call my colleague Dr. Darden. I find it far more appropriate to refer to him as the Reverend Cochran. It sure is only on Sunday mornings that I hear that many quotes from the Bible. I can understand why Cochran is so taken by the Bible. It has the answer to a lot of things. Even a situation like this. As Jesus says: You don't make your words true by embellishing them with religious lace. In making your speech sound more religious, it becomes less true. This quote comes from a paragraph named empty promises. And that is what Cochran's speech is about. Luring you away from the truth with empty promises.[107]

We here see how it is possible always to end up in the offensive position, no matter what part of the opponent's claims you are countering.

The new rhetorical situation demanded an answer from the prosecution to the accusations and allegations put forward by the defense. It is, however, important not to get bogged down in details, neither to your own evidence, nor to the defense team's innumerable allegations. The prosecution's dilemma was that they feared to omit evidence or counter-arguments, which could have been decisive in the jurors' verdict. To solve this problem it is beneficial to use *Preterition*.

Preterition is the pretended sacrifice of an argument. The argument is briefly outlined while the speaker is announcing that he will not use it. The sacrifice of the argument satisfies the properties, while it also suggests that the other arguments are sufficiently strong to make this one unnecessary.[108] In this case it could have been done like this:

> We are not going to get into the fact that the nurse that drew the blood from Simpson has stated that he made a mistake when he estimated the amount of blood he drew, and that therefore, there is no missing blood.
>
> We are not going to waste time wondering why Simpson cannot remember when he got a scar-producing cut. Neither are we going to bore you with the details of how this team of well-paid defense lawyers has gone out of their way to create a theory that could somehow acquit this wealthy man. We will not get into the impossibility of more than a dozen people, that in many cases didn't know each other, lying in order to frame Simpson. We are also not going to wonder about why people that on earlier occasions overlooked Simpson's violent behavior towards his wife, now suddenly want to frame him. We are only going to ask you why people of different races, including black, would be involved in a racist plot against Simpson?

It is here seen how this technique makes it possible to briefly mention one's counter-reasoning, evidence, and refutations while at the same time opening up the opportunity for strengthening and backing one's focus and main allegations.

This technique could also have been used successfully when dealing with the aspect of Mark Fuhrman's racist remarks. It could have given the prosecution an opportunity to deal with the issue, without focusing upon it:

> We are not going to get into Fuhrman being treated for halluci-

nating about violent behavior in the past. Neither are we going to stress the sad fact that this man somehow thought that he was impressing this young aspiring screenwriter by using derogatory terms. We are going to spare you the details of how none of what this frustrated individual claims he has done, seems to have taken place.

But we are going to ask you why a former black police officer would contribute to this racial conspiracy by claiming that Simpson confessed to him that he had dreams of killing his wife. We are not asking you to believe Fuhrman; we are asking you to believe the other fifty people involved in this case.

A common way of reasoning is to point out what has happened on earlier occasions. Analogies can point out inconsistencies in your opponent's argumentation, and thereby move the burden of proof over to the opponent.

The defense team used this technique often when they wanted to move the burden of proof to the prosecution concerning their conspiracy and contamination claims. This was done by mentioning situations where such acts had taken place.

The trick in moving the burden of proof is that an analogy argument demands a reaction. If the audience accepts the comparison, and the opponent does not react, the one that applied the analogy has scored a point.

When one counters an analogy argument, one can apply three strategies:[109]

(1) One can question the previous case, and question the lessons that the debater wants to convey to the current issue.
(2) One can question how appropriate the connection is between the example and the issue at hand.
(3) One can come up with a contra analogy that is able to top the previous analogy.

An example of the second strategy could sound something like this:

Scheck compares the handling of the blood samples in this case with tests from Selmark, where cross-contamination occurred

> because blood samples were handled at the same time as the reference sample. First of all, I would like to make it totally clear that the blood sample from Simpson wasn't handled at the same time as the reference samples, but before the blood samples were even taken out of their plastic bags. Second of all, I would like to make it totally clear that when the cross-contamination occurred at Selmark, the DNA from the "real killer" was still present in the blood samples. It had not just vanished as the defense claims in this case.

The prosecution could have started by "vaccinating" the jurors against Cochran's arguments concerning racism, that is to say, prepared the jurors for the defense's potential use of such arguments and thereby made them more-or-less immune to these arguments. Like a vaccination, you give them a touch of the disease, just enough to make them immune against the disease itself. This could have been put into the opening statement to plant the seed in the jury's mind from the beginning. The opening statement would have been a good place to apply the vaccination technique, since it is always harder to get your message through when your audience has already been convinced of something else. Christopher Darden could have said:

> Ladies and gentlemen, we are going to show you that O.J. Simpson is guilty of this horrible double murder. During this trial we are going to show you that he left so many traces and fatal pieces of evidence behind, that the only way the defense team is going to get him acquitted, is by turning this case into a case about racism.

This would probably have caused some objections from the defense team, but it could definitely have been argued that they were just stating what they were going to show during the trial itself. And, as with the defense's opening statement, the words would have been said and couldn't be taken back.

You can vaccinate against an argument even though it may not be used by the opponent. But you should be aware, that you may give your audience or opponent an idea that they otherwise may not have thought about. It is worth noticing that this issue may come up in the deliberation between the jurors. By having touched upon the subject, one makes sure that one is heard on the subject.

The anticipation of an argument is a sign of competence. The effect of a speaker foreseeing an argument is that the argument will not diminish the confidence felt for the speaker when it is put forward by his opponent. An anticipated argument, however effectively it may be advanced, has lost its critical power, since it has already been mentioned and rejected by the opponent.

After the rhetorical situation has been changed, or an attempt at changing it has been made, there are several techniques one can use in order to take the sting out of the arguments advanced. A way of lessening the strength of arguments is to emphasize their routine, easily foreseeable character, making them old stuff to the hearer. It could sound something like this:

> I guess this is what defense lawyers defending a murder has to say: "My client was framed." And what else is there really to say when all the evidence points at him! You all know that this is what a person in Simpson's situation has to say. But, let's look at the realities in this case …

The advantage of this technique is, first of all, that the audience is reminded of similar circumstances where the method the opponent employs has been used. Not only does it help in classifying the arguments as manipulative, it also deprives the audience of the feeling of being part in "finding the truth." The audience cannot listen to the opponent's argumentation, and have a feeling that they together with him or her are finding the truth. This means that there isn't the same degree of commitment to the conclusion reached in the argumentation. Secondly, this approach does not demand that one has to anticipate the situation. This method contributes to strengthening the impression of one's own competence and thereby one's ethos.

An argument can lose its force if it can be shown, by labeling it with a technical term, that it belongs to the category of arguments that the theoreticians have picked out and classified as overbold. The audience, thus enlightened and enabled to recognize the banality of the argument and to appreciate that it is a device, will retroactively modify its appraisal of its strength. Conversely, the one attacking it will have given useful evidence of his competence. It could sound something like this:

> What Scheck is doing here by throwing all these allegations around, is what is called "the cluster bomb" technique. The idea is that all these allegations and claims are going to cause the opponent to run frantically around trying to respond to all of these. At the same time it is meant to confuse the jury, so that they will overlook the main issue, and their weak points.

A comparison of Cochran and Hitler's ways of reasoning would have been brilliant in this connection. I will discuss further the similarities between Hitler's reasoning and Cochran's reasoning in the chapter, "Cochran and Hitler."

One may go further than just to predict and classify the opponent's arguments. A further step may be taken to draw the opposite or a different conclusion from his or her reasoning. This antidote against the opponent's reasoning may be highly effective as the opponent's arguments are used to favor oneself. In this way it is, in addition to incriminating one's opponent, possible to create a coherent view of the world, something that appeals to most people, as many are of the opinion that truth should be unambiguous and relatively simple. This could have sounded something like this:

> Cochran says that the police are incompetent and partial in their judgment in this case. And you know what, he is right! They should have stopped this spousal abuse long before it turned into a murder case. If they had not been so star-stricken they could have prevented this rich man's abuse of this young woman from turning into a double homicide

I am not going to get into the specifics of the evidence, such as whether a photo of Simpson wearing a pair of Bruno Magli shoes or a bloody fingerprint would have mattered. Even though mistakes were made, the prosecution still had an overwhelming amount of evidence. If you can make the blood evidence go away, even the part of it that was collected before any blood was drawn from Simpson, who says they couldn't have counter pictures of Simpson wearing Bruno Magli shoes? It is not necessarily any different from having pictures of Simpson wearing the same kind of gloves. The problem with the new evidence, or the evidence that was not introduced in the case is that we don't have the defense team's response. If the prosecution is not able to correct the basic flaws in their argumentation, the amount of evidence is irrelevant.

If you, for instance have not tackled the problem of your audience thinking that there is a conspiracy going on, further evidence will just confirm this belief. That is why the basic bone structure has to be in place.

It is important to know that the highest degree of objectivity, in itself, is not the goal within practical argumentation. We need *opinions* that spring from our filings, to make our audience feel that what we are talking about is *interesting* and *relevant.*

Of course it is not possible to say with certainty to what extent a different argumentation on the part of the prosecution would have changed the new rhetorical situation. We can only note that the prosecution made no appreciable attempts at changing the new rhetorical situation except for a few statements presented in their rebuttal on the last day of the trial. This might be due to a combination of them not knowing what to do and a denial of the existence and justification of what the new situation called for.

What characterizes an effective argumentative speech or text is the ability to stress one's theme right from the beginning. During the rest of one's speech or text, one needs to state the reasons for one's position, documenting and clarifying it. It is important to make sure that your audience understands the relevance the particular argument has to your main theme. It is not enough merely to repeat one's claim, one has to get into the details with reasoning. Above all one should avoid sounding inconsistent.

In the end one has to gather the threads to support the overall theme in the case. Argumentation is most effective if one gives thorough information about the reasons for one's opinion, and not claim that one's opponent is wrong in everything he says.

Traits that characterize a winner are being obliging and the ability to clearly stress the main disagreements in a polite way. One needs to debate in a friendly way, at the same time as one stands firmly upon the central issues in one's point of view. One should not try to hide that one, first and foremost, wants to influence others to think the same as oneself. In general one should be more interested in showing that what one is saying is right, than showing that one's opponent is wrong.

In other words, you need to be firm, without being hostile. You need to point out where you disagree, and why you are right, without threatening the opponent's integrity and pride more than necessary. This has to be done in a way that shows that what the audience ends up thinking about the issue means a lot to you. The winning traits-*preciseness, firmness, energy, and engagement*-characterize what we in general view as *believability*.

We have now been looking at some of the ways Marcia Clark could have responded to the new rhetorical situation. In the next chapter we are going to have a look at the similarities between Cochran's argumentation and the argumentation techniques used in Adolf Hitler's, *Mein Kampf*.

18. COCHRAN AND HITLER

The hearer always sympathizes with one who speaks emotionally, even though he really says nothing.

Aristotle

The strategies used by Cochran to manipulate his audience are not new. They have been used in the past to move whole nations, even into war. An example in the twentieth century is Adolf Hitler and Nazi Germany. It is ironic that Cochran in this case uses Hitler as an example as they both use many of the same manipulative strategies.

Hitler's book *Mein Kampf* and Cochran's book *Journey to Justice*, are both descriptions of these men's struggle for their cause. They are both at war against an enemy, Hitler, the Jews, Cochran, the police. They demonize them and want to beat them by any means available.

They both, at least initially, worked within the democratic system, but they had no scruples about what rhetorical means they were willing to deploy in order to win the vote of their audience. This lack of ethical inhabitation stems from putting the cause before the means.

Since their audience was basically the same type, a frustrated and economical disenfranchised German population of the 1930s and frustrated and economical disenfranchised inner-city blacks of the 1990s, they end up employing the same rhetorical tactics, since they are the most effective with this kind of an audience.

In Hitler's *Mein Kampf*, we see how Hitler, like a medicine man, concocted a panacea which is capable of healing disruption and disputes in a sick democracy and unite people under a banner. All in the name of democracy Hitler found his panacea, his cure for "all that torment you".[110]

If we replace Hitler's race theories with Cochran's racism theories and put the police and public authorities where Hitler put the Jews, we clearly see that Cochran and Hitler used the same concepts in a similar way. As soon as Hitler has identified his enemy, all "evidence" becomes self-affirmative. If indisputable evidence was found to prove that the Jewish worker [*the police*] was deeply opposed to "the international capitalist Jew conspiracy" [*racist conspiracy*], Hitler answered with unbeaten certainty: This is just an example of how wily the "Jewish plot" [*the police conspiracy*] is.[111]

In this way it was possible for Cochran to strengthen his position, paradoxically inversely proportional to the amount of evidence against Simpson.

Hitler and Cochran use the religious aspect in similar ways to their own advantage. Every time they get to an important aspect they use associative tricks in order to move on. They do that every time they come across a strategically important moment, all the way to a vision of the end of the world, out of which they re-emerge with their watchwords: "I do now believe to be acting with the mind of the almighty Creator when I say: *In resisting the Jew [the police] I fight for the Lord's Creation*."[112]

How is it possible to succeed in exploiting religion in this way and convert what in reality is an economic question, rich vs. poor, into a religious question? In this respect it is significant that Hitler succeeded in doing it in Germany in the 1930s with its severe economic problems and Cochran succeeded in the U.S.A. in the 1990s with its marked polarization of material benefits. This materialization of a religious pattern is, an extremely effective propaganda weapon in a time when religion has lost clout due to centuries of capitalist materialism.[113]

By acting as a doomsday prophet, Cochran, like Hitler, avoids having to come up with a distinct logical analysis of the course of events. As they were both able to produce a noneconomic interpretation of the economic problems, their messages were highly effective in deflecting attention away from the economic factors in the conflict.

Hitler's race theories and Cochran's racism theories provide a noneconomic interpretation of an economic phenomenon. But how can it be that indeed the religious aspect is so suitable for this purpose?

The idea of the church which primarily deals with questions of "personality," with questions of moral improvement, naturally focuses on the necessity for an action of the will against the individual's immediate desires. Thus its opposition to a purely "environmental" understanding of people. Thus its focus on the "person". Thus its tendency to seek noneconomic explanations of economic phenomena. Hitler's ideas of noneconomic "reasons" for conflicts are influenced by this.[114] This thought pattern can therefore also be used by Cochran to explain away economic issues such as Simpson's wealth, and the standard treatment of poor (black) defendants.

Cochran and Hitler use the church's resistance to social explanations for economic conflicts, but it is still surprising that these jurors were able to feel a community with a person like Simpson who, in his extreme wealth, lived in a world completely different from their own. On this Hitler writes in *Mein Kampf*: "The longing for unity is so strong that people are always ready to meet you halfway if you offer them a notion of unity even if it has nothing to do with reality."[115]

Both Cochran and Hitler used an endless amount of repetitions. Many of Cochran's repetitions have almost become sayings in American society, such as: "If it doesn't fit, you must acquit," or "It just doesn't fit." It is possible that an equally important appeal was not so much the repetition *per se* but the fact that Hitler and Cochran through the repetition arranged a complete philosophy of life for people who had only experienced the world in fragments.[116]

On the subject of repetition Hitler writes:

> The receptivity of the great masses is very limited, their intelligence is small, but their power of forgetting is enormous. In consequence of these facts, all effective propaganda must be limited to a very few points and must harp on these in slogans until the last member of the public understands what you want him to understand by your slogan. As soon as you sacrifice this slogan and try to be many-sided, the effect will piddle away, for the crowd can neither digest nor retain the material offered.[117]

> ...the most brilliant propagandist technique will yield no success unless one fundamental principle is borne in mind constantly and with unflagging attention. It must confine itself to a few points and repeat them over and over. Here, as so often in this world, persistence is the first and most important requirement for success.[118]

We see how the important points of the prosecutions argumentation could get lost in the almost one year-long trial.

Both Hitler and Cochran offer a "curing" union via a made-up devil made gradually convincing by means of ordinary marketing and repetition techniques. The quotation below from *Mein Kampf* furthermore shows that besides the purely logical reasons there may be another reason why Cochran wanted to make the whole police force and the public authorities, collectively appear as a homogeneous group in collusion with Fuhrman and the devil:

> ...efficiency primarily dependent on the ability to avoid the dispersed attention of the people and instead focus it on one common enemy. The more uniform the militant will, the greater magnetic effect and impact. It is to the merits of the true great leader when different opponents emerge as one as weak and unstable characters otherwise will be confused by the variety of opponents and maybe thereby have doubts about their own cause.
>
> As soon as the tottering masses are faced with too many enemies, objectivity intervenes and advances the question whether in reality only the enemies are wrong and their own nation or movement right.
>
> At the same time the first paralysis occurs. Therefore, a number of different enemies must always be viewed as one in order that the masses perceive the war as being against one party. This reinforces the belief in your own goals and the firmness towards the enemy.[119]

Looked at from the outside, it may be hard to understand how a juror can reject so many indicators and arguments that point in a direction other than one's own conviction. If we look at how we understand our surroundings based on paradigms we, up to a certain point, keep defending our way of viewing the world and either reject conflicting elements or try to force them into our own philosophy. A change in paradigm usually does not happen gradually, but jerkily, as at a religious revival.

A new paradigm is accepted less because of its previous merits than because of the promises connected to the future. Based on this we can say that it was even harder for the prosecution to make the jurors change their paradigm, as based on the worldview offered by Cochran, where they were promised a better future with peaceful coexistence and equal opportunities for all. This must be seen in connection with the fact that the prosecution "merely" wishes justice for two people who lost their lives.

What characterizes a fanatic is that he or she thinks that the aim legitimizes the means. Every action or means is legitimate to use in order to achieve a certain end result. Even to kill people or otherwise destroy people's lives becomes of minor importance compared to the desired aim. In this quote from *Mein Kampf* we see this shine through in Hitler's thoughts about propaganda and its use: "Is propaganda a means or an end? It is a means and must therefor be judged with regard to its end. It must consequently take a form calculated to support the aim which it serves."[120]

In Cochran's quest to win in the O.J. Simpson case, we see the same willingness to apply every propagandistic means necessary in order to achieve the end goal, to have his client acquitted and thereby defeat the police. As Cochran describes it in his book *Journey to Justice*, winning the Simpson case was the ultimate victory over the LAPD.

This quote from *Main Kampf* illustrates Hitler's deliberate use of emotions and his awareness of the importance of understanding one's audience: "The art of propaganda lies in understanding the emotional ideas of the great masses and finding, through a psychologically correct form, the way to the attention and thence to the heart of the broad masses."[121]

Both Hitler and Cochran understood the importance of the

emotional appeal, that you have to appeal to people's emotions in order to get some interest or action out of them. Furthermore, both Hitler and Cochran understood their audience well enough to be able to appeal successfully to them at an emotional level. We don't have a written statement from Cochran stating his thoughts on this matter, but we can see a very secure and massive use of the emotional appeal in Cochran's argumentation, not least in his closing statement in the Simpson case. On the use of emotion Hitler states:

> To overcome this barrier of instinctive aversion, of emotional hatred, of prejudiced rejection, is a thousand times harder than to correct a faulty or erroneous scientific opinion. False concepts and poor knowledge can be eliminated by instruction, the resistance of the emotions never. Here only an appeal to these mysterious powers themselves can be effective...[122]

Hitler states that you have to appeal to emotions in order to combat emotions. In the Simpson case, where two people were brutally murdered, strong emotions are evoked by the nature of the case. Cochran also chose to combat those strong feelings with counter-emotions.

We have been looking at how you implement some of these rhetorical techniques. But what about the ethical aspect of all of this? This is what we are going to look at in the next chapter, "Decent Argumentation."

19. DECENT ARGUMENTATION

The characters which accompany wealth are plain for all to see. The wealthy are insolent and arrogant, being mentally affected by the acquisition of wealth, for they seem to think that they possess all good things; for wealth is a kind of standard of value of everything else, so that everything seems purchasable by it.

Aristotle

Following the trial there was a great deal of discussion in the U.S. both publicly and within legal circles, as to whether Johnnie Cochran's defense was within the framework of what can be considered decent argumentation. Some claim that a defense lawyer may do anything to win his client's acquittal, that this is actually demanded of the defense lawyer. If this is correct, it would indeed mean that no form of legal ethics existed. A defense lawyer would be comparable to a prostitute who without bounds sells her services to the highest bidder. Though there may be quite a few people who share this view, I do think it is going too far.

The scope for how far a defense lawyer may go is very wide, especially within criminal law, as it is a human being's life or freedom that is at stake. There are, however, certain things that are required by statute and in turn others that are recommended that one follow, taking into account good legal ethics.

Defense lawyers are under an obligation to not intentionally mislead a jury. This has been specified accordingly:

A lawyer may not:

(1) Knowingly advance a claim or defense that is unwarranted under existing law, except that he may advance such a claim

or defense if it can be supported by good faith argument for an extension, modification, or reversal of existing law.
(2) Conceal or knowingly fail to disclose that which he is required by law to reveal.
(3) Knowingly use perjured testimony or false evidence.
(4) Knowingly make a false statement of law or fact.
(5) Participate in the creation or preservation of evidence when he knows, or it is obvious, that the evidence is false.[123]

At the same time, defense lawyers are under an obligation to defend their clients vigorously. The question is whether this latter requirement also includes having your client acquitted. Can the duty to defend your client and vigorously advocate his case be translated into doing everything to have your client acquitted?

Recently, several debaters have put forward the argument that a lawyer also has a duty to society. In any event, there is no doubt that Johnnie Cochran and Berry Scheck were on the verge of what is unacceptable.

Due to Cochran's behavior, and a number of irregularities in the procedure, the case was very close to being retried. To give an example: In the defense team's opening statement, Cochran and the rest of the defense team said that they were going to present two witnesses during the trial that they had not informed the prosecution about. Legal procedure dictates that you have to inform the opposite side about what witnesses you are going to call to the stand during the trial. On top of this, Cochran criticized the prosecution for not having mentioned these witnesses to the jury, insinuating that the prosecution wanted to hide their existence. Besides that the prosecution was not made aware of these witnesses existence, it can be said that it is not the duty of the prosecution to call attention to the opponent's witnesses.

It later turned out that the defense chose not to call these witnesses to the stand. There has been some speculation as to whether the defense simply wanted to raise doubt in the jurors' minds about Simpson's guilt at the outset of the trial and that they never had any real intention of calling these witnesses to the stand, as they did not seem credible. The defense admitted having made a mistake in not informing the prosecution of the existence of these witnesses. This was a violation of the legal procedure and it nearly got the defense into serious trouble. Even though the defense apologized in the presence of the jurors and the prosecution got the opportunity to explain, it may be claimed that the damage to a certain extent had been done. If intentional, this act would fall within item two on the above list.

An example of an irregularity committed during the trial was that at a certain point Judge Ito's wife, who is employed in the police department, got involved in the trial itself. That happened when Fuhrman made some derogatory statements about her on the tapes previously mentioned. It was a question of whether to call her as a witness in the case. In that case, Judge Ito could no longer preside at the trial since a judge cannot adjudicate a case in which one of his own family members or close friends is involved. It was also a question of whether he could keep a neutral position in the case after hearing the derogatory remarks about his wife.

Initially, the prosecution demands that he resign, but that would imply a retrial of the case and at that point the case had been going on for more than six months. Therefore, the prosecution changes its mind and the trial continues, but only after both parties have agreed not to call Judge Ito's wife as a witness.

Not only the lawyers have to live up to certain standards, the jurors as well have a number of duties. This includes an obligation to take into consideration all the evidence before they deliver a verdict. They are made aware of this by the judge at the beginning of the trial.

The judge explains to the jurors that the lawyers' individual statements must not be viewed as the truth, but on the contrary as a biased pleading in the case. However, Cochran is under an obligation to not intentionally mislead the jury. Seeing that Johnnie Cochran, in his interpretation of the law to the jurors, says that if there is some of the evidence that they are not prepared to accept, reasonable doubt has been raised about the accused's guilt and therefore they have to disregard all the other evidence, it is fair to argue that Cochran intentionally misleads the jury and encourages them to disregard their legal obligation. This is seen in Cochran's statement: "If it doesn't fit, you must acquit."

That Cochran succeeded in misleading the jurors is seen by a juror stating after the trial that, "If one thing doesn't fit, you must acquit."

Scheck eased his way into claiming the same thing by stating:

> Each fact which is essential to complete a set of circumstances necessary to establish the defendant's guilt must be proven beyond a reasonable doubt. Each essential fact. That is what is special about a circumstantial evidence case. For each essential fact they have to prove it beyond a reasonable doubt. If they fail, if there is a reasonable doubt about an essential fact, you must acquit. Those are the rules.

This later enabled Scheck to say: "There is really no doubt either that they played with this sock, is there? And if that can happen, that is a reasonable doubt for this case period, end of sentence, end of case."

It is fair to claim that in this case Cochran and Scheck intentionally misinterpreted the law because the fact that one piece of circumstantial evidence is not proved beyond a reasonable doubt does not mean that the rest of the evidence loses its importance.

One of the reasons why Cochran was allowed to go as far as he did could be that he, at one time, as district attorney, had been the superior of the judge and the two lead prosecutors involved in the case.

According to American legislation, lawyers are not allowed to enter perjured testimony. But on the other hand, lawyers must observe professional secrecy, which forbids them to communicate their knowledge.

If Simpson had confided in him, and had he known that O.J. Simpson committed the murders, Cochran would not have been able to defend Simpson the way he did. Under the code of ethics governing American lawyers, Cochran would in that situation have had to either, withdraw from the case or just let Simpson tell his own version of what happened.

We cannot as a matter of course demand that argumentation should be objective. But we can put up the criterion that it be decent. Decent argumentation means that no indecent argumentation tricks aimed at deceiving the audience are deployed. Indecent argumentation methods are the lie, the suppression, and the distortion. A distortion is when you for some reason deliberately twist the truth, and thereby give your audience a false impression.

The question here is whether this particular situation-a lawyer who defends his client in court-does not call for some other criteria of what is regarded as decent. It cannot be said that suppression necessarily is an outright indecent quality in a defense lawyer. He is under an obligation to defend his client's case to the best of his abilities while at the same time, to a certain extent, upholding his professional secrecy.

On the other hand, I do believe that the lie, and in certain circumstances the distortion, in a legal setting, are covered by the concept of indecency.

In argumentation one can talk about how symmetrical a communication is i.e. the balance of strength between the opposite parties involved in a dispute. The less asymmetrical the communicative relations is, the less grave the indecency. It is rare that the relationship is completely symmetric. In a legal action no one will expect the lawyer to provide information that is directly prejudicial to his client. In principle, the situation is symmetric and the responsibility for the disclosure of evidence rests upon the parties' lawyers. But here also the demand for decency applies and support must not be the result of deception.

The part where Fuhrman and Vannatter are turned into a synonym for Hitler is indeed a fine example of a distortion balancing on the edge of what is reasonable. Another example of distortion, which balances on the borderline between lie and distortion, is when Cochran asserts that the incidents of domestic disturbances between Simpson and Nicole were not violent.[124]

One can also discuss whether it is decent to convert a murder case into something else in order to have one's client acquitted. It is a distortion of what the case is really about into something which is more favorable. Again here it may be asserted that Cochran intentionally tried to mislead the jury. It is in these situations that it may be difficult to find the borderline between an intentional attempt at misleading the jurors and a mere defense of a client's case to the best of one's abilities.

Moreover, it may be questioned whether Cochran does not intentionally advocate a defense which is outside the scope of the statutory authority. Statutory authority is the scope within which a case must be to warrant a charge or liability. If it falls outside the statutory authority, the accused is not liable and cannot be held liable for whatever it is he is charged with. In cases where, for example, an employee causes injury to another person outside of working hours his employer can usually not be held liable for any injury. To encourage the jurors to acquit Simpson in order to send a message and protest against racism and incompetence within the police is arguable outside the statutory authority.

This balancing act which Cochran and Scheck performed has the possibility of distortion, as it may be difficult to establish whether his intentions really are indecent, or whether it is simply a reflection of his understanding of the situation. For that very reason distortion must be held to be a particularly subtle form of indecency. It is a more dangerous form of reasoning than lie and suppression, indeed, because it is often difficult both to comprehend and attack. The concept of decency is dependent on the sender. Whether the reasoning is decent or not is primarily dependent on the sender's attitude to the audience. Indecent argumentation may be viewed as argumentation where the sender seeks to win support by deceiving the audience. If, for example, the sender makes support for his point of view conditional on whether the audience in the circumstances is unable to grasp the arguments, he has misused his privilege as a sender. An example of this could be a doctor that argues medical issues with a patient, using arguments that he knows are not true, but that he also knows his patient will not be able to recognize

You can question the effects of trying to raise racist feelings in the jury by calling two of the white officers involved in the case "twin devils of deception," a synonym for white devils. Cochran here makes it particularly subtle by covering the message up in a code that most whites would not be able to decode.

Although Cochran based his case on racism, he and Fuhrman are actually the involved parties in this case, who voiced any racists opinions. If we take into consideration that Fuhrman's statements were uttered several years prior to the case, Cochran is actually the only one stating racists opinions during the case itself. The jury being mainly Afro-American, he would, of course, also be the only one benefiting from it.

When does the indecent or partly indecent argumentation become a real problem? Indecent argumentation becomes dangerous argumentation if the sender speculates in a communicative relationship that lacks symmetry. This means that the two parties are not an equal match, and that the strongest party therefore can get away with manipulative strategies. Indecent argumentation becomes truly alarming when support is actually won for it. Then we can talk about demagogy and the like.

In addition to the purely strategic and technical similarities between Cochran and Hitler's reasoning methods we may assert that the demagogic aspect in many ways is similar in their reasoning methods as well. In all circumstances, initially they were both successful in their reasoning.

Now we are going to have a chance to judge for ourselves if Cochran and Scheck exceeded the lines of ethical argumentation based upon the standards of the legal community. You decide for yourself on which side of the line the specific deeds and statements belongs.

Ethical Lawyers are under an obligation to defend their clients vigorously.

Unethical (1) A lawyer may not knowingly advance a claim or defense that is unwarranted under existing law, except that he may advance such a claim or defense if it can be supported by good faith argument for an extension, modification, or reversal of existing law.

Cochran's statement to the jurors that they need to police the police through their verdict.

Ethical Lawyers are under an obligation to defend their clients vigorously.

Unethical (2) A lawyer may not conceal or knowingly fail to disclose that which he is required by law to reveal.

The defense team did not disclose certain witnesses to the prosecution that they intended to call during the case, a thing that you are procedurally bound to do. Since the prosecution didn't know about these witnesses, it enabled Cochran to say that the prosecution was trying to hide them from the jurors.

It ended up looking even more like a trick, when the defense team never presented these witnesses to the jurors. The significant part about this was that these witnesses were the basis for several of Cochran's claims in his opening statement.

Ethical Lawyers are under an obligation to defend their clients vigorously.

Unethical (4) A lawyer may not knowingly make a false statement of law or fact.

Cochran and Scheck's claim that if there is one part of the evidence that the jury members disregard, they have to disregard the entire load of evidence.

Ethical Lawyers are under an obligation to defend their clients vigorously.

Unethical (5) A lawyer may not participate in the creation or preservation of evidence when he knows or it is obvious that the evidence is false.

Scheck's claim that the dog hair, from Nicole Brown's Akita that were on the glove found at Simpson's estate were the soft belly hairs from the Akita. This was suppose to prove that the hair had not gotten on the glove by Simpson brushing up against something, but that the glove was initially found on the ground at Nicole Brown's house, where the dog supposedly lay on it, and then transported to Simpson's estate by Fuhrman.

Akitas are a double coated dog that have soft hairs all over their body which are found in a softer inner coat which they constantly shed. Therefore the hair on the glove could easily come form the dog being touched as the killer left the scene.

Scheck's claim that all the blood evidence had either been planted or contaminated. If we just look at the contamination issue, the entire original DNA from the "real killer" had to be totally deteriorated. This also means that all the control tests would had to have failed at the same time as contamination had to have taken place within each blood sample.

In a sense Cochran and Scheck were in the same dilemma as law and rhetoric in general: That there aren't significant and adequate ethics to hold them in place. Law and rhetoric have to find this route together by using concrete borderline cases to define the width and borders of this path.

On January 20, 1942, a small group of high-ranking Nazis held a conference at Wannsee, near Berlin, to discuss and lay out the plans for the "Final Solution to the Jewish Question," that is, for the destruction of European Jewry. Among the many noteworthy facts about this conference (now known as the Wannsee Conference) is that over half of the conference participants had Ph.Ds. In studying just this one small but highly significant detail from the Holocaust, we learn that education without compassion can sometimes be a very dangerous formula.

20. THE SUBSEQUENT CIVIL CASE

Those who either are, or seem to be, highly prosperous do not think they are likely to suffer anything; wherefore they are insolent, contemptuous, and rash, and what makes them such is wealth, strength, a number of friends, power.

Aristotle

In the subsequent civil case O. J. Simpson was sued for being liable for Nicole Simpson and Ron Goldman's deaths. In the state of California there is no maximum amount of damages that a person may be held liable to pay as a sanction for a criminal act he has committed. In this respect the jurors must take into consideration the extent of Simpson's liability in committing the crime and to what extent the amount will be financially damaging to him. In addition, the amount must be commensurate with the act committed.

In the civil case the jurors found O. J. Simpson liable for the deaths of Nicole Simpson and Ron Goldman and therefore liable to pay damages to the victims' families. The jury awarded $33.5 million in compensatory and punitive damages.

The jury consisted of six women and six men nine of them were white, one was of Spanish origind one of Asian origin, and the last was half-black, half-Asian. Originally, there was one black woman on the jury, but the defendants demanded that she be disqualified when they found out that her daughter had been working for the prosecution during the criminal case against Simpson. She was then replaced by an Asian man. As it was now a civil case, it was heard in a different part of Los Angeles. Therefore, the demographic composition of the jury was different as jurors have to be selected from the district where the case is heard. It not only meant that the jury, to a far larger extent, consisted of whites, as opposed to the majority of black jurors in the criminal case against Simpson, it also had an impact on the jurors' social class and their educational background. The plaintiffs stated that they were very pleased about the composition of the jury and they stressed that at least four of the jurors had some higher education. Presumedly, the plaintiffs meant that it would be harder for the defendants to "sell" a simplistic picture to people with higher educational levels, than to people with no or poor education. Those with low self-esteem also are more likely to see the world as a struggle between "us" and "them" and are more likely to feel threatened by others.[125]

Moreover, it can be said that they neither share the experiences, disillusions or rage that some blacks carry. Therefore, the defense lawyers' defense in the first trial is no longer an appropriate response to the rhetorical situation since *it is no longer recipient related.*

For several reasons the defendants' situation is even more disadvantageous than was the case for the defense in the criminal case. The strategy conceived by Cochran and the rest of the defense team can no longer be used, but at the same time they are partially stuck with it as the case has been so publicized. What Cochran said during the first trial had an advantageous effect on the jury, but in turn was outright provocative to many other people, including many whites. As one white woman states: "The real message is that a rich and famous man can batter his wife-to the point of death-and get away with it. If he is black and she is white, a big majority of African-Americans will find an excuse to cheer him on."[126]

Or as one columnist stated: "Now, many white Americans - including this one - are as sobered by this decision as black Americans were angered by the Rodney King verdict."[127]

Two other factors made the defendant's position considerably worse in the civil case than in the criminal case. First of all, the requirements as to when guilt is proven are stricter in a criminal case than in an action for damages. In the U.S. the accused's guilt must, in a criminal case, be proven beyond reasonable doubt, whereas in an action for damages it is sufficient merely to show by the preponderance of the evidence that the defendant committed the act. Secondly, the defendant cannot, as in a criminal case, remain silent. This means that the plaintiffs' counsel could question Simpson under oath, also prior to the opening of the case, in what is called a deposition. The statements made by the defendant during deposition may be used against him during the trial. Simpson also had to testify during the trial itself and therefore could not improve his image and personality through an eloquent lawyer. The symbiosis between Simpson's image and looks and Cochran's intelligence and eloquent behavior was no longer possible.

That Simpson incriminated himself while making his statement in court is best seen from some of the statements made by the jurors after the trial:

> One white male juror said, "I had trouble believing what he was telling me. It seemed like he was just waiting to get the questions done before denying the allegations against him." ..."He really should have gotten his story straight before he got up there [on the stand]," another female juror said. Another juror said he had problems with Mr. Simpson's credibility and his repeated denial he owned Bruno Magli shoes of the type that left a bloody sole print at the murder scene.[128]

The photos of O.J. Simpson in a pair of Bruno Magli shoes which proved that he had owned such a pair, was not available at the criminal trial. This evidence was not introduced before Simpson had already denied in the civil case that he had owned such a pair of shoes.

In the civil case Simpson was caught lying and, therefor, in that case he himself had to suffer the consequences of violating the ethical requirement. In addition, Simpson proved to be neither particularly eloquent nor a good tactician, as is evident from this quotation:

> Ironic, isn't it, that both cases hinged on an N word? Attorney Daniel Petrocelli asked Simpson how many times he had hit his wife. He answered "*Never*". Nobody believed him. When Simpson was asked if he had ever worn Bruno Magli shoes like those whose bloody prints were discovered at the crime scene, he replied, "I would have *never* owned those ugly-ass shoes." Those

photographs proved otherwise, and Simpson learned an invaluable lesson about the civil trial's N word-never say never.[129]

Petrocelli fully exploited the possibilities in the civil case to catch Simpson in lies about events and facts, which he could later prove wrong. In a sense, it was the same strategy that Cochran and the other defense lawyers had used when they caught Mark Fuhrman lying about his racist statements.

Petrocelli to a far greater extent relied on the police and backed their image, morals, and ethics as opposed to what the prosecution did in the criminal case. Mr. Petrocelli was quoted as saying his strategy was to try "a tight case" and put on as many police witnesses as possible, thereby forcing Mr. Simpson to contradict them all.[130]

Not only did Petrocelli endeavor to keep a tight focus on his argumentation, he also supported the image and morals of the police indirectly by demonstrating how many police officers must be under suspicion to warrant a rejection of the accusations that the case against Simpson was a plot. Where Cochran focused on the weakest link in the chain, Mark Fuhrman, and then developed his conspiracy theory from there, Petrocelli, in reverse, focused on the credible people in the police and let their good reputation strengthen the credibility of the rest of the police force.

Petrocelli put great emphasis on conducting a focused prosecution, which is seen from the evidence he omitted to produce during the trial. The plaintiffs uncovered a great deal of evidence they did not use simply because they needed to compress their case and present the jury with the strongest and most uncontrovertible facts. Among the unused evidence: the notes of a West Los Angeles therapist who had separately treated Nicole Brown and Ron Goldman and who wrote down Nicole's account of being beaten by Simpson in the days just before the murders; and the recollections of a Connecticut limousine driver who described to the plaintiffs during deposition how, during a trip from a board meeting at the Frostier Group, a knife company, the former pro football star used one of the complimentary knives he had just been given to demonstrate in the back seat how a person could kill someone. That conversation took place during the week before the murder. Petrocelli felt that both of those people were credible, but their stories just did not fit into the thesis he was engineering.[131]

That Petrocelli actually did succeed in restoring the ethics, morals, and image of the police and thereby make the jurors trust the police is seen from some of the statements cited from the jurors after the trial.

The jurors said they had considered the defense's allegations that the police had planted evidence against Mr. Simpson and had uniformly rejected them. Several of the panelists said they attached considerable importance to the DNA blood evidence and the bloody glove found by police behind Mr. Simpson's estate the night of the murders, but that their conclusion that Mr. Simpson committed the murders was based on the accumulation of circumstantial evidence.[132]

There is no doubt that from the outset the odds of the two cases were not the same, but it is nevertheless interesting to see how the plaintiffs in the civil case handled the argumentation much more expediently from a rhetorical perspective. We cannot know with certainty how the outcome of the two cases would have been had different rhetorical strategies been employed, but we can note that in the criminal case the prosecution employed faulty rhetorical strategies and lost to a unanimous jury. In the civil case, the plaintiffs showed far more competence in rhetorical reasoning and won. This is not solely based on the amount of damages awarded but also on the fact that once again the jury was unanimous in its verdict.

21. LONG-TERM EFFECTS FOR THE PARTIES INVOLVED

In regard to moral character, since sometimes, in speaking of ourselves, we render ourselves liable to envy, to the charge of prolixity, or contradiction, or, when speaking of another, we may be accused of abuse or boorishness, we must make another speak in our place.

Aristotle

The O.J. Simpson case has had far-reaching implications for how Americans view the legal system. Originally, it was intended that this case should enhance Americans' sense of justice and demonstrate to the public what a fine legal system they had. These were the reasons why permission was given to transmit live on TV from the courtroom to the entire American population along with the rest of the world. That was the attitude shared by many leading lawyers and judges within the American legal system. It was also one of the first statements Judge Ito made at the outset of the trial. But the trial had the diametrically opposite effect. Moreover, it had far greater impact on people's sense of justice than could have been expected at its opening. As a former public prosecutor and now a professor at a university said: "The Simpson case keeps coming up because it played such a big role in shaping people's feelings about the justice system... I thought it was going to be a chance for people to see on television just how strong the system is. It ended up being bitterly adversarial, dragging out, a trial that seemed to have no focus and a jury that deliberated in just a matter of hours..."[133]

Yet only one party in the trial lacked focus. Throughout the entire trial, the defense keep a clear focus, which was to change the rhetorical situation and discredit the police and the public authorities. That this was not seen or accepted as a targeted strategy may be due to the fact that it was outside the scope of the logic, deductive paradigm, and, therefore, was not understood or accepted as relevant, acceptable, or even existing.

The O.J. Simpson case even affected the president's 1996 state of the union address. As President Clinton said:

> I call on American men and women in families to give greater respect to one another. We must end the deadly scourge of domestic violence in our country. And I challenge America's families to work harder to stay together. For families who stay together not only do better economically, their children do better as well. ...I say again, the era of big government is over. But we can't go back to the era of fending for yourself. We have to go forward to the era of working together as a community, as a team, as one America, with all of us reaching across these lines that divide us - the division, the discrimination, the rancor - we have to reach across it to find common ground. We have got to work together if we want America to work.[134]

The long-term effects of the Simpson case are most evident in the reaction of the public to subsequent high profile cases. An example is the Louise Woodward case, where an English au pair was charged with the murder of a baby she was employed to care for. At first, she was found guilty of murder in the first degree, which caused a storm of protests, both in England and the U.S. Later the jury's verdict was reduced by the judge to involuntary manslaughter. How deeply the Simpson case had affected Americans is seen from this quotation: "Nearly 100 protesters hoping to influence the judge marched outside the courthouse chanting 'Free Louise.' Among the signs they held was: O.J. Innocent, Louise Guilty? What's wrong with this picture?"[135]

Not only in America but also throughout the world the Simpson case has affected people's attitude to the American legal system, not least because people abroad could follow the trial live on TV. In connection with the Woodward case, it was much debated in the English press, which was harsh in its criticism of the American legal system.

British newspapers condemned the Massachusetts murder conviction of an English au pair as another mistake by an American justice system that blundered in acquitting O.J. Simpson. "Stitched up by the system that freed O.J. Simpson," the mass-circulation Daily Mirror declared next to a photo of an agonized Louise Woodward as she heard the verdict in a Massachusetts courtroom.[136]

However, it is not only the overall view of the American legal system that was influenced by the Simpson case. The case had great implications for the individual parties in the case. If we look at the defense, which at first came out as winners, the case has had far-reaching effects. Effects on their image and perceived ethics and morals (ethos), because large parts of the population viewed the outcome of the case the result of manipulation and distortion of what the case was really about. These likely consequences have already been advanced publicly as is seen from this commentary on the result of the Woodward case: "The Mirror said the jury may have been antagonized by Woodward's defense lawyer, Barry Scheck, who helped defend Mr. Simpson when he was acquitted in 1995 of murdering his ex-wife and her friend."[137]

The defense lawyers who initially won the Simpson case may have lost in the long run by harming their profession in the future. Seeing that their ethos has been weakened, people no longer believe what they say having been revealed as manipulators. They will, therefore, be under constant suspicion of deception. This is an implication that they probably did not consider from the outset. The case was indeed exceptional due to the wide press coverage it received. In normal circumstances the new jury would not have known what had been going on in the previous case, but as it had been shown on TV and there had been so much public debate about it, it had a large effect.

It may be claimed that Cochran knew how to take advantage of the television media during the trial. During the trial there was some debate as to whether he, through the television media indirectly, said things to the jurors that he was not allowed to say in court, by making statements in the media of which the jurors might indirectly learn, when visited by their family and friends. He is now paying the price of the case being publicly displayed. It was probably not the first time that Cochran used such a tactic. But, it was the first time that "everyone" got to know about it.

The cases Cochran takes in the future, have to be very strong and clear-cut, and preferably consist of mainly African American jurors, for Cochran to stand the same chance of winning a case. There is a high price to be paid if you are perceived to be dishonest or without ethics therby damaging or losing your ethos.

In the Woodward case, matters were not improved by the fact that the defense, which Barry Scheck was a member of, gambled and chose a tactical maneuver which could easily be viewed as too smart and manipulative. The defense demanded that the jurors only be allowed to find Louise Woodward guilty of murder of the first degree or acquit her completely. Therefore, the jurors could not find her guilty of manslaughter, which had been the wish of the prosecution. The defense had arranged some mock trials in which the jury acquitted her of all charges, given only these two options. Therefore, they chose to gamble in that case. This, combined with Barry Scheck's reputation as a manipulator, probably had a strong provocative effect on the predominantly white jury. The problem has been discussed among the defense lawyers following the conviction: "Woodward's lawyers said the judge should have asked prospective jurors about possible bias against Barry Scheck, a member of the defense team who fought in court on behalf of Mr. Simpson..."[138]

Following the trial the defense had to go to the judge and appeal to him for a reduction of the judgment to involuntary manslaughter, something the judge may do, but is rarely done. The defense assumed full responsibility and, in the end, the judge did reduce the conviction to involuntary manslaughter.

Like Cochran, Scheck seems to have a cause that he burns for. Scheck's cause is not to rid the LAPD of racism, but to use the new DNA technology to free the wrongly convicted. Quoting a *Time* magazine article:

Barry Scheck along with his partner Peter Neufeld has established a law clinic named the "Innocence Project" that uses DNA to free the wrongly convicted. Prisoners send in requests to the clinic to take up their case. They then have law students read through the trials and draft legal motions. Out of a 100 requests 70 percent are rejected. Out of the remaining 30 percent, they manage to free 60 percent.

While DNA makes headlines by exonerating people of crimes they were convicted of years ago, the same technique is enabling police across the country to track down and put away criminals who might otherwise have gone free. DNA is the biggest thing to happen in crime solving since fingerprints-and it's likely to be a lot more useful. Fingerprints can be used only when a perpetrator happens to leave a clean imprint. But DNA can be taken from hair, sweat or saliva. It even has a convenient tendency to fall off skin, leaving genetic markers behind.[139]

By contradicting the DNA evidence in the Simpson trial, Scheck now has somewhat of a credibility problem, which did not go unnoticed by *Time* magazine's audience:

> What you failed to mention about Barry Scheck ["Nation," Sept. 13] is that this is the same Barry Scheck who convincingly argued in the O.J. Simpson trial that DNA samples can be contaminated and made useless (or at least open to "reasonable doubt") as scientific evidence in a criminal trial. Through his own arguments, we are left with two possible conclusions: either Scheck is freeing potentially guilty people through the Innocence Project, or he successfully defended a double murderer he knew to be guilty. I don't know whether to laud this man or deplore him.[140]

Scheck tries to defend himself by claiming that it is easier to exclude someone by the use of DNA, than it is to determine if somebody is the guilty culprit. This argumentation sounds a bit weak, when you have a DNA match.

The Timothy McVeigh case was another high profile case in which the Simpson case played a major role. McVeigh was charged with, and later convicted of, having blown up a federal building in

Oklahoma City. The explosion killed 168 people. The defense team in this case was very conscious of the influence the Simpson case had on people's sense of justice probably because they wanted to advance some of the same arguments and follow a tactic similar to the one employed in the Simpson case. The two cases were very similar in the sense that, like the Simpson case, huge amounts of evidence against McVeigh had been collected. How important the defense lawyers found this aspect of the case is seen in this comment:

> The man on trial may be Timothy McVeigh, but it often seems like this is the third O.J. Simpson trial rather than the first Oklahoma City bombing trial. During the first week of jury selection, nearly every prospective juror was asked about the Simpson criminal and civil trials. The questions included how much they saw of the trial coverage, and what they felt about the players and the verdict. At one point, an attorney for Mr. McVeigh asked a jury candidate so many questions about the Simpson case that U.S. District Judge Richard Matsch snapped: 'We're not trying O.J. Simpson."[141]

That the jurors actually had marked opinions on the Simpson case can be seen from the statements below. It is also worth noting that some of the experts who gave evidence in the Simpson case would be called as witnesses in the McVeigh case as well. It is probably reasonable to assume that certain parts of the American population would think that the Simpson case had effected their ethos as well:

> Despite claims by jurors that they won't let the Simpson case influence them, they still had strong opinions about the case-all negative. Nearly all of their opinions were based on the televised criminal trial that resulted in Mr. Simpson's acquittal. They were not based on the blacked-out civil trial that ended with Mr. Simpson being held liable for the two murders. Mr. McVeigh's prospective jurors were particularly hard on Mr. Simpson's criminal trial judge, Lance Ito. "I didn't think the case was handled very well on the part of the judge," said No. 294, a man who runs a window washing

> company. He believed Mr. Simpson is guilty. Other jurors thought the Simpson criminal defense team got away with too much. "I felt like they brought race into the trial to get him off because the jury was predominantly black" said prospect No. 552, a cardiac unit nurse. Mr. McVeigh's defense likely will make a Simpsonesque challenge of the reliability of scientific evidence tested by the FBI crime lab. Some of the same FBI scientists who testified against Mr. Simpson will appear at Mr. McVeigh's trial.[142]

The reason McVeigh's defense lawyers were so interested in the potential jurors' knowledge and opinions in the Simpson case, is that it is not possible to use a well-known manipulative trick in self-defense. Therefore it could limit the argumentation strategies available for the defense in the McVeigh trial.

The Simpson case also had implications for the subsequent civil case where the use of video cameras was forbidden and it was widely discussed within the legal circles whether to forbid TV transmissions from the courtroom completely.

Another major consequence of the Simpson case was that in its wake a number of acquittals occurred in cases where black jurors refused to find the accused guilty as a protest against racism, abuse of power, and incompetence. This was a direct consequence of Cochran's appeal in his closing statement to send a message that one would not tolerate racism, abuse of power, and incompetence. This created a lot of anxiety within the legal circles as it undermined the legal system. It ceased, however, after a few months but based on this, we can see how strong Cochran's appeal was on certain parts of the black population and how basic the chords that he touched upon.

When it comes to the prosecution, the Simpson case had far-reaching implications as well. Even though they lost the case, they won in the long run by the way the public embraced them. Millions of copies of Christopher Darden and Marcia Clark's books have been sold, far more than the other books that have been published about the trial. Marcia Clark received the highest retainer ever for a nonfiction book, $2 million. Among other things Marcia Clark became the host of her own TV show called *Lady Law*. Clark and Darden have become celebrities because of the trial and have received widespread marks of sympathy from large parts of the American public. Even though they in a sense proved they were not particularly competent, people thought they had their "hearts in the right place." In other words, their ethoses were strengthened by demonstrating themselves as "good people" even though they lost some by proving to be "not competent enough." This indicates that in the long run, being regarded as a good and decent person carries heavier weight than professional competence. This in turn shows how important a broad-based ethos is to our abilities to function in a social context. That it is one of the basic structures in our rhetorical capabilities.

Johnny Cochran also worked as a TV host. Cochran didn't suffer as greatly as many of the other lawyers on the Simpson defense team, because his own did not reject him. Still, Cochran has limited his ability as a trial lawyer, since he no longer has a credible ethos to jurors who are not black. As time goes by, his ethos may even weaken in the black community, if they feel that he has manipulated them.

Cochran, in his need to justify himself, advocates in his book *Journey to Justice* that he helped clean up the police. This fits in with the war metaphor, from which Cochran saw the case. In war there are casualties, therefore it is justifiable to get a guilty man off if one can win the war against the police.

Several of the other defense lawyers in the Simpson case also felt it necessary to defend their participation on the Simpson defense team. They have stated that since we have no trouble accepting that wealthy people eat better food, live in bigger houses, and can afford better doctors than ordinary people, we should have no trouble accepting that wealthy persons get better legal representation than poor people do.

The reason we accept that rich people get better houses, etc., is because we accept that we have to play by the rules of society. But when you can pay your way out of not having to follow the basic rules of our society i.e., you are not allowed to kill then the rich are no longer playing by the rules. Therefore, there is no longer any basis for accepting equality. We basically only accept that people have different means, as long as we all are equal under the law.

The problem also arises on the other end, where poor people get worse representation than others. People in the mainstream generally do not get so emotional about this because it doesn't feel so personally threatening to many of us. Rhetoric opens up possibilities for bettering this situation.

If rhetoric were a mandatory course in law school, even average lawyers would be aware of these techniques. This could help to level the playing field, and thereby prevent some of the wrong convictions given on the basis of incompetence of the defense lawyer.

The lawyers prosecuting Simpson also had to pay some personal costs. Christopher Darden seemed to suffer the most; being a black prosecutor, he has experienced racism from both blacks and whites. Cochran particularly labeled him as being naive, an opportunist, and a traitor. Cochran had to discredit Darden to be able to appeal freely to the black jurors on the basis of race. The trial was so rough on Darden, who had been a public prosecutor for thirteen years, that he resigned and went on to teach at a university. Marcia Clark also resigned as a public prosecutor. As she says, "I could have continued being a DA, but I knew what would happen. I wouldn't be able to try cases for a long, long time. Either the defense would try to get me removed, for fear the jury would be biased in my favor or my own office would be afraid to deploy me, because a jury might be biased against me. As I saw it, the Simpson trial had ruined me as a prosecutor."[143]

In most arguments time is a significant factor. The arguments which have won support should preferably preserve it the next day. When taking into account the time aspect, neither the prosecution nor the defense came out of the trial marked winners. This is due to the fact that both the prosecution and the defense devised wrong objectives of and quality criteria for their argumentation. The prosecution essentially considered good rhetoric to be logical argumentation and the defense considered successful rhetorical argumentation to be effective argumentation. Both the prosecution's, as well as the defense's, strategies and criteria for judging their argumentation are expressions of a misunderstanding or a distortion of what good rhetoric includes.

The rejection of formal validity and effectiveness as universal quality criteria is linked to the fact that argumentation in practice is situation bound. If we require nothing else from an argument than that it be effective, we rule out all other relations in the communicative situation than the recipient relation. And if all we require from an argument is formal validity, we completely disregard the communicative aspect. Argumentation must always be judged based on the specific context, since good argumentation is always an expression of the demands of the entire communicative situation. Of course it is always important whether our argumentation finds support when we look at the quality of the argumentation, but it is not enough to look solely at its effectiveness, since argumentation cannot exist detached from time and place. That is to say, other aspects must be taken into account, not least the time aspect or the long-term consequences.

Over time we tend to move towards a truer and more distinct understanding of a situation. This is because it takes more energy to manipulate and lie than it does simply to say things as they are, or as we understand them. Over time, an imbalance between truth and lie will therefore seek to level itself unless it is continuously provided with new energy. This new energy could be in the form of an allegation that keeps suppressing the truth every time it tries to stick its head out of the sand. The time aspect combined with the inherent strength of "truth" can cause a very high price to pay for deliberately manipulating or misleading people even where such strategy to start with was successful. Secondly, it may over time, move towards a truer picture of our surroundings, both in regard to the events that have taken place and to future events.

Are there any purely personal consequences to be paid by the individual for deliberately manipulating and deceiving others seen in relation to how we perceive our surroundings? We may say that, by so doing, it is easy to get a cynical attitude. Like an ax that is dulled as it chops a tree, we are hurt by the social and psychological consequences of what we have done. If we look at a person's life as consisting of a *physical*, a *psychological*, an *emotional*, and a *spiritual* dimension, we may say that the cynic has lost the spiritual dimension of life. By a spiritual dimension I mean religiousness, spirituality, or simply a feeling that life has a higher meaning.

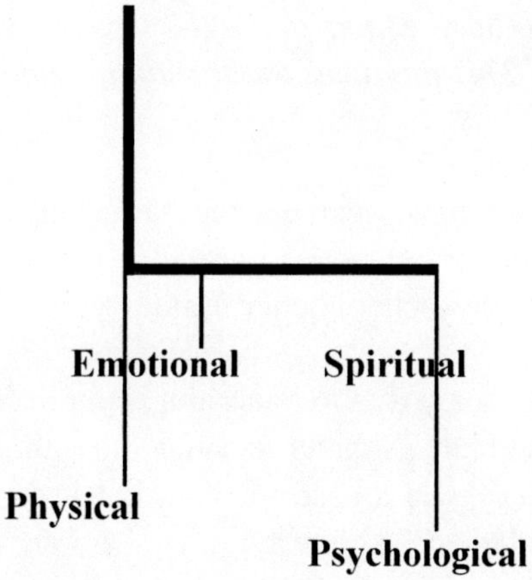

The four dimensions of life can be seen as the four legs of a chair that we sit on. If one leg is gone, there is no stability.

That cynicism and religiousness are contrasts can be seen in people who have either had a very cynical attitude to life or a profoundly religious basis and who, if they "lose" faith in their philosophy of life, often move from one extreme to another. In all circumstances, to lose the spiritual dimension of life is a high price to pay for neglecting your ethical conviction. Being smart and being wise is not the same thing. A smart person may want to win however possible, a wise person factors in the long-term consequences.

It is never impossible to reach your audience, as long as you do it on their premises.

It create a hazardous situation, in the American landscape that there is a lack of training in rhetoric and communication within law schools. It has created a "laissez faire" situation where way too many situations are determined by coincidence.

This is an unacceptable situation when one takes into consideration to what an extent American law is created by court cases, and how people's economy, freedom, and in some cases, even life are at stake. It is necessary that we not only teach lawyers about the law and how to apply it, but also how to present their case in the best possible way.

Too much lottery within the legal system undermines people's sense of justice. This threatens the foundation upon which American society is built.

Lawyers may have learned the law, but they have learned absolutely nothing about how to argue in court. In essence people don't come out of law school better trial lawyers than they were when they entered.

Just like a doctor, a rhetorician's aim is not necessarily to cure his patient, but to help him as far as he can in the right direction. Rhetoric can not necessarily win a case for you, but it can help you present your case in the best possible way.

As you have seen, the rules of effective communication have not changed since the birth of democracy and the creation of law and rhetoric as scholarly disciplines. We as a society have unfortunately moved away from the knowledge and wisdom of what good reasoning contains, a knowledge that was acquired before the birth of Christ.

As Cicero used his knowledge to protect the republic against Catelina's attempts to harm the democracy, we too should cherish this knowledge in order to protect our society. This applies equally to the law as to politics.

I have spoken; you have heard; you know the facts; now give your decision.

Aristotle

BIBLIOGRAPHY

American Bar Association Model: *Code of Professional Responsibility,* **Canon 7; Disciplinary Rules 7-102.**

Albrectsen, Bent: *USA's sorte protest (America's Black Protest) The Danish Newspaper "Politiken,"* **6 March 1997, p. 10.**

Aristotle: *The Art of Rhetoric.* **The Loeb Classical Library, Harvard University Press, London, 1994.**

Associated Press: *Give life back to O.J. jury told, The Blade,* **28 January 1997.**

Associated Press: *Simpson trial mood floods McVeigh process, The Blade,* **6 April 1997.**

Associated Press: *Nanny verdict outrages media, public in Britain, The Blade,* **2 Nov. 1997.**

Associated Press: *Nanny's lawyers ask change, The Blade,* **4 Nov. 1997.**

Atkinson, Max: *Our Master's Voices,* **Routledg, London, 1984.**

Beck, Joan: *A Sad Day for Justice. Simpson Trial Sends a Disturbing Message to Women, Chicago Tribune,* **Thursday, October 5, 1995.**

Bitzer, Lloyd F: *The Rhetorical Situation. In: Philosophy and Rhetoric,* Supplementary Issue, 1992, **The Pennsylvania State University, University Park, PA.**

Brown, Amos C: *Hitler, Fuhrman and Cochran, San Francisco Chronicle,* **October 5, 1995.**

Bugliosi, Vincent: *Outrage The five reasons why O.J. Simpson got away with murder.* **New York, London, W.W. Norton & Company, 1996.**

Burke, Kenneth: *Retorikken i Hitler's "Min Kamp" (The Rhetoric in Hitler's "Mein Kampf"), Rhetorica Scandinavica,* **no. 4, 1997, pp. 9-20.**

Burke, Kenneth: *A rhetoric of motives.* **Berkley and Los Angeles, University of California Press, 1969.**

Carlsen, Per Juul: *Paranoide teorier og underholdende sammensværgelser (Paranoid Theories and Amusing Conspiracies), The Danish Newspaper "Politiken,"* **2 March 1997, p. 16.**

Cicero, Marcus Tullius: *De inventione De uptimo Genere Oratorum Tupica,* **Harvard University Press, London, 1993.**

[Cicero]: *Rhetorica Ad Herennium* - **Harry Caplan - London - William Heinemann LTD - 1977.**

Clark, Marcia with Teresa Carpenter: *Without a Doubt.* **Viking Penguin, New York, 1997.**

Cochran, Johnnie: *Journey to Justice,* **One World, Ballantine Books, New York, 1996.**

Cohen, Adam: *The Frame Game, Time,* **March 29, 1999, vol. 153, no. 12, pp. 54-56.**

Cohen, Adam: *Innocent, After Proven Guilty, Time* **,Sep. 13, 1999, vol. 154, No. 11, pp.26-28.**

Cohen, Adam: *Gangsta Cops, Time,* **March 6, 2000, vol. 155, no. 9, pp. 30-34.**

Coolley, Armanda; Bess, Carrie; Rubeen-Jackson, Marsha: *Madam Foreman. A Rush to Judgment?* **Beverly Hills; Dove Books, 1995.**

Darden, Christopher: *In Contempt,* **Harper Spotlight, New York, 1996.**

Darden, Christopher: *Justice is the color of the beholder, Time,* 17 **February, pp. 38-39.**

Dilworth, Donald C.: *California courts address perception of racial and ethnic bias, Trial,* **April 1997, pp. 86-87.**

Eiby, Tine: *Vi mødes i retten (See you in court),* **The Danish newspaper "Weekendavisen," 13-19 September 1996, p. 5.**

Estrich, Susan: *Not the Facts: Having a Jury Rule on Social Problems, Los Angeles Times,* **Sunday, October 1, 1995.**

Fuhrman, Mark: *Murder in Brentwood,* **Regnery Publishing, Inc., Washington, D.C., 1997.**

Goldberg, Hank M.: *The Prosecution Responds. An O.J. Simpson Trial Prosecutor Reveals What Really Happened,* **1st ed. New Jersey, Birch Lane Press, 1996.**

Goodman, Ellen: *An apartheid of perceptions, The Boston Globe,* **Thursday, October 5, 1995.**

Harris, Davis A.: *Driving While Black, Toledo City Paper,* **April 1999, pp. 15-18.**

Hicks, Elliot G.: *Why Black Americans See Different, The Charleston Gazette,* **Thursday, October 19, 1995.**

Hindsholm, Søren: [Cicero] *Retorik til Herennius,* **Gyldendal, Copenhagen, 1998.**

Hitler, Adolf: *Mein Kampf,* **Houghton Mifflin Company. Boston, 1927 (1971).**

Jamieson, Kathleen Hall: *Eloquence in an electronic Age. The transformation of political speechmaking,* **Oxford U.P., 1988.**

Jamieson, Kathleen Hall: *Dirty Politics. Deception, Distraction and Democracy,* **New York, Oxford University Press, 1992.**

Jørgensen, Charlotte: *Saglig Argumentation er ikke altid Sagain (Objective Reasoning Is Not Always the Answer), Sprint,* **no. 2, 1988, pp. 22-27.**
Jørgensen, Charlotte; *Onsberg, Merete:* *Praktisk argumentation (Practical argumentation)* **1st ed. Copenhagen, Teknisk Forlag A/S, 1992.**

Jørgensen, Charlotte; Kock, Christian; Rørbech, Lone: *Retorik Der Flytter Stemmer. Hvordan man overbeviser i offentlig debat. (Vote Sliding Rhetoric. How to persuade in the public debate),* **1st ed. Copenhagen, Gyldendal, 1994.**

Knudsen, Peter Øevig: *Kærligheden kan ikke diskuteres (Love can't be discussed)*, The Danish newspaper "*Weekendavisen*" 30 Jan. - **5 Feb. 1984, p. 4.**

Lafferty, Elaine: *The Inside Story How O.J. Lost, Time,* **Feb 17, 1997, pp. 28-40.**

Lange, Tom and Philip Vannatter: *Evidence Dismissed, The Inside Story of the Police Investigation of O.J. Simpson.* **Pocket Books, a division of Simon & Schuster Inc., New York, 1997.**

Lassiter, Christo: *The O.J. Simpson Verdict: A Lesson in Black and White,* **Michigan Journal of Race And Law, 1996.**

Liewellyn, Jeffrey M.: *Letters to the Editor. Time,* **October 4, 1999, vol. 154, no. 14.**

Løgstrup, K. E.: *Den Etiske Fordring (The Ethical Requirement),* **2nd ed., Copenhagen, Gyldendal, 1991.**

Miall, David S.: *Metaphor as a Thought-Process,* **JAAC 381, 1979-80, p.21.**

Park, Roger C.: *Character Evidence Issues in the O.J. Simpson Case-Or, Rationales of the Character Evidence Ban,* **University of Colorado Law Review, Fall 1996.**

Perelman CH. and Olbrechts-Tyteca, L.: *The New Rhetoric. A Treatise on argumentation,* **University of Notre Dame Press, London, 1969.**

Peterson, Eugene H.: *The Message, The New Testament Psalms and Proverbs in Contemporary Language.* **Navpress, Colorado, 1995.**

Pittsburgh Post-Gazette: *Everyone Has Own Opinion of the Verdict,* **Wednesday, October 4, 1995.**

Proffitt, Steve: *Simpson trial revealed very different fears within the races, Los Angeles Times,* **Wednesday, October 11, 1995.**

Prystowsky, Richard J.: *Education with Compassion. The Path and Goal of Holistic Teaching, Living, and Learning," Paths of Learning,* **vol. 1, number 1999.**

Schiller, Lawrence; Willwerth, James: *American Tragedy. The Uncensored Story of the Simpson Defense.* **1st ed, New York, Random House, 1996.**

Simonsen, Margit: *Når Det Kilder På Indersiden af Livet (When It Tickles on the Inner Side of Life),* **Copenhagen Institute of Philosophy, Pedagogic & Retorik, 2000.**

Skyum-Nielsen, Peder: *Fyndord (Maxims).* **1st ed. Copenhagen, Hans Reitzels Forlag, 1992.**

Spence, Gerry: *O.J., The Last Word,* **New York, St. Martin's Press, 1997.**

The Gospel of Matthew, verse nineteen. Holy Bible, King James.

Times-Post News Service: *Awards exceed expectations of plaintiffs, The Blade,* **11 Feb. 1997.**

Tobin, Jeffrey: *The Run of his life: The People v. O.J. Simpson,* **New York and Toronto, Random House, 1996.**

Toulmin, Stephen: *The Uses of Argument,* **Cambridge University Press, 1958.**

Uelmen, Gerald F.: *Lessons from the Trial. The People v. O.J. Simpson.* **Kansas City, Andrews and Mcmeel, a Universal Press Syndicate Company, 1996.**

U.S. News & World Report, Oct 16, 1995, vol 19, n. 15 p. 53(2).

U.S. News & World Report, March 24, 1997, vol. 122 n. 11.

Vico, Giambattista: *On the Study Methods of Our Time.* **Translated with an Introduction and Notes by Elio Gianturco, Cornell, New York, 1990.**

Warc, B.L.; Linkugel, Wil A.: *They Spoke in Defense of Themselves. On the Generic Criticism of Apologia. Quarterly Journal of Speech,* **no. 59,**

1973, pp. 73-283.

Walton, Douglas N.: *Informal logic: A handbook for critical argumentation,* **Cambridge, Cambridge University Press, 1989.**

Index

NOTES

[1] This case can be looked up under Court of Common Pleas, Franklin County, Ohio. Case no. 97CVC-10-0953. Blanche Harmon v Mt. Carmel, Columbus, Ohio.

[2] U.S. News & World Report, March 24, 1997 v. 122 n. 11, p. 46.

[3] Christo Lassiter: The O.J. Simpson Verdict: A Lesson In Black And White, p.9.

[4] Thomas Jefferson in 1787

[5] Coolley, Bess & Rubeen-Jackson: Madame Foreman, p. 91.

[6] Coolley, Bess & Rubeen-Jackson: Madame Foreman, p. 138.

[7] Donald C. Dilworth: California courts address perception of racial and ethnic bias, p. 86.

[8] The reality for young blacks may be even worse than the statistics suggest. The report includes only the small fraction of lawbreakers that end up in court, and its focus on men obscures an even more disturbing increase in female convicts. While six times as many black men as women are behind bars or on probation or parole, the percentage of African-American women enmeshed in the legal system nearly doubled in the last five years.

The reaction to the study resembles the racial split in attitudes about Simpson's acquittal. Many whites say the statistics merely reflect that fact that a disproportionate number of criminals are young black men. Many blacks say the numbers are the product of a legal system that is tilted against them in ways ranging from overt racism among police officers and judges to sentencing rules that intentionally or not penalize members of minority groups much harder than whites. U.S News & World Report, Oct 16, 1995, v.119, n.15, p.53 (2). Ted Gest: *A shocking look at blacks and crime.*

[9] Christo Lassiter: The O.J. Simpson Verdict: A Lesson in Black and White, p. 16.

[10] Jørgensen, Kock and Rørbech: Retorik der flytter Stemmer, p. 336.

[11] Adam Cohen: The Frame Game.

[12] Adam Cohen: Gangsta Cops.

[13] David A, Harris: Driving While Black.

[14] David A. Harris: Driving While Black.

[15] Elliot G. Hicks: Why Black Americans See Different.

[16] David A. Harris: Driving While Black.

[17] Pittsburgh Post-Gazette: Everyone Has Own Opinion of the Verdict.

[18] Jeffrey Toobin, The Run of His Life, pp. 354-355.

[19] Christo Lassiter: The O.J. Simpson Verdict: A Lesson in Black and White, p. 1.

[20] Christo Lassiter: The O.J. Simpson Verdict: A Lesson in Black and White, P. 18.

[21] Coolley, Bess & Rubeen-Jackson: Madam Foreman, p. 100.

[22] Stephen Toulmin's reasoning model.

[23] Hank M. Goldberg: The Prosecution Responds, p. 320.

[24] Christo Lassiter: The O.J. Simpson Verdict: A Lesson in Black and White, p.50.

[25] Stephen Toulmin's argumentation model.

[26] Roger C. Park: Character Evidence Issues in the O.J. Simpson Case-Or,

Rationales of the Character Evidence Ban.
[27] Roger C. Park: Character Evidence Issues in the O.J. Simpson Case-Or, Rationales of the Character Evidence Ban.
[28] B.L. Ware & Wil A. Linkugel
[29] Ware & Linkugel: They Spoke in Defense of Themselves.
[30] Armanda Coolley; Carrie Bess; Marsha Rubeen-Jackson: Madam Foreman. A Rush to Judgment? p. 103.
[31] Armanda Coolley; Carrie Bess; Marsha Rubeen-Jackson: Madam Foreman. A Rush to Judgment, p. 111.
[32] Lloyd F. Bitzer: The Rhetorical Situation, Philosuphy and Rhetoric, p. 5.
[33] Week of March 13th 1995. Fuhrman is questioned again; this time the questions are pointedly focused on racial slurs that were reportedly overheard and asserts that the bloody glove was planted because Fuhrman is a racist.
[34] Perelman & Olbrechts-Tyteca: The New Rhetoric, pp. 465-466.
[35] Gerald F. Uelmen, Lessons from the Trial. pp. 173-174.
[36] K.E. Løgstrup: Den Etiske Fordring, p. 18.
[37] Lafferty, Elaine: The Inside Story How O.J. Lost, p. 36.
[38] Jørgensen, Kock & Rørbech: Retorik Der Flytter Stemmer, p.39.
[39] Coolly, Bess & Rubeen-Jackson: Madam Foreman, p.97.
[40] Coolly, Bess & Rubeen-Jackson: Madam Foreman, p.97.
[41] Coolly, Bess & Rubeen-Jackson: Madam Foreman, pp. 88-89.
[42] Hank M. Goldberg: The Prosecution Responds, p. 344.
[43] Kenneth Burke: A Rhetoric of Motives, p. 56.
[44] Schiller & Willwerth: American Tragedy, p. 660.
[45] Amos C. Brown: Hitler, Fuhrman and Cochran.
[46] Gerald F. Uelmen: Lessons from the Trial, p. 167.
[47] Coolly, Bess & Rubeen-Jackson: Madam Foreman, p. 156.
[48] Coolly, Bess & Rubeen-Jackson: Madam Foreman, pp. 193-194.
[49] Coolly, Bess & Rubeen-Jackson: Madam Foreman, pp. 201-202.
[50] Vincent Bugliosi: Outrage, p. 189.
[51] Coolly, Bess & Rubeen-Jackson: Madam Foreman, p. 90.
[52] Steve Proffitt: Simpson Trial Revealed Very Different Fears Within the Races.
[53] Peder Skyum-Nielsen: Fyndord, p. 125.
[54] Aristotle: Rhetoric, p. 287.
[55] Aristotle: Rhetoric, p. 289.
[56] Max Atkinson: Our Masters' Voices, pp. 159-160.
[57] Gerald F. Uelmen: Lessons from the Trial, p. 158.
[58] Johnny Cochran: Journey to Justice, p. 263.
[59] Judge Ito dismisses a thirty-eight-year-old Latino postal worker who had previously been involved in an abusive relationship. Week of April 3erd: A sixth juror is removed for failing to reveal a history of spousal abuse.
[60] Coolley, Bess & Rubeen-Jackson: Madam Foreman, p. 35.
[61] Coolley, Bess & Rubeen-Jackson: Madam Foreman, p. 128.
[62] Johnny Cochran: Journey to Justice, p. 257.
[63] Johnny Cochran: Journey to Justice, p. 49.
[64] Johnny Cochran: Journey to Justice, p. 125.
[65] Johnny Cochran: Journey to Justice, p. 359.

[66] Reverend Duane Tisdale, from "The Friendship Baptist Church."
[67] Giambattista Vico: On the Study Methods of our Time.
[68] Susan Estrich: Not the Facts: Having a Jury Rule on Social Problems.
[69] Jørgensen, Kock & Rørbech: Retorik Der Flytter Stemmer, pp. 142-144.
[70] Mark Fuhrman: Murder in Brentwood, p. 131.
[71] Mark Fuhrman: Murder in Brentwood, p. 3.
[72] Darden asked Heidstra, "The second voice that you heard sounded like the voice of a black man, is that correct?" Cochran nearly jumped out of his chair. "Objected to, Your Honor," he sputtered. "I object." The defense caused such a commotion that Judge Ito excused the jury and told Heidstra to step outside for a moment. Darden patiently recounted to the judge that an acquaintance of Heidstra's, Patricia Baret, had told Detective Tom Lange that Heidstra told her that "he heard the very angry screaming of an older man who sounded black." Thus, Darden explained to Ito, he had every right to ask the question. But Cochran was not to be mollified. "I resent that statement," he thundered. "You can't tell by someone's voice when they're black. I don't know who's made that statement, Baret or Lange. That's racist." Cochran continued his tirade: "This statement about whether somebody sounds black or white is racist, and I resent it, and that's why I stood and objected to it. I think it's totally improper in America, at this time in 1995, just to hear this and endure this." Hank M. Goldberg: The Prosecution Responds, pp. 381-382.
[73] Mark Fuhrman: Murder in Brentwood, p. 283.
[74] Mark Fuhrman: Murder in Brentwood, pp. 126-127.
[75] Mark Fuhrman: Murder in Brentwood, p. 320.
[76] Marcia Clark: Without a Doubt, p. 451.
[77] Mark Fuhrman: Murder in Brentwood, p. 287.
[78] Mark Fuhrman: Murder in Brentwood, pp.286-287.
[79] Mark Fuhrman: Murder in Brentwood, p.291.
[80] Hank M. Goldberg: The Prosecution Responds, p. 301.
[81] David S. Miall: Metaphor as a Thought-Process, p.21.
[82] Jeffry Tobin: The Run of His Life pp. 260-261.
[83] Mark Fuhrman: Murder in Brentwood, p. 229.
[84] Jeffrey M. Liewellyn, Letters to the Editor, Time, April 5. 1999.
[85] Gerry Spence: O.J. The Last Word, pp. 24-25.
[86] American Bar Association Model: Code of Professional Responsibility, Canon 7; Disciplinary Rules 7-102.
[87] Vincent Bugliosi: Outrage, p. 180.
[88] Vincent Bugliosi: Outrage, p. 205.
[89] Gerald F. Uelmen: Lessons from the Trial, p. 115.
[90] Authentic dialog reported in the Massachusetts Bar Association Journal.
[91] Gerald F. Uelmen: Lessons from the Trial, p. 169.
[92] Gerald F. Uelmen: Lessons from the Trial, p. 169.
[93] Hank M. Goldberg: The Prosecution Responds, pp. 319-320.
[94] Marcia Clark: Without a Doubt, p. 462.
[95] Christo Lassiter: The O.J. Simpson Verdict: A Lesson in Black and White, (FN128).
[96] Perelman & Olbrechts-Tyteca: The New Rhetoric, pp. 483-484.
[97] Marcia Clark: Without a Doubt, p. 7.

[98] Marcia Clark: Without a Doubt, p. 253.
[99] Marcia Clark: Without a Doubt, p. 117.
[100] Jeffrey Tobin: The Run of His Life, pp. 114-115.
[101] Lange & Vannatter: Evidence Dismissed, p.251.
[102] Marcia Clark: Without a Doubt, p. 468.
[103] Schiller & Willwerth: American Tragedy, p. 661.
[104] Associated Press: Give life back to O.J, Jury told.
[105] Associated Press: Give life back to O.J. Jury told.
[106] Margit Simonsen, Copenhagen Institute of Rhetoric. Has developed ground-breaking theories about the persuasive aspects of humor. See theses: When it tickles on the inner side of life.
[107] Eugene H. Peterson: The Message, The New Testament Psalms And Proverbs In Contemporary Language. p. 21, Matthew 5: 29-44.
[108] Perelman & Olbrechts-Tyteca: The New Rhetoric, p. 487.
[109] Douglas N. Walton: Informal Logic: a handbook for critical argumentation, p. 262.
[110] Kenneth Burke: Retorikken i Hitler's "Min Kamp", Rhetorica Scandinavica, 1997, vol. 4. p. 9.
[111] Kenneth Burke: Retorikken i Hitler's "Min Kamp", Rhetorica Scandinavica, 1997, vol. 4. p. 10.
[112] Kenneth Burke: Retorikken i Hitler's "Min Kamp", Rhetorica Scandinavica, 1997, vol. 4. pp. 11-12.
[113] Kenneth Burke: Retorikken i Hitler's "Min Kamp", Rhetorica Scandinavica, 1997, vol. 4. p. 10.
[114] Kenneth Burke: Retorikken i Hitler's "Min Kamp" , Rhetorica Scandinavica, 1997, vol. 4. p. 13.
[115] Kenneth Burke: Retorikken i Hitler's "Min Kamp", Rhetorica Scandinavica, 1997, vol. 4. p. 15.
[116] Kenneth Burke: Retorikken i Hitler's "Min Kamp", Rhetorica Scandinavica, 1997, vol. 4. p. 19.
[117] Adolf Hitler: Mein Kampf, pp. 180-181.
[118] Adolf Hitler: Mein Kampf, p. 184
[119] Kenneth Burke: Retorikken i Hitler's "Min Kamp", Rhetorica Scandinavica, p. 10.
[120] Adolf Hitler: Mein Kampf, p. 177.
[121] Adolf Hitler: Mein Kampf, p. 180.
[122] Adolf Hitler: Mein Kampf, p. 471.
[123] American Bar Association Model: Code of Professional Responsibility, Canon 7; Disciplinary Rules 7 - 102.
[124] Schiller & Willwerth: American Tragedy, p. 656.
[125] Kathleen Hall Jamieson: Dirty Politics, p. 66.
[126] Joan Beck: A Sad Day for Justice.
[127] Ellen Goodman: An apartheid of perceptions.
[128] Times-Post News Service: Awards exceed expectations of plaintiffs.
[129] Christopher Darden: Justice is the Color of the Beholder, p. 38.
[130] Times-Post News Service: Awards exceed expectations of plaintiffs.
[131] Lafferty, Elaine: The Inside Story of how O.J. Lost, p. 33.
[132] Times-Post News Service: Awards exceed expectations of plaintiffs.
[133] Associated Press: Simpson trial mood floods McVeigh process.

[134] State Of The Union Address, January 23, 1996.
[135] Associated Press: Nanny's lawyers ask change.
[136] Associated Press: Nanny verdict outrages media, public in Britain.
[137] Associated Press: Nanny verdict outrages media, public in Britain.
[138] Associated Press: Nanny's lawyers ask change.
[139] Adam Cohen: Innocent, After Proven Guilty, pp.26-28.
[140] Jeffrey M. Liewellyn, Letters to the Editor.
[141] Associated Press: Simpson trial mood floods McVeigh process.
[142] Associated Press: Simpson trial mood floods McVeigh process.
[143] Marcia Clark: Without a Doubt, p. 480.

Winning with Words

by
Maria Louise Staffe

Available at your local bookstore or use this page to order.

--1-931633-75-4 - Winning with Words - $18.95 U.S
Send to: Trident Media Inc.
801 N. Pitt Street #123
Alexandria, VA 22314
Toll Free # 1-877-874-6334
Please send me the item above. I am enclosing
$___________(please add $3.50 per book to cover postage and handling).
Send check, money order, or credit card:

Card #___________________________ Exp. date ________

Mr./Mrs./Ms.______________________________________
Address____
City/State___________________________Zip____________

Please allow four to six weeks for delivery.
Prices and availability subject to change without notice.

Printed in the United States
1471000002B/332